*To all who have sailed with me from North Greenland
to Antarctica and from Fiji to Helsinki. Joyous times were had by my
family and me, and I hope by all who have helped me sail various
Palawans over tens of thousands of miles during a period of 55 years.*

A South Pacific Adventure with Sailor, Explorer, Aviator and Former IBM Chief Executive Tom Watson

PACIFIC PASSAGE

By Thomas J. Watson, Jr.

This book is printed in Hong Kong

ISBN 0-913372-68-4

Design by Clare Cunningham

PHOTO CREDITS:

Page 8:	The Natural History Museum, London, England
Pages 16-18	Drawings courtesy of Sparkman & Stephens, New York
Page 21:	Photos by Dana Jinkins, Concepts Publishing
Pages 54-55	The National Maritime Museum, Greenwich, England
Page 56	Courtesy of the G. W. Blunt White Library, Mystic Seaport Museum
Page 61:	The Natural History Museum, London, England
Page 104:	The Natural History Museum, London, England
Page 129:	The Natural History Museum, London, England
Page 139:	The Natural History Museum, London, England
Page 150:	The Natural History Museum, London, England
Page 155:	The Natural History Museum, London, England
Page 175:	The Natural History Museum, London, England
Page 178:	The Natural History Museum, London, England

Images on endsheets: The Natural History Museum, London, England
Image on back of dust jacket: The Natural History Museum, London, England

All other images in this book are photographs taken by Tom Watson and by members of *Palawan*'s crew.

The painting shown on pages 54-55 was done in 1773 by William Hodges, artist aboard *Resolution* during Cook's second exploration of the Pacific. It shows two types of Tahitian voyaging canoes.

Cataloging-in-publication data:
Watson, Thomas J., 1914-
    Pacific Passage / by Thomas J. Watson, Jr. —
Mystic, Conn. : Mystic Seaport Museum, c1993.
        p. : col. ill. ;   cm.
    Originally published: Logbook For Helen.
[S.l. : s.n., ca. 1980].

    1. Palawan IV (Ketch).   2. Voyages and travels - 20th century.
3. Islands of the Pacific - Description.   I. Title.

G530.W37 1993

Table of Contents

Foreword   *6*

Preface   *8*

CHAPTER 1:
Heading: The South Pacific   *12*

CHAPTER 2:
Planning: Crew, Equipment and Stores   *24*

CHAPTER 3:
Cocos: Once a Pirate Haven   *32*

CHAPTER 4:
Darwin's Laboratory: The Galapagos and Wildlife   *40*

CHAPTER 5:
Polynesia: Myth and Mystery   *54*

CHAPTER 6:
Where Past is Present: Easter Island Rendezvous   *64*

CHAPTER 7:
Pitcairn: Climax of the *Bounty* Saga   *80*

CHAPTER 8:
Les Isles Oubliees: The Gambiers and Mangareva   *88*

CHAPTER 9:
Tuamotus: The "Dangerous" Archipelago   *100*

CHAPTER 10:
Society Islands: Tahiti at Last   *112*

CHAPTER 11:
The Cook Islands: Atolls and Reefs   *130*

CHAPTER 12:
Samoa: Pago Pago and Apia   *140*

CHAPTER 13:
Feasts and New Friends: The Kingdom of Tonga   *152*

CHAPTER 14:
The Adventure's End: Fiji and Farewells   *164*

Epilogue   *176*

Foreword

The author of this delightful story of a cruise to the South Seas modestly plays down his role as one of the outstanding sailor-adventurers of our time. He alludes to two other sea adventures in this account — a circumnavigation of Newfoundland in 1971 and a cruise to Greenland in 1974 when he took *Palawan III* to 77° 38' north — the farthest north that any yacht had been on the west coast of Greenland to that time. These cruises, as impressive as they are, seem now to have been surpassed by Tom Watson's more recent accomplishments. In 1984-85 he sailed a new *Palawan* from Helsinki via Lisbon to Cape Horn, then to the Antarctic Peninsula, and finally through the poorly charted waters of the Chilean archipelago. In 1986 he sailed from Corner Brook, Newfoundland, up through treacherous Hudson Strait to Churchill on the western shore of Hudson Bay, in the process weathering some severe North Atlantic gales in an area replete with icebergs. After a number of more leisurely Caribbean cruises, when Tom was in his middle sixties he sailed *Palawan V* singlehandedly from Bermuda to Antigua in the Lesser Antilles and then back to Bermuda again.

It was no surprise that in recognition of these achievements the Cruising Club of America saw fit to award him their 1986 Blue Water Medal. This honor is given annually to the amateur sailor of any nationality who makes the most noteworthy voyage in that year and displays exceptionally meritorious seamanship in the course of the adventure. The C.C.A. Blue Water Medal is a sort of Nobel Prize for cruising sailors, and as a recipient Tom Watson joins such distinguished mariners as Eric Tabarly, Sir Francis Chichester, Major H.W. Tilman, Rod Stephens, Vito Dumas and Alain Gerbault.

How does anyone in a single lifetime achieve such recognition in the sailing world at the same time that he has achieved so many other things? During Tom Watson's tenure as CEO, the IBM that his father passed on to him became one of the most successful and respected companies on the world, and after his retirement from IBM he served as our Ambassador to the Soviet Union. And all during these several careers he actively pursued a lifelong interest in aviation which included flying everything from balloons to jet aircraft.

Perhaps the secret of Tom Watson's success in so many diverse activities can be found between the lines of this intriguing tale. First is his readiness to accept challenges of all kinds, both physical and intellectual; second is his consuming interest in people from all walks of life and his sensitivity to their feelings and potentials, and third is an enthusiasm for researching the history and ethos of the peoples and places he has either visited or plans to visit. All of these characteristics add depth and interest to his accounts of adventures like this one.

Most of us are seduced by the romance of the South Seas, and it is safe to say that readers will delight in the way this narrative weaves together the experiences of *Palawan*'s crew and the mores and history of each island visited, comparing things as they were to contemporary conditions and philosophizing about the changes taking place. The author obviously has a great admiration for the Polynesians who explored and settled such a vast area of the Pacific with none of the aids to navigation that we consider essential today. With his talents as a writer and photographer he effectively brings to life the magic and the mystery of the great voyages that peopled Oceania and the spectacular beauty of many of these islands as they are experienced today.

Another fascinating aspect of this story is its rather intimate view of the little world of *Palawan IV* and her company. Tom Watson discusses very frankly his views on family, friends, and the people he meets, as well as his own apprehensions at various stages of the adventure. And it becomes clear that even with a crew of all ages, sexes and backgrounds, and inevitably a few tense moments, his subtle and continued efforts to create a "happy ship," that cruising ideal, are very successful. This is no mean achievement considering the long periods at sea and all hands confined to a limited space.

For anyone contemplating a voyage to this intriguing part of the world, *Pacific Passage* contains some excellent practical advice on equipping and provisioning a yacht for a long cruise away from most sources of supply. It should also be a helpful guide in selecting potential ports and landfalls from Panama to Fiji. Having made a few modest cruises with the author, I can confirm his meticulous preparation for any conceivable contingency, with the result that the comfort and well-being of anyone lucky enough to be a member of one of Tom Watson's crews is guaranteed. An important result of this thorough planning has been that over the years, with seven different *Palawans*, and with the successful completion of a number of long offshore races and a variety of exotic and hazardous long cruises, no serious accidents or injuries have occurred.

The Pacific passage described in these pages was well-planned, well-executed, all but perfect in its unfolding and, of course, full of the powerful romance of the South Seas. I suspect that Helen and her friends will all their lives look back on this adventure as one of the high spots of their youth, even despite some minor difficulties with "the old man."

— *Edwin Thorne*

Preface

Sailing and flying are what I like best. If I had lived a hundred years ago, I imagine I would have chosen to be a ship's captain. If I had been born ten years earlier I hope I would have been a pioneer aviator. As it is, since being introduced to the art when I was twelve, I have gone sailing whenever I could lay my hands on a sailboat or join someone else for a sail. Since 1932 I have flown nearly 100 different aircraft types, military and civilian, accumulating about 19,000 hours.

When I was in my early twenties my father owned a 65-foot schooner, aboard which I discovered the thrill of voyaging. My first trips took me eastward to Halifax and to Bras d'Or Lake, but even such short voyages were immensely satisfying. I was exhilarated by the sense of anticipation in probing places unknown to me, by the mystery of what comes next, and by the challenges of navigation and the wiles of the weather. Even now, as I write this during a passage from Florida to Mexico and on to Belize and the River Dulce in Guatemala, I am just as excited by making a new landfall, seeing a new horizon, and reaching a remote and unspoiled port, as I was in finding Cape Breton Island in 1936.

Perhaps sailing is also important to me because a businessman is never free of his job. He works as hard as he can for as long as he can and then somebody else takes over. There are moments of great satisfaction, but the journey is never-ending. At sea, however, a voyage has a destination, and upon reaching port a skipper and crew can relax with a glowing sense of completion and accomplishment.

Looking back, I can say that sailing has been an important bond in our family. Living together in the tight quarters of a boat, working together toward a common goal, and discovering together the wonders of the sea have, I am sure, deepened the love and resilience of our family. Certainly the presence of my sister Helen and my daughter Helen on this passage to Polynesia made it one of the most memorable cruises I have ever taken.

Why did I wish to make this four-month voyage into the South Pacific? I suppose I was in quest of a seafaring people whose voyaging abilities had always been a wonder to me. When I was joined by some of my closest sailing companions and my spirited daughter and her friends, this visit to the seas and islands of the world's greatest sailors became an important voyage of rediscovery for me.

To record my memories of the cruise, I wrote this text, with the help of Pamela Constable, as *Logbook for Helen* — inspired by ornithologist Robert Cushman Murphy's *Logbook for Grace*. I published a few hundred copies and gave them to Helen and her friends, never intending the work for a broader audience. But at the urging of friends and strangers alike, I have revised the text a bit for publication by, and for the benefit of, Mystic Seaport Museum, which I have been associated with for many years, mostly as a trustee. Marcia Wiley, the Museum's publications staff, and designer Clare Cunningham have all contributed to put the book into the final form in which you see it.

Much has happened in the 16 years since I wrote *Logbook for Helen*. Among my reasons for making this Polynesian cruise was to see if I would feel comfortable spending the rest of my life sailing and perhaps writing some yarns about that sailing. Although I enjoyed every moment of the trip and was satisfied with my efforts to record it in print, I discovered that I needed more varied activities to occupy myself.

They say chance favors the prepared mind. When I returned to IBM as chairman, but not chief executive, after a heart attack in 1970, I found myself with no great path ahead of me. IBM was in good hands, and I knew that I would be fully retired from the company in January 1974, when I would turn 60. I had begun to think that I might live for a number of years, whereas during the year or two after the heart attack I lived from day to day. So I mixed a few cruises on the boat with the sun of Antigua.

Then one day, in the summer of 1977, as I was sitting in my home in Maine, gazing across Penobscot Bay toward Deer Isle, the phone rang. It was Secretary of Defense Harold Brown, an old friend, calling to ask me to join him and Secretary of State Cyrus Vance in working with the Carter administration. "At this time in my life I'm in a position to sit in a chair as I am now doing and look out across the bay and decide where I am going to sail my boat tomorrow. I can't imagine what I could do to help people in Washington," I told him.

Nevertheless, Secretary Brown persuaded me to come down and talk. A short time later President Carter nominated me to head the General Advisory Committee, which President Kennedy had established in 1961 as a blue-ribbon panel to work toward the control of nuclear weapons. This tremendously interesting job was part-time, but I spent most of my time between the monthly meetings learning about the next subject or worrying about how I would perform in front of the very distinguished and very able committee members, including McGeorge Bundy and the president's security advisor, Brent Scowcroft.

After a year and a half of chairing the General Advisory Committee I began to hear rumors that I might be nominated as ambassador to the Soviet Union. This was not a job that I would ever seek, nor did I consider myself likely to be selected, but one night, when I was staying in my brother's embassy in Paris, my wife Olive posed a totally hypothetical question: would I ever consider being an ambassador? "Absolutely not," I replied. "All of the requirements of an ambassador are talents that I don't have. However, if the country was the Soviet Union, then I would have to give it some thought." And so, as these rumors persisted, I began to think.

I discovered that the policy of administrations is to float the name of a potential nominee in order to smoke out any sins in the possible nominee's background before the president puts the nomination forward. In response to my name, there were few protests, and before long I was in the Great Hall of the State Department, being sworn in as U.S. ambassador to the Soviet Union.

I spent a year and a half in Moscow and found the work very interesting. However, shortly after I arrived the Soviets attacked Afghanistan and the generally frigid relationship between the U.S. and the Soviet Union turned into outright hostility. I learned a great deal as ambassador there, but the circumstances left me few opportunities for the sort of positive contributions to U.S.-Soviet relations that I had hoped to make. When Ronald Reagan became president in January of 1981 I tendered my resignation.

In April 1981 my good friend Andrew Heiskell, former head of Time, Inc., took me to dinner and proposed that I make the commencement speech at Harvard. Although I felt inadequate for the task, I knew it would give me a chance to publicize the grave dangers inherent in the nuclear arms race from the best platform one could possibly have, so I agreed. The speech was such a success that for the next eight years I accepted every invitation I received to speak on the urgent need to resolve the nuclear threat through creative treaty negotiations. When we started our treaty efforts in 1958 there were a few dozen weapons on both sides. By the 1980s we had worked the count up to about 9,000 per side. Clearly, something was wrong with the process.

During my decade-long involvement with international diplomacy and efforts to control nuclear weapons I did manage to find time to satisfy my love for sailing. In 1980 I commissioned *Palawan V*, a 50-foot Paul Luke ketch, which I sailed alone from Bermuda to Antigua and back. However, it became obvious to me that Olive and I could not be comfortable in such a small vessel as we got older. Therefore,

I had Sparkman & Stephens design a larger, sturdier boat. Built in aluminum like my previous two boats, *Palawan VI* was launched by Abeking and Rasmussen in 1984. As related in the epilogue, I made several voyages to distant waters in this boat. I was proud, indeed, when the Cruising Club of America awarded me the Blue Water Medal in 1986 for the long voyages I made during the decade.

After recovering from a cancer operation in 1989, I was determined to get back to the sailing, skiing, and acrobatic flying that I hope keep me mentally alert. In 1990 I received *Palawan VII*. Designed by Ted Hood and Ted Fontaine and constructed at Ted Hood's yard in Taiwan, she is a 75-foot sloop, large enough so that we and our guests can be very comfortable. The designer and the type of boat were selected by my blessed wife Olive who has patiently followed me for 51 years. It was her turn to pick a boat suited to her needs and that is what we have in the new *Palawan*. In the meantime, with the assistance of gifted *Fortune* editor Peter Petre, I had written an autobiography that emphasized my relationship with my father and with IBM. Published as *Father, Son & Company*, the book spent 14 weeks on the best-seller list.

So now, at 79, I am still reasonably strong and in good health. It gratifies me to have witnessed the apparent end of decades of nuclear standoff. Yet much remains to be done. I endowed the Thomas J. Watson, Jr. Institute for International Studies at Brown University to help promote the search for solutions to problems in world affairs in the future.

As we look toward the future, with the company of our spirited children and grandchildren, there is always something to occupy our interest, our hearts, and our love. I trust that I have done my best to pass on to them a safer world and to impart to them the values and the sense of discovery that I have gained in a lifetime of sailing.

— Tom Watson, Jr.
January, 1993

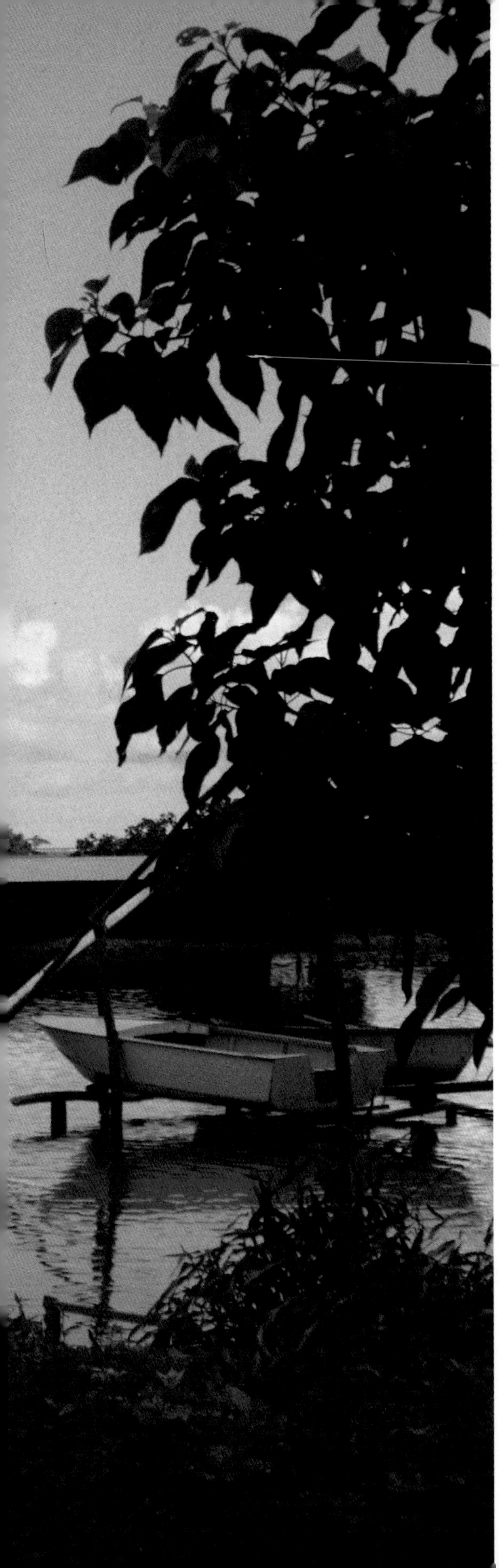

CHAPTER 1

HEADING:

The South Pacific

My watch says 3:10 A.M. Jimmy Madden, the navigator, estimates we won't reach Cocos until about 0945. Yet, worrisome questions interrupt my dreams. What if the fixes and times are off and we strike Cocos in the dark? What about my responsibility as a skipper? If I hang over Jimmy's shoulder at the start of the voyage when we're both rusty on navigation, will I be hurting more than helping?

Most sensible thing to do is relax, multiply and divide in my head, and convince myself that reaching Cocos before dawn is an impossibility. By now, I'm fully awake and beginning to ponder broader questions. What am I doing in the middle of this windless but uneasy and extremely hot patch of ocean? Why did I ever think I could play skipper, father, doctor, psychologist and disciplinarian to eight people aged 20 to 74 while crossing 9,000 miles of open sea in a 68-foot boat?

My love affair with the sea began when I was 12. My parents had taken my brother, my sisters and me to Cape Cod for the summer. They rented a catboat and hired a Harvard student — Don Murchie of Dedham, Massachusetts — to teach me sailing and tutor me in math. He didn't succeed too well at the second task, but was very successful at the first. By the end of the summer I understood the rudiments of sailing and had discovered the magic of the sea that has provided me, over the past 50 years, with some of the happiest moments of my life.

A few years later I received a copy of Joshua Slocum's book *Sailing Alone Around the World*, the story of a sea captain in his sixties who "retired" from the sea in 1895 and sailed his 37-foot yawl, *Spray*, around the world singlehanded. In those days this was an astounding feat. When I read it I wanted to leave college to follow his track. However, a year or two later such dreams were put on hold when Hitler marched into Poland and America's eventual entry into the war became obvious. I joined the U.S. Army Air Corps and spent the next five years piloting various types of military aircraft all over the world. Far from satisfying my wanderlust, these experiences heightened it.

It wasn't until a decade later, when I was married with three children and with a growing business to run, that I finally returned to the water. By then, we had moved to Greenwich, Connecticut, where I met Paul Campbell and spent two sum-

LOG ENTRY: JANUARY 31, 1976

Sea unsteady but windless. Engine rumbles noisily as usual; the mainsail, hoisted as a steadying sail, occasionally slats — all sounds that I've heard before during hundreds of nights at sea. Why am I awake? Suddenly, I remember. Cocos Island, 500 miles from the Pacific mouth of the Panama Canal, lies somewhere ahead.

mers racing in Long Island Sound on his 36-foot sloop, *Julie*. I learned much from Paul, not only about sailing but also about leadership. He was good at both. In 1949 I began to build and race boats of my own: the first, a 15-year-old Geiger sloop called *Tarbaby*. Later I built a series of sailboats, each named *Palawan*, and from 1950 on I missed few major East Coast ocean races.

Palawan, incidentally, is the name of a beautiful atoll of palms and white sand just south of the Philippines where I spent five memorable days just before the end of WWII. I decided then that if I were ever to own a boat, I would name her for this delightful island. Furthermore, it's good luck for a boat to have seven letters in her name. For this and other reasons all of our boats have been named *Palawan*, and all have been happy ships.

During the next 20 years, I raced the first three *Palawans* extensively; there's no better way to learn the sea. We raced up and down Long Island Sound, to Bermuda and Annapolis, in the Buenos Aires-Rio Race in 1968, in two transatlantics (to Marstrand, Sweden, in 1960, and to Copenhagen, Denmark, in 1966), and in the Fastnet and the Admiral's Cup Series at Cowes, England, as part of the American team in l969. Between 1966 and 1970, *Palawan III* started in 37 races and placed either first, second, or third 22 times. Then, suddenly, in the fall of 1970, this strenuous, pleasurable activity came to a halt.

I had a heart attack.

The doctors told me that there was no apparent physical reason for my illness and that the best way to avoid a recurrence would be to slow down my business activities. IBM, the company of which I was chairman, had never been more prosperous, the management team was excellent, and I saw no reason not to step down before the company's mandatory officer retirement age of 60. Certainly the prospect of unlimited time to enjoy my family, to do some work in the not-for-profit world and perhaps sail to faroff places, was very appealing. I decided to do it, and immediately felt that a great weight had lifted from my chest. Thirteen years of following a dynamic and successful father as chairman of IBM had been a greater strain than I had realized.

With the triumphs and regrets of business life now behind me, I wanted to make the most of the carefree days ahead. It was time for the dreams inspired by Slocum's book and others to become realities; it was time to make those leisurely cruises to out-of-the-way places. During my recuperation, I did a lot of reading with that in mind, and, in particular, became fascinated with the journals of Captain James Cook. In one I was amused to find a comment I could almost have written myself. It was in Cook's letter to a friend upon being retired to a desk job after a decade of roaming the seas:

"My fate drives me from one extreme to another. Months ago the whole southern hemisphere was hardly big enough for me, and now I am going to be confined within the limits of Greenwich Hospital, which are far too small for an active mind like mine. I must confess it is a fine retreat and a pretty income, but whether I can bring myself to like ease and retirement, time will shew." Less than a year after Cook penned this complaint, he obtained the command of two ships and was off on his third and last great sea adventure. Well, I thought, if James Cook could fight his way out of the doldrums of impending retirement and take to the sea again, so could I.

During the previous several years, I had also developed an interest in prehistory and in an archaeological process called carbon-dating, which, for example, has permitted dating Indian artifacts found near my summer home in North Haven, Maine, back to 5,000 B.C. Formerly, Maine Indians were believed to have arrived in 1,000 A.D. The carbon-dating technique has also been used extensively to study another fascinating race — the ancient Polynesians who first peopled the Pacific islands, navigating their canoes thousands of miles across a great ocean triangle a good many centuries before European navigators dared to sail out of sight of land.

As I lay in my hospital bed, I began to envision a voyage that would not only retrace the paths of the Europeans — principally Cook — across the Pacific, but would also allow me to visit and study the places where its earliest inhabitants settled and created a lasting oceanic culture. At first, my plan was to sail around Cape Horn, leaving the Pacific and the Polynesians for later. When my 20-year-old daughter, Helen, pleasantly surprised me by asking if she might come along, she persuaded me that we would both enjoy a leisurely sail from the Panama Canal through the Pacific islands much more than a rough passage through cold and rainy Patagonia. She was astute enough to realize that while rounding the Horn might be a great accomplishment for an

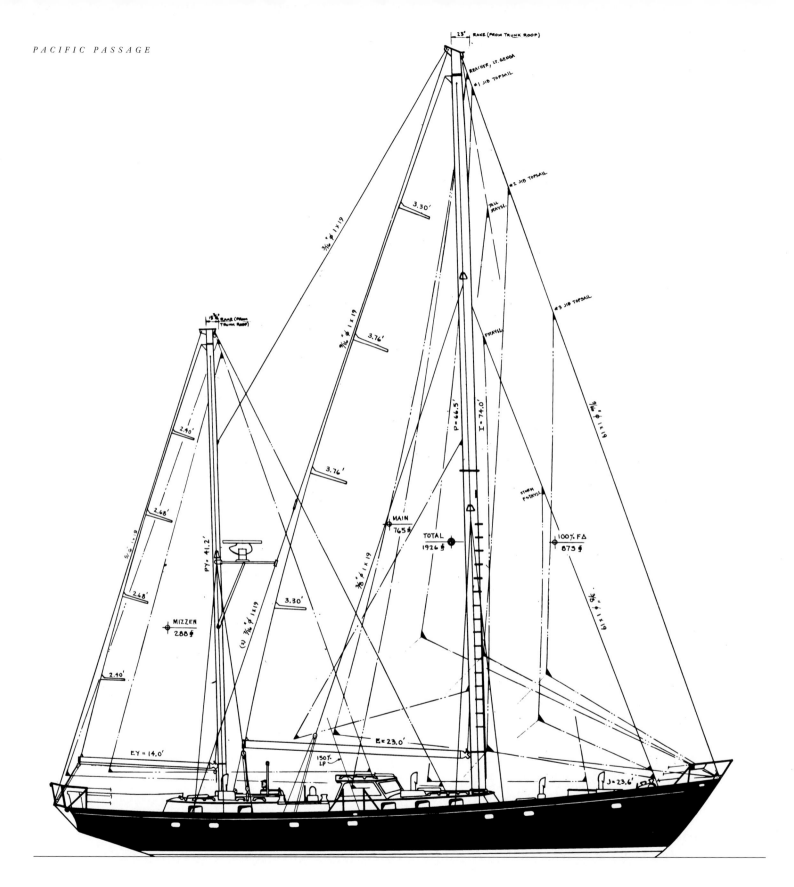

Our fourth Palawan *was built in 1972 for distance cruising with ample comfort, capacity, and self-sufficiency at sea. She logged 60,000 miles during our seven years with her.*

LOA: 67' 6"
LWL: 50' 6"
Beam: 17' 6"
Draft: 6' 8" (centerboard up)
Displacement: 98,000 pounds
Sail Area: 1926 square feet

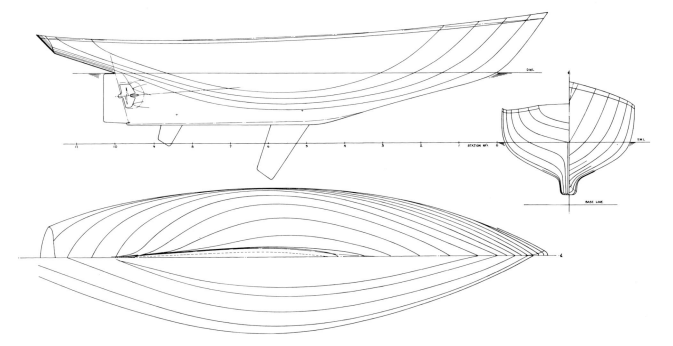

ambitious sailor, it might be simply uncomfortable for the less-dedicated such as herself and others aboard. She was so persuasive that it was easy to accept her suggestion.

Before leaving the hospital, I had given a lot of thought to a new boat and had blocked out the basic lines of a comfortable long-range cruiser with Olin Stephens of Sparkman & Stephens, who had designed my three previous *Palawans*. Finally, in March 1971 I gave the building contract to Abeking and Rasmussen of Bremen, West Germany. While awaiting the new boat, and to make sure I was choosing the right leisure activity for my retirement years, I sailed *Palawan III* — the boat I had raced for the past five years — around Newfoundland. This voyage was a two-fold success. I found that I was physically fit to handle a boat and that I enjoyed cruising as much as, or more than, ocean racing.

My ideas for *Palawan IV* were specific. In keeping with my plans to travel to distant places with minimal and sometimes inexperienced crew, the boat had to have an easily handled rig. She had to be roomy enough to accommodate seven or eight people in comfort; she had to be capable of operating far from civilization for long periods of time and to cruise long distances

under power. She also had to be sturdy enough to take whatever punishment any ocean might have to offer. In the Pacific we were bound to encounter long, windless stretches; but we needed a seaworthy design for the inevitable storms one encounters from time to time.

She also had to be a boat that Paul Wolter, our professional since 1958, was comfortable with. As he had with the completion of *Palawan II* and the supervision of the construction of *Palawan III*, Paul played a large part in the development of *Palawan IV*. As the plans progressed, his experience and advice were invaluable, specifically in calling my attention to the importance of using mock-ups to test design ideas. For instance, when we had looked at the plans for the galley of the 58-foot racing *Palawan*, standing space seemed confined and Paul felt a slight angle of heel would throw the cook onto the stove. So we made a full-sized mock-up of the galley area, and tilting it showed that he was absolutely right. To have built it as originally planned would have been a disaster. This experience led us to a decision to mock up the entire vessel. Where we found it impractical to mock up a whole section, we modeled a half or a quarter of it, tilted it 30 degrees

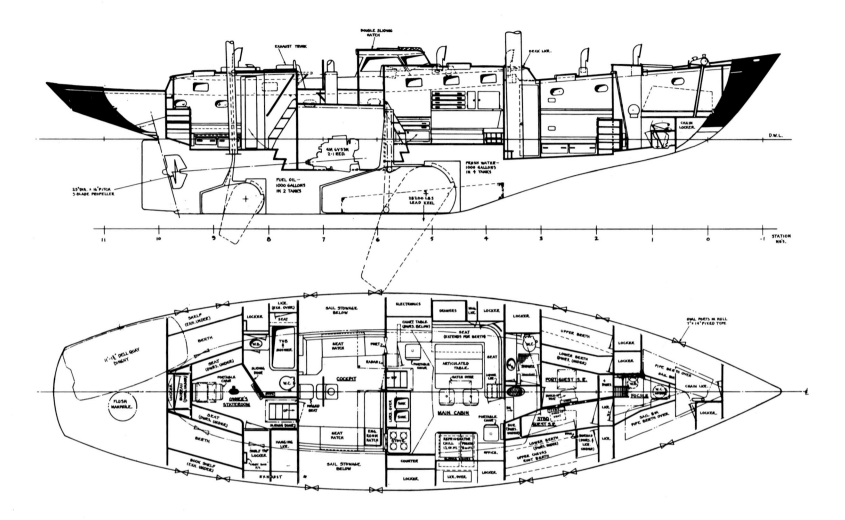

in each direction and each time simulated working, moving around, and trying the bunks in the various sections. When building *Palawan IV* this procedure, which took place in my garage during the winter months following my release from the hospital, saved many dollars in construction time and error and contributed greatly to our comfort and safety at sea.

The resulting boat, completed in 1972, was a centerboard ketch of slightly over 50 tons, built of aluminum with a teak deck. Her dimensions were 68 feet length overall, 18 feet beam, and 7 feet draft with the board up, 11 feet with the board down. She accommodated seven comfortably in three cabins with two heads and a fo'c'sle toilet. She carried 1,926 square feet of sail in jib, main, and mizzen, which would provide a good turn of speed

under full sail in anything over a 10-knot breeze, while her split rig would enable a variety of sail combinations to suit crew and conditions and facilitate shortening sail if necessary. With a 170-horsepower engine and a 1,000-gallon fuel capacity, she could, if needed, power 1,300 miles, and the 1,000-gallon water capacity meant that we could supply eight people with two gallons of water a day for two months at a stretch.

All of my boats except the first two have had a center-cockpit layout. The pluses are obvious: it permits more usable space in the stern than does a conventional design and enables a large, comfortable owner's cabin aft. It also permits putting the engine in an easily accessible area under the cockpit floor, leaving space on either side for the galley, head, navigation station, or stowage.

A disadvantage is that it puts the crew somewhat more forward in the way of spray and wind. Over the years we have found that we can see the sails just as well from this position, and when hard on the wind the helmsman usually sits to leeward in order to see the jib adequately. A center cockpit does present some problems of forward visibility, but since I was now cruising rather than racing and did not need the larger sail area of a genoa, I usually used a double-head rig with high-cut (smaller) yankee jib-top-sails in order to have a clear view of both sides of the bow.

The boat had a partial deckhouse covering half the cockpit — quite low to keep her from looking like a motorsailer, but high enough for two people to sit out of the weather on either side. From the cockpit, the main companionway, with its sturdy rails, descended to the cabin, where two vertical stanchions and many handholds along the overhead below decks kept one from being thrown around when moving about in a seaway. Right under the companionway was a large stowage area for foul weather gear.

A particularly nice feature below decks was the interior finish, which was absolutely beautiful. The panelling was teak that had been rubbed to a rich satin finish, producing a warm, cozy feeling. Whether one came below from tropical sun or from sun reflected by ice fields, the dark interior was soothing and restful.

Beneath the cabin sole, Sparkman & Stephens had contrived an ingenious stowage area about three feet deep above the fuel and water tanks. It was accessible by lifting the floorboards. We called this area "the cellar," and in it in labeled boxes we stowed anything that was not needed on a daily basis: spare parts, boxes of canned goods, soft drinks, sails, and other gear. It was an enormous space, and although we had a huge supply of provisions and extra gear, we never managed to fill it.

The design of *Palawan IV* had the added safety feature of water-tight compartments. The boat was divided into three sections: a watertight compartment at the end of the fo'c'sle, another at the forward end of the engine room, and another aft of the engine.

According to what I had read, during the February-September period in the central Pacific there was little possibility of encountering any weather more threatening than a light rain shower or two en route. At that time of year, a hardy soul with a little luck could cross the Pacific between 20 degrees north and 20 south in a decked-over canoe — as Captain Voss did in *Tilikum*. And it's well-established that thousands of Polynesians in open canoes had roamed that ocean since before the time of Christ.

But the sea is unpredictable. More than 95 percent of the time I've spent on the ocean has been safe and pleasant; it was the other five percent that haunted me as we readied the boat for the Pacific. Those few hours of terror in 45 years of sailing kept me awake more than a few nights as I contemplated taking eight people — three of whom had never sailed before — into the world's largest ocean.

The first of these terrifying moments occurred when I was 21, cruising the Nova Scotia coast in my father's 65-foot schooner, *Poseidon*. We were about 50 miles off Halifax one brisk night when I awoke with the distinct feeling that we had slowed down and were riding lower. Frantically pulling up the floorboards, we found the bilges full of cold Canadian water. It took us an hour while furiously pumping to locate the broken scupper pipe that was intermittently letting a two-inch stream into the hull. We quickly plugged the hole, congratulating ourselves on saving the boat, and never spoke of the terror that I know gripped us all. The incident has been memorialized on every boat I've been in charge of since. I post a diagram of the location of every through-hull fitting (intakes and outlets) in several locations below decks to enable one to locate a leak quickly. I also carry a small hand ax to chop through the interior wood — the ceiling as the boat-builders call it — to locate a hole between the ceiling and the hull.

My second encounter with fear at sea came in 1953, during a cruise from Maine to New York. With Hurricane Carol reported coming closer and closer, we hurried across Massachusetts Bay, entered Nantucket Sound, and then pushed on to Martha's Vineyard. Once there, we realized that the storm would reach us by noon the next day. How could we protect *Palawan* from the predicted 100-knot winds? With great luck we were able to pick up a mooring with a rode of heavy line, indicating that the anchor or cement block on the bottom was substantial. As a backup we set our heaviest anchor to windward, and spent the evening double-tying the mainsail stops and stowing all loose gear and lines below.

Early the next morning my wife and children moved ashore and a friend and I remained on board, working out a strategy for survival. Soon the wind began to pick up and in a few hours we had a raging hurricane on our hands. During the day the winds gusted to well over 100 knots. But there was no time to let terror get the better of us. We were too busy running the engine to ease pressure on the mooring line and anchor, renewing chafing gear on the anchor rode, and maneuvering under engine to slue the boat sideways out of the paths of other boats as they broke loose from their moorings and charged by. Reluctantly, we had to refuse to help others, for if we had passed anyone a line we would have destroyed our own chances for survival.

Ironically, we almost lost *Palawan* near the end of the storm. Leaves blown into the harbor had found their way into the cooling system intake, making it impossible to keep the engine running. By this time, however, the wind was diminishing and we could do without the engine. When it was all over, only seven of the fifty-odd vessels that had been anchored in the harbor the night before remained afloat.

Another frightening experience, and a night of which I am not particularly proud, came during the 1964 Bermuda Race. We were about 100 miles off Bermuda when the wind began to blow, finally reaching about 70 knots. I was horribly seasick, and as it blew harder, I found it increasingly difficult to face the wildness of the deck. Consequently, I spent a good portion of that night lying at the foot of the companionway, embarrassed but too sick or scared to move.

Two years earlier we went through a brief hurricane returning from the Bermuda Race with two of my children and several friends aboard. We had cleared St. George's Channel in the morning and by nightfall were about 60 miles off the islands, when Bermuda Harbor radio began forecasting strong winds in our area. We battened things down for a rough night, and the wind, blowing at about Force Six by midnight, had increased to a full gale by dawn. By noon it was gusting to well over 70 knots.

The crew was below except for our professional, my son Tom, and myself, and we had our hands full. We had moved progressively down to a reefed mainsail, storm jib, no mainsail, then no sail at all, and finally we began to prepare for a full hurricane. We had oil ready in one of the heads to pump overboard if necessary to calm the seas, and running before the gale with bare poles, we trailed astern two long loops of rope, which were secured on opposite sides of our taffrail. These helped greatly to slow the boat and quiet the seas, so that the cockpit filled less frequently. But to carry the ropes from the foredeck, where they were stored, to the stern was a major task. I found I couldn't stand against the wind, but had to crawl forward slowly, snapping and resnapping my safety harness as I went. The roar of the wind was monstrous, and the only way to communicate with anyone else on deck was by hand signal.

Had I been sailing with an experienced crew, the episode wouldn't have been particularly frightening, but seeing the horrified looks on the faces below — where seven people had nothing to do but listen to the machine-gun hammering of halyards on the mast — dramatically heightened my awareness of the danger. The thought that these people were totally depending on three of us for survival was sobering. However, by late afternoon the wind had died down, by midnight the seas had moderated, and by the next morning, as we all ate a huge breakfast, the memory of the storm was fading.

If the chances of running into a storm at sea were any greater, I probably would have chosen a different hobby. But a good bout with the elements every few years has added some thrills to my life and taught me much about dealing with emergencies and emotion. Certainly a busy, relatively organized businessman could face no greater test of tolerance than to confront the inside of a tossing yacht during a major storm, as this log notation makes clear:

The cabin is constantly in motion — rising, falling, rolling; the floor is wet, cushions on the settees are wet; foul-weather gear, sou'wester hats and boots tangle with dirty wet blankets in a corner along with crumbled saltines, a spoon or two, spilled pea soup, and a pair of parallel rules. The air stinks of bacon grease, coffee dregs and vomit. In the sink there's a grease-encrusted frying pan and several stained coffee cups. Beneath them, used paper towels and more smell. In the heads, toilet articles have fallen from lockers and rattle around on the floor. Crew or passengers who stumbled in to use the facilities have not taken careful aim, with resulting odor and stains. Salt spray has worked its way down through the ventilators, soaking towels and toilet paper and making the floor slippery. Even the heartiest seagoing stomachs have now given in to seasickness; no one has the energy to clean up the mess. Everything just sits.

Above, Palawan's navigation area at the foot of the companionway; at left, the galley to starboard of the nav station; at right, one of the two berths in the owner's cabin.

Given 48 hours of sun and calm, the mess will disappear, and the storm that has so recently shattered crew morale will become something to joke and reminisce about later. But while it's raging, it's feared by the knowledgeable hands aboard who remember tales of the victims of other storms.

Years ago, for instance, Miles and Beryl Smeeton pitch-poled (end-for-end) in their 50-foot *Tzu-Hang* near Cape Horn, narrowly escaping death, only to repeat the horrifying experience in the same area a few years later, again escaping. In the summer of 1976, a well-equipped ocean-racer returning from Hawaii was rolled through 360 degrees and dismasted by a rogue wave. The crew survived only by summoning Coast Guard help on a jury-rigged ham radio. Other such stories abound.

A responsible sailor is always alert at sea. Even when sitting on deck sipping iced tea in the afternoon, he knows that, if it decides to, in three short hours or less, the sea can take you from sunburn to chilblains and from heaven to hell.

Palawan IV was delivered at Bergen, Norway, in June l971. Our shakedown was a family cruise to show daughter Helen and some friends the beauties of Scandinavia, as we had done for our other children in 1958. Later, I invited most of my old racing crew to cruise from Cowes to Lisbon, where *Palawan* spent the fall. The boat was brought home via the Caribbean, to Camden, Maine, in the spring of 1972. The following spring she set off on her first major adventure, sailing up the west coast of Greenland and far beyond the Arctic Circle, a storied cruise in itself. Finally, after a year of less-eventful cruising in Maine, we began in earnest to plan the Pacific voyage, and I started to assemble a crew.

Before setting out on a voyage I try to read as many books as possible written by those who have sailed the same area, and to consult personally with those who have done so in recent years. One man who knew a great deal about both sailing and the Pacific was my old friend Robin Balfour, Lord Riverdale, of Sheffield, England. A businessman of note and a former commodore of the Royal Cruising Club of Great Britain, this remarkable 75-year-old had crossed the Pacific twice and received his country's highest cruising awards for his voyages.

Early in the fall of 1975, I journeyed to England to visit with him, and when I arrived at his modest, comfortable home in Sheffield, I found that he had thoughtfully prepared a complete agenda, along with some slides from his cruise to Fiji and beyond in 1968. To my surprise, instead of sitting down to begin our discussion, he asked whether I would first care to take a walk on the moors. What a walk it was! For over an hour Robin and his wife Christian led me up hill and down dale at a vigorous pace through brush, over stone walls, and along muddy paths, hardly letting me stop to admire the view when the clouds lifted enough to see across the valley. I was puzzled by this breathless episode, but soon forgot about it in my absorption with his ensuing presentation.

Upon returning to the house, we sat for five hours — with a pause for lunch — while Robin told me everything he knew about navigating the Pacific, offered advice on what supplies to take and what weather conditions to expect, and made suggestions about sightseeing. We should avoid the Marquesas Islands, he said, because they are somewhat upwind of our track and therefore hard to reach from the Tuamotus, and also because the demoralization and poverty there outweighed the beauty and tranquility of the countryside. We should be careful not to bring cockroaches on board with supplies because they could easily infest the ship. We should expect sharks everywhere, he added, but need not worry much about them within the lagoons, where they would not attack without provocation. He also gave me tips on how to enter unmarked passages through coral reefs, how to catch fish, what to take for trading with the islanders, and how to protect camera equipment from the high humidity.

I was overwhelmed by his knowledge and the effort he had made to help me. Then he took me aside at lunch while Christian was in the kitchen and said, in a low, conspiratorial tone, "I say, Tom, do you suppose there'd be a berth on that vessel for me?" I realized then the purpose of that fast walk on the moor: my plans had stirred up his desires to go voyaging again, and the sly old fox had been trying to show me that he still had enough stamina to handle anything that a voyage across the Pacific might produce. The idea took me completely by surprise, so at first I was noncommittal. "You know, if I came with you, you'd have to make it sound as though I was vital to the voyage, or I'd never be able to convince Christian that I should go," he added. I promised that if we decided to ask him along, I'd write him a letter indicating that his presence on board was a necessity.

I thought about the matter a great deal and finally decided

that Robin would be an ideal addition to the crew. Despite his age, he was obviously in fine health and spirits. An amiable fellow with an imposing build, a pug nose, and a face like John Bull himself, he was a man for all seasons — sailor, hunter, raconteur, and manager of a steel company. He was well-educated and highly articulate. I could easily imagine him keeping everyone entertained around the cabin table during long sea passages.

Throughout the voyage, I never regretted having asked Robin to join us. There were times when he was a bit difficult, as we all are occasionally. I sometimes felt he was too quick at second-guessing me with advice as I was about to execute a maneuver of the ship, and his stories about the adventures of his boat *Bluebird of Thorne* were numerous. But I have wonderful memories of him. He shared the aftercabin with me, and, lying in our bunks, we sometimes talked about fathers. It was obvious that both of us had been greatly influenced by our dads.

Robin was an amazing man aboard: always full of information, punctual and enthusiastic, and, as he later wrote in an article for the British Cruising Club, his age difference made him a kind of catalyst for the rest of the crew.

In late January 1976, when our crew of eight assembled at the Panama Canal to join the boat, it consisted of myself; Robin Balfour; my old sailing companion Jimmy Madden and his daughter Anne; Paul Wolter and his young assistant David Flanagan from Camden, Maine; Carter Christensen — a friend of Helen's from Greenwich; and Eleanor Lazarus, a young woman from Cincinnati who had been with us on other cruises. Daughter Helen would join us at Easter Island.

All of us had been reading about the Europeans who first explored the Pacific, and despite the bustle of the send-off party and customs run-through, we could not help but think of Vasco Núñez de Balboa, the Spanish explorer who founded a colony on the isthmus and trekked for weeks over the mountains of Panama, intrigued by tales of a vast sea that might provide a western route to the Indies. Finally, on 25 September 1513, as John Keats wrote (mistaking Cortez for Balboa), he

> *star'd at the Pacific — and all his men*
> *Look'd at each other with a wild surmise*
> *Silent, upon a peak in Darien.*

Although Balboa later lost favor with the Spanish royalty and was eventually executed on trumped-up charges of treason, his discovery opened the way for generations of adventurers, who roamed the new ocean in search of unknown lands and trade routes. First came Fernando Magellan, who discovered a twisting strait through the tip of South America in 1520 and became the first European to lead an expedition that circled the globe. Although Magellan was killed before the expedition reached its conclusion, it was he who named the vast western ocean the "Peaceful Sea." Then came the Dutchmen: Jakob Le Maire and Willem Cornelis Schouten, who set out in 1615 to challenge the Dutch East India Company's empire by approaching Indonesia from the Pacific, becoming the first to round Cape Horn; Abel Tasman, who found New Zealand in 1642; and Jacob Roggeveen, who discovered Easter Island in 1722. A century of exploration by French and British navigators followed: Sir Francis Drake circled the world again in 1577; Frenchmen Louis Antoine de Bougainville and John de la Perouse explored many islands between 1766 and 1788; and Samuel Wallis discovered Tahiti in 1767.

This era of sea adventurers was finally capped by the three world voyages of Captain James Cook, a stern humanitarian who both conquered scurvy and charted many Polynesian islands and the coasts of New Zealand and Australia. He sailed south until he encountered ice at three different places, thereby setting to rest the popular theory of a huge habitable "southern continent." Captain Cook's explorations ended when he was killed by Hawaiian natives in 1779. To my mind, Cook was the greatest naval commander in history. Despite the crudeness of eighteenth-century wooden ships and the lack of repair facilities, the extent of his voyaging was prodigious even by today's standards. He rarely lost a man, and the high reenlistment rate among his crews testified to his abilities as a leader.

Although our well-built and well-provisioned ketch would experience few of the hardships these early explorers had faced, we were nonetheless apprehensive as we set out from Panama on the afternoon of 28 January 1976 to cross a basin that covered one-third of the world's surface. As we looked at our charts, I think everyone wondered whether we would actually be in Suva, Fiji, on the fifteenth of June, as planned. I know I did.

PLANNING:

Crew, Equipment, and Stores

During the year preceding our departure, not a day went by when I was not attending to some detail of planning for the voyage, and I often awoke at night to jot down reminders. I made hundreds of notes concerning charts, navigation gear of all kinds, port procedures, tools, crew, emergency equipment, food, medical supplies, safety equipment, and myriad other items. Reading continually about the places we planned to go, I gathered advice about dangers that might await us, sightseeing areas, and special items to bring other than necessities, such as jewelry to trade, and Frisbies, suggested by daughter Susan, which were tremendous hits. All of this and more I recorded in a Cruise Preparation Notebook divided into appropriate categories. Eventually, as our departure date neared, I prepared Crew Bulletins based on the information I had gathered, and sent a copy to each crew member.

In general, the Bulletins discussed details of the voyage: the route, the expected dates of departure and arrival, the crew that would rendezvous at Panama, and how they — and the boat — would get there. I stressed the necessity for "packing light," in a medium-sized duffle and one slender hanging bag, all personal gear or medicines needed, and I asked the crew to have any shots deemed necessary by their personal physicians. I also wanted information on any medical frailties or diet needs that I ought to know about as skipper, and I indicated the need for sun protection in clothing, hats, and lotions in the South Seas climate. The Bulletins described communications en route, mail drops along the way, and other information that families at home might wish to have handy during our long absence.

One of my own most important responsibilities was to see that we had aboard the most up-to-date Pilot Charts available from the U.S. Hydrographic Office. Of prime importance for long-distance cruising, Pilot Charts were first compiled in the late 1840s by Matthew Fontaine Maury, an American naval officer and hydrographer, who spent years collecting data about the world's oceans and published the first textbook on oceanography. Now updated and issued every month, these surprisingly accurate charts show the general conditions to be expected — currents, winds, percentage of storms and storm tracks, water and air temperature, icebergs — for all the oceans of the globe.

They are the cruising sailor's bible.

I spent several evenings going over the Pacific editions of these charts and concluded that as long as we reached Tahiti after March fifteenth, and returned to Panama before November, we would probably encounter the best weather that could be expected in the course of a 20,000-mile sail anywhere in the world. There would be doldrums, or very light breezes, from the Canal to the Galapagos Islands; a brisk and dependable southeast trade wind from there to the Gambiers; less dependable winds up through the Tuamotus to Tahiti; and a mixed bag west to Fiji.

Although the charts indicated that the winds would rarely blow more than 30 knots, this did not rule out the possibility of a heavy Pacific storm any time of year, and we made detailed preparations for this danger. But the favorable odds against our encountering a real storm helped reassure me about the prospect of putting to sea with a crew of four relatively inexperienced young women, four men over 50, and only one strong and experienced young hand.

For navigating within various island groups, I knew that the most up-to-date coverage would come from charts prepared by the country that had owned or governed each area for the longest time. So I sent to England for charts of the Galapagos and Easter Island, to France for charts of the Gambiers, Tuamotus, and Tahiti, and to England and New Zealand for those of the Cooks, Samoa, Tonga, and Fiji.

Our navigational equipment was also chosen carefully and included depth sounder, Decca radar, and single-sideband (SSB) radio. There were a number of radio aids on our track, but for the most part they were aeronautical and we could not rely on our *Radio Aids Book* for information about them. We knew that Loran would be useless in the Pacific because there was no signal transmission, but our Decca 101 radar was to prove extremely valuable in piloting near shore. Mounted high on the mizzenmast, it could pick up traces of land at 18 miles, and we eventually discovered that it would even pick up the sea breaking on offshore reefs at a range of a mile or two.

Although the ship carried two eight-man life rafts and 20-day emergency food and water supplies for each, we knew we would have little chance of being rescued in the lonelier reaches of the Pacific unless we could report our position immediately and reasonably accurately. Strongly affected by the sun, SSB works well at very long range only a few hours each day, but it was comforting to know that in an emergency, unless we sank very fast, we could probably reach KMI Oakland (California) from anywhere on our route. As a backup, I arranged to report to my office in New York our position just before leaving each island, and our estimated time of arrival at the next.

Crew safety was an area of heavy responsibility. In 40 years of ocean sailing I had learned some of the mishaps that can occur at sea, and many of the safety innovations added to *Palawan IV* were developed to prevent them ever happening to me again on *Palawan*.

I especially feared losing a crew member overboard through a careless misstep, an unexpected ship movement catching someone off balance, or a large wave sweeping the cockpit in a storm. I was haunted by memories of an incident that occurred several decades ago during a transatlantic race, in which an experienced owner/skipper was sitting on the cabin top enjoying an after-breakfast cigarette when a lurch of the ship threw him into the sea. One of his sons jumped in immediately to help him and the other launched a dinghy to row after the two men in the water. This left the ship manned by an inexperienced crew, and in their haste to jibe and return for a rescue, they broke the main boom, preventing them from getting the boat under control in time to help the men in the water. The boat was eventually brought back to port under jury rig, but all three men in the water drowned.

In a more recent mishap much closer to home, a crewman on *Palawan II* fell overboard one night during a race on Long Island Sound. The spinnaker had collapsed momentarily, and as it filled again the navigator, who was standing between the rail and sheet, was knocked overboard by the sheet as it became taut. Fortunately, he was picked up unhurt after some 30 minutes in the water. Although I was not on board at the time, I have never forgotten the incident.

Mindful of such disasters, we worked out a variety of safety methods to insure that no similar accidents would befall anyone on the Pacific cruise. First, we established a firm rule that the night watch stay in the cockpit at all times unless ordered by the watch captain to move around on deck. Everyone had to wear a safety belt clipped to a strong part of the ship while on deck at night.

In this center-cockpit boat, the long distance to the stern made it difficult to reach and throw a life ring overboard promptly. Therefore, our safety equipment included a device that I had first used on the previous *Palawan*. Long tubes were welded into each side of the stern, inside of which were emergency buoys with 10-foot plastic masts, each topped with a large red flag. The buoys were hooked in turn to life rings fastened to the taffrail in welded stainless rod cages, which also contained whistles, dye markers, and strobe lights. The entire contraption was rigged so that if someone went overboard, the helmsman or anyone in the cockpit could pull a nearby cord to release the life ring, pull the buoy out of its tube, and activate the light. Without the light, it would be almost impossible to locate anyone in the water at night.

Another incident that taught me a lesson happened one squally night off the New Jersey coast during the Newport-to-Annapolis Race. We were on a port tack when suddenly we saw the red light of a yacht on starboard tack very close at hand on a collision course. Since she had the right of way, I shouted, "Ready about" and put the wheel down hard, only to have a winch override jam the genoa sheet, making it impossible to release it. After a few tense moments, we were able to clear the stern of the right-of-way yacht, but it took us 20 precious minutes to straighten out the problems on deck. From then on I've always made sure that there are sharp knives in scabbards taped prominently at the base of the mainmast and in the cockpit, ready for instant use to cut a jammed or fouled line.

Also in the interest of safety we carried four anchors in total: our normal C.Q.R. 100-pound anchor attached to 300 feet of chain; a backup yachtsman anchor of about the same weight folded in the bilge; a plow anchor weighing about 75 pounds; a 50-pound Danforth; and, of course, rodes and 30-foot chain leads for each.

While we had an ample tool supply, we did not carry out-of-the-ordinary heavy tools. However, I did make sure to carry a banding mechanism, which we had used in the past to apply half-round pieces of aluminum to mend broken spars. This is a very useful emergency repair device.

To be certain that I hadn't overlooked a safety detail when planning for the Pacific, I spent days aboard *Palawan IV*, looking her over and trying to imagine how various emergencies might arise and how we would cope with them. Beginning at the bow, I checked the plow anchor and chain. The anchor was held in place by a pair of stainless steel chocks that guided the chain into an electric windlass. When the anchor shank was seated on the bow with the plow extending overboard, it was all very neat. But I failed to consider what would happen if the bow were driven underwater at 10 knots, and whether the guard was heavy enough to hold the anchor in place against that tremendous force. Later, I found out. One rough night during the Pacific cruise, the anchor bent the chocks and the first stanchion as it was carried aft by a heavy sea. Only quick crew work prevented the dangling anchor from tearing a hole in the bow. Another lesson learned.

Checking the rigging, I considered what the consequences would be if the headstay broke. We carried extra 3/8-inch galvanized wire and a method of bolting this wire into breaks in our rigging, but we were inexperienced in doing this. To guard against headstay failure, I would have to make sure the intermediate stay and companion runner were always set up and hope this would be enough to save the mast. I examined the turnbuckles for cracks or other signs of wear, the wire rigging for hooks or breaks, and the winches and cleats to make sure they were strong enough.

The hull was a very strong monocoque construction — the aluminum forming the sides was carried across the entire deck — but there were still weak spots. Standing in the cockpit, I could imagine a towering wave astern driving full force against the sliding panels that close the companionways, and I decided to have screw-on aluminum plates ready to install to strengthen both those areas in heavy weather.

The after end of the deck was not as safe as I would have liked, but there was no other way to organize it. The two rigid dinghies had to be fitted into each other and lashed to the deck, and during the voyage the bottom dinghy became the inevitable repository of much extra deck gear. In a very severe storm I planned to throw both dinghies overboard, if they weren't swept off first by a breaking wave. Forward of them, a barrel containing one of our three inflatable life rafts was located in an accessible but vulnerable position.

During the three years that the boat had been at sea, we had installed several additional stanchions and handholds on deck to which lines could be hooked to secure crew to the ship. We had also added handholds and footholds below, so that now we could move about on deck and below, well-supported in all conditions.

Also of top priority for our well-being at sea were our medical supplies. The two biggest health hazards on board were Jimmy, with an irregular heartbeat, and me, five years past my heart attack, but we were well supplied with the appropriate medications for each of us should the need arise. We also had to be prepared to treat coral cuts, bruises, heat rashes, sprains, and Man-o'-War stings as well as major problems such as acute appendicitis (massive doses of antibiotics) or a compound fracture.

I had consulted several doctors who helped me compile a medical supplies list that included everything from aspirin to scalpels. We had morphine and Demerol to cope with extreme pain and a substantial quantity of ampicillin, an antibiotic for infection. For coral infections we were advised to take a supply of Gentian Violet, and we were well equipped to contend with tropical sores, fevers, lack of salt, and heat prostration, should the need arise. Although none of us was prepared to perform an operation on the cabin table, we did have surgical equipment for setting broken bones and taking stitches. However, if someone had an attack of appendicitis, or gall or kidney stones, we planned to use massive doses of ampicillin, ice bags, and morphine to keep the pain tolerable, the diesel engine to get us to port as quickly as possible, and the SSB to solicit advice; in extremis, we would resort to the ship's *Bible*.

In the past, I have coped with a few medical emergencies — torn hands, bruised eyes, and the like. Fortunately, during the Pacific voyage we encountered nothing more serious than a few scrapes, a twisted ankle, the skin rashes and infections the women developed in the very humid weather, and a persistent carbuncle on Carter's foot.

While reading Captain Cook's journals, I was thankful that, although many of the health hazards of sea voyages of his day remained the same today, we had more convenient remedies than he had. In particular, I was grateful that we did not have to cope with scurvy, which we now know is caused by a lack of Vitamin C.

In Cook's time this disease took more sailors' lives than any other single cause. Luckily for those who sailed with the enterprising captain, he was very curious about scurvy and determined to wipe it out on his ships. Suspecting that the disease was caused by a lack of fresh food, he experimented with various preventives, forcing his crews to consume sometimes distasteful potions of malt, vinegar, carrot marmalade, or lime juice. He also developed something called "portable soup," a distillate of dried vegetables boiled in water, which he insisted his men eat. As a last resort, he insisted they eat grass soup, for which he sent his men ashore to collect island grasses.

Cook's methods and odd menus were not always popular with the meat-and-potatoes seamen, but he applied typical ingenuity to this problem, particularly in getting them to eat sauerkraut. As he told it, "The men at first would not eat it until I put in practice a method I never once knew to fail with seamen, and this was to have some of it dress'd every day for the Cabbin table, permitting all the Officers without exception to make use of it." Soon the crew was howling at this undemocratic treatment and clamoring for their fair share of the "sour krout." The result of Cook's persistence was that his ships lost almost no men to scurvy, although it was still a serious problem on all other ships of the Royal Navy. It was to be another 100 years before an antiscorbutic diet became a part of the published orders of the British Navy.

Now, as then, shipboard morale is directly affected by the quality of the provisions on board and the way they are prepared. "Fate cannot touch me today; I have eaten well," was a favorite saying of Major Tilman, a renowned mountain climber and long-distance sailor, and over my years of ocean racing the habit of careful provisioning has become well-ingrained in me. In building *Palawan IV* for long cruises, I made sure there was ample storage space for dry, refrigerated, and frozen foods.

Almost all the dry provisions were stored in the "cellar." Items used frequently, such as dried soup, were kept in plastic bins in part of the cellar near the refrigerator-freezer. The rest were placed in compartments, and their locations were recorded in a notebook. As each item was used, it was checked off so that when we had to restock we would know what we needed.

Planning provisions for eight people for six months on board may seem a staggering task, but years ago Paul Hammond, a fine ocean-racing sailor and teacher, gave me the menus and matching order lists he had developed for long races. I have gradually refined them until, now, although we eat very well, cooking aboard *Palawan* is a relatively simple routine. With a crew of eight, galley duty rotates among the crew and we assign a cook and a dishwasher for each meal; by the time you've prepared a meal for eight at sea, you're usually exhausted.

When provisioning for the Pacific voyage, I took the order list for a one-month race and multiplied by six, keeping the meals simple but varied. Breakfast might consist of bacon and eggs; lunch, pea soup and ham sandwiches; and dinner, roast beef or spaghetti with canned green beans and cake. The menus described exactly how to make each meal, which had been made dozens of times before with the same utensils on the same stove. However, you'd be surprised at the individual touches that are added to a particular menu by different cooks. We carried numerous herbs and sauces to encourage originality, usually with good results. Generally, a rivalry builds up so that everybody strives to produce meals that are tasty and neatly served.

Also, over the years one learns a few tricks that make galley duty easier. We've discovered that eggs keep a long time in cool storage, but egg powder works almost as well and is less messy to handle. Instead of fresh butter, we carried two 2 1/2-gallon drums of margarine — when crumbs gathered on the top layer, we scraped them off carefully and chilled the margarine to be used, which tasted like fresh butter.

Eventually, everyone contributed to our lore of galley hints, especially Paul Wolter, who devised a method of baking bread in a pressure cooker. I don't know the details, but he follows a very simple recipe that calls for mixing the yeast with flour and salt water, and halfway through the baking he turns the bread over in the cooker so that it browns evenly. It smells and tastes delicious, and we were never without bread on *Palawan* no matter how far or long offshore.

With order lists in hand, we bought all our dry stores in Camden, Maine. En route among the islands, we were able to buy fresh fruits in open-air markets, and our supplies were further supplemented when my sister Helen brought 100 pounds of vegetables with her when she flew from Ecuador to join us at Easter Island. She also brought 60 pounds of bacon from Fred Lazarus, Ellie's father. Although we were able frequently to get frozen fish from Japanese trawlers, we could get good meat only in two places in the Pacific — Papeete and Suva — so our freezer was a great convenience. I took ten frozen meat meals (for eight) — including steak, roast beef, chicken breasts, and chops — down to Panama, and I brought an additional supply of meat when I returned to Tahiti after a flying trip home. Throughout the four-month cruise, we ate about two fresh-meat meals a week and two of canned meat. The other three dinners were either omelets, spaghetti, or fish. Most of the dry stores lasted the entire voyage, but we restocked the low items in Fiji.

Our major supplies list included:

Canned vegetables	29 dozen cans
Canned fruit	40 dozen cans
Tuna fish	60 cans
Other canned meats	482 cans
Beef stew	22 pounds
Chicken breasts	90
Powdered eggs	86 dozen (equivalent)
Canned margarine	105 pounds
Velveeta cheese	44 pounds
Baking potatoes	170
Dried fruit	36 boxes
Powdered milk	250 quarts
Dried soup	280 packs
Spaghetti	24 pounds
Sugar	30 pounds
Cheesecake mix	48 boxes
Hershey bars	14 dozen
Instant coffee	24 jars
Beer	17 cases
Mayonnaise	25 jars
Napkins	2,100
Soap bars	48

Whenever I despaired of ever getting the supplies all together and stowed, I thought of Captain Cook and how much more difficult it was for him to supply his ships without the facilities and convenience foods we have today. Moreover, the supplies taken

aboard in Cook's day were crudely packaged and subject to mold and infestation. Compare my order list to Cook's provisions on the bark *Endeavour* for 70 men at sea for one year (which he stretched to two and a half years by adding local supplies):

Bread in bags	21,116 pounds
Bread in butts	13,400 pounds
Flour in barrels	9,000 pounds
Beer in puncheons	1,200 gallons
Spirits	1,600 gallons
Beef (salted)	4,000 pieces
Flour in lieu of beef	1,400 pounds
Suet	800 pounds
Raisins	2,500 pounds
Pease in butts	187 bushels
Oatmeal in butts	10 bushels
Wheat	120 bushels
Oil	120 gallons
Sugar	1,500 pounds
Vinegar	500 gallons
Sourkraut	7,800 pounds
Malt in hogsheads	40 bushels
Salt	40 bushels
Pork	6,000 pieces
Mustard seed	160 pieces

Stopping at ports along the way, Cook added quantities of fresh meat and bread, as well as native onions, yams, plantains, turtle meat, chickens, hogs, taro, wild celery, and a variety of local fruits. Often he had to throw out huge quantities of bread and water that had become contaminated. In one report on the state of provisions aboard *Endeavour* in 1769, Sir Joseph Banks wrote to Cook that many provisions were lasting well, but that the ship's biscuits were as usual, harboring five kinds of vermin. "I have often seen hundreds nay thousands shaken out of a single bisket," he said. "We in the Cabbin have however an easy remedy for this by baking it in an oven, not too hot, which makes them all walk off, but this cannot be allowed to the private people [passengers] who must find the taste of these animals very disagreeable." And in 1777 Cook reported having to condemn 686 pounds of bread, "so much eaten and dirtied by weevils, cockroaches, rats and other vermin as to be wholly unfit for men to eat, occasioned by the prodigious number that are in the ship, which destroy everything they can get at." How petty our few galley mishaps seem compared to the hell of cooking at sea in the 1770s!

For the record, we had little trouble with cockroaches. Our first one appeared at Easter Island. Knowing their ability to multiply, Paul and David immediately sprinkled roach powder throughout the food stowage area. After that we saw only random roaches, kept at the powder, and never had to fumigate the ship. Happily, we had no rats, mice, or beetles. The boat was totally fumigated on return to Camden, Maine.

Obtaining cooking fuel on the way loomed as a problem until we eliminated it by buying two Primus stoves. We could carry about 30 gallons of alcohol in the ship's stove tank, and we had 20 one-gallon containers in the hull, but we could not rely on alcohol for daily use because it would be used up rapidly, is expensive, and often is unobtainable in the Pacific. So we resorted to the Primus stoves, mounting one in a bracket above the regular stove, with the other stowed as a spare. We also took along repair parts such as new burners and gaskets. Despite constant minor repair problems, our Primus produced a very hot flame and performed well. Because the flame was concentrated and non-adjustable, we found it helpful to insert an asbestos ring for simmering.

As mentioned previously, *Palawan* carried 1,000 gallons of water. With stern discipline, we kept consumption down to less than two gallons a day per person. Although we kept the pressure system on, we were careful to use only one of four tanks at a time so that we would not run completely out of water accidentally. We found water supplies in the Pacific adequate but infrequent. Panama City water, heavily treated with chemicals, tasted unpleasant, and we weren't able to pump it out completely and resupply until we reached Mangareva in the Gambiers. Good water was available at all major ports, and although we were prepared to treat the water ourselves with purification pills, we never had to do so.

I have never had in any of my boats the kind of fungus growth in water tanks that seems occasionally to bother others. *Palawan*'s builders, Abeking & Rasmussen, had enamelled the

inside of the tanks and provided very accessible cleaning openings, so the tanks remained fresh at all times. With some gifts of fresh water along the way, our tanks never got far below half-supply, and we never had to resort to catching rainwater.

Our fuel capacity was also 1,000 gallons, and we found fuel available in ample quantity at the Panama Canal, the Galapagos, and Tahiti. It could also be obtained with some difficulty at Easter Island, where the natives had a racket going. Although they didn't charge much for the fuel, they charged an exorbitant amount for ferrying it out to the boat in a motorboat. Then we had to wrestle the two 50-gallon drums from the launch onto *Palawan*'s deck ourselves. Their delivery fee did not include a helping hand.

As for repair facilities, we knew they would be limited. Beyond the Canal there was minimal service in the Galapagos; blacksmithing, welding, and brazing at Easter; minimal facilities at Mangareva; and then nothing until Tahiti, where there was a top-notch shipyard. From there on there were no reliable repair sources until Samoa, which had an extensive shipyard, and then there was nothing until Fiji. From the outset, our policy was to carry as many spare parts as possible.

Like our provisions lists, our spare parts list had also been developed over years of ocean-racing experience. As for sails, we had back-ups for everything except the mainsail — an extra would have been difficult to stow, and with our split rig we could conveniently use other sails if anything happened to the main. We had spare lines in quantity, galvanized iron wire for repairing the rig, and an auxiliary tiller in case the wheel steering mechanism broke. Below decks we had everything from kerosene lamps to use if the electrical system gave out, to plywood for repairing a porthole if the glass was broken. As it turned out, we had few mechanical problems other than a leak in the gearbox oil cooler. We patched it up once, but it later rendered our gearbox inoperative.

While all of the above was being tended to, I also carried on a continuous and voluminous correspondence with officialdom to comply with customs formalities and obtain the necessary visas and prior clearances into various ports. However, finally, with all papers in order, all supplies accounted for, and all crew members on hand, *Palawan IV* was ready to sail into the Pacific.

CHAPTER 3

COCOS:

Once a Pirate Haven

During those first few days at sea, while the crew settled into shipboard routine, but before they became complacent because of the mild weather, I made a point of reviewing with them the safety procedures I had outlined in the Crew Bulletin. For races as well as cruises, I usually post these instructions in the main cabin and ask crew members to initial them when they have read them; then we review them together.

As far as I was concerned, of greatest importance were man-overboard drills to familiarize everyone with our specially rigged life-ring buoy devices, which could be released from the cockpit. Although the ocean seemed harmless as I spoke, I tried to explain how difficult it could be to return quickly to pick anyone up from the water. *Palawan* would probably be running before the trade winds in high, breaking seas with the spinnaker flying and the boom vanged out, and the quick release of the life rings and marker buoys would be essential to a rescue. So we practiced releasing these contraptions until the crew could drop one almost beside an imaginary victim astern within seconds. One must, of course, douse a spinnaker to return for a pickup, but with a powerful engine such as we have, the other sails can be overpowered and don't need immediate tending other than trimming. One very important caution, however, is to be absolutely sure that there are no lines trailing overboard to wind around the propeller when the engine is started, especially when performing a rescue. We spoke of this danger again and again.

I also repeated my warnings about stepping outside the cockpit at night, and the need for using a safety belt at all times in heavy weather, especially on deck at night. I stressed the importance of always having "one hand for yourself and one for the ship." We reviewed instructions in rigging for storm conditions, in the location and use of emergency equipment — how to cut stays or unpin turnbuckles in case of a dismasting — and in the use of axes to chop holes in the wood paneling below decks to reach and patch a hole in the hull.

We reviewed the contents and use of the medical kit and special medications available. Most important, I asked that medical problems, however minor, be reported to me at once. Then we made sure everyone knew how to use the fire extinguishers and the ship's communications equipment for emergencies. Everyone was

---

LOG ENTRY: FEBRUARY 1, 1976

Most of us are strangers to one another. First two days at sea somewhat awkward as we learn to live together. Paul and David spend much time analyzing possible mechanical failures and stowing supplies; Robin Balfour tries to teach Carter about the sea during their watches together. She makes little comment. Does her silence mean she is — or is not — receptive? At 75, Robin has a quicker mind and healthier appetite than most men at 60. He's as neat as a pin in the cabin, dresses colorfully in lavalavas and pareus acquired on previous Pacific cruises, and is always there with a song or story. Jimmy is working inordinately hard on his charts; I'm afraid he'll burn out, but I don't know how to tell him without hurting his feelings. Anne, who has done her homework on the Pacific, has been

entertaining us with tidbits about the various islands ahead. Everyone, I think, has begun a journal.

The GM diesel hums smoothly, the sun beats down relentlessly and the sea is undisturbed by the slightest ripple. So far, everyone is cheerful and willing, but this is the honeymoon, not the marriage.

instructed in launching the life rafts and the location of the specially packaged food rations and 15-gallon water containers to be put in them. Having read at least two reports of killer whales sinking small vessels near the Galapagos, I had also added an "abandon ship" practice to the list. With variations and refinements, this is essentially the same briefing I have been giving crews for over 40 years, and they are always attentive during these sessions.

The safety drills helped everyone to get to know the boat and her gear as well as the procedures and, I felt, helped less-experienced crew members feel a little more at home. Fortunately, we never had to use any of the emergency routines, but at sea the moment of need is not the moment to begin instruction.

I also felt the concentration on safety would help take everyone's mind off him- or herself. From long experience with other crews in other oceans, I'm aware that small cross currents of personalities tend to become magnified at sea, and I could see poten-

Running under power — Ellie Lazarus on deck.

tial areas of minor conflict here. Paul wasn't used to having so many voluble young women around, and they made him slightly uncomfortable. Carter, who knew next to nothing about sailing, was already starting to bristle whenever I tried to give her seagoing advice. Dave was going to have to be very careful not to spend too much time with any one girl on board; and Lord Riverdale, for all his colorful garb and enthusiasm, was beginning to dwell overlong on his past adventures — and we were only two days out!

Hoping to keep things smooth for the sake of all, I silently promised to hold my tongue when the inevitable moments of annoyance and stress arrived. Shocking frankness or a thorough showdown are acceptable and often useful devices in business management, but they simply do not work at sea. Frictions and unpleasantness must be tiptoed around or praised away except in extreme cases. This may not seem like the most efficient method of running a ship, but I have learned over many years that it's the only way to ensure a pleasant cruise.

The point was forcefully brought home to me during a cruise to Nova Scotia in 1935, when I must have been issuing orders like a Captain Queeg. As soon as we arrived in Halifax the entire crew of personal friends registered in a hotel and announced that they planned to return home by train unless I could be a little more sympathetic to their feelings.

A few years later, in another kind of ship, I again faced a potential mutiny. In 1942, as copilot of a B-24 Liberator bomber on a mission to Russia, China, and back through Siberia and Alaska, I was also in charge of maintenance. After we had flown more than 100 hours together, the enlisted crew confronted me at 3:00 A.M. in a restaurant in Cheng-tu, China, and told me flatly that they thought I was autocratic, snotty, unsympathetic, intolerant, and difficult to communicate with. This was a pretty serious problem, especially since our commanding general had asked me to lead the return mission in a few months with the same crew. During the month it took us to get home I tried very hard to change, and in the end the crew agreed to risk flying with me again.

These and other experiences over the years, including occasional emphatic admonishments from my wife of 47 years, have shown me what personal traits to guard against. Throughout my business career, I was often impatient, ignoring the human element in my desire to reach a particular goal with dispatch. My only saving grace was an ability to sense when I was wrong and to apologize promptly. Furthermore, unless you work entirely alone, as a painter or author does, you need the cooperation of a number of other human beings in order to get a job done. Eventually, I developed a rule of thumb: press as hard as you can, short of causing team members to balk or boil over. Wherever possible, work with and compliment them. And when you are wrong, admit it.

Just after dawn on our third day out, Carter spied Cocos Island about 25 miles away, under a heavy cloud. This was our first Pacific landfall, and although by now I had conquered the misgivings that plagued me the first night, I still experienced a small surge of relief as the island emerged on the horizon.

Cocos is a typical volcanic island. It rises abruptly from the sea to a height of 2,100 feet and covers an area of about eight square miles. There are steep cliffs on all sides, which enabled us to see the island from a distance in spite of its shroud of rain and mist. Also typical is the cloud cap that sits above it, formed when moisture-laden sea wind sweeps up on thermals over the hot land mass. As the system cools in higher altitudes, rain drenches the island, creating an almost impenetrable undergrowth and running off in cascades to the shore.

As we drew closer, my binoculars picked out first a small schooner, then a yawl, and finally a seaplane, all anchored in Chatham Bay. As the hook went down, the stories of the mysteries that surround Cocos and rumors of the treasures buried there ran through our minds as we gazed at the rugged outline of this tiny outcropping in the sea. Finally, eager to explore our first Pacific island and bathe in its waterfalls, we put a dinghy over and headed for shore. The shallow beach was surrounded by steep, uneven cliffs, the rocks bearing a graffiti of the names and dates of visiting ships for the past 200 years. We read the names, dug our toes in the sand, and played in the falls, enjoying the luxury of leisurely freshwater showers.

Watching us from a distance as we got our bearings ashore, the skipper of the schooner eventually waved and approached us along the beach. He was Arthur Hammond — slight, sandy-haired, in his mid-thirties. Guardedly sociable, he seemed the stereotype of a singlehander: when short of funds he worked at odd jobs in whatever port he found himself until he had enough money to take off. Then he cruised alone until his money ran out, repeating the process as needed. This time, he said, he was headed for the Galapagos, Easter Island, and Tahiti, and hoped to wind up in New Zealand.

My mind wandered as he spoke. What kind of man is the solo world voyager? He didn't seem especially anxious to talk a great deal, although he was perfectly willing to respond to questions. Actually, he turned out to be one of those unique characters one meets on an airplane, ski lift, or cruising boat: we saw him for just a few minutes; yet he impressed us profoundly, perhaps because he was doing exactly what he wanted to do, and was doing it well. His boat was shipshape and organized, and he was seeing the world as he wanted to. Other world sailors we met later seemed more like drifters; Hammond seemed armed, loaded, and moving.

Inshore of *Palawan* lay the flying boat *Calypso*, from which four men were unloading equipment. They had flown out from their base in Costa Rica and would live aboard the plane while completing a reef photography project. One of the four was Jacques Costeau's son Philippe, who was directing the expedition. Another member of the group was a young botanist who had spent four weeks on Cocos, and who waxed almost poetic about its flora and fauna. We weren't so excited by the flora — mostly dense jungle — but he was right about the fauna. The island is a refuge for huge colonies of birds — boobies, terns, gulls, frigate birds, finches, flycatchers, and cuckoos — which wheeled and dipped overhead and waddled over the rocks on shore, at ease and unmindful of us.

Except for several short-lived penal and agricultural colonies set up during the past century, Cocos has never been inhabited for any length of time. It's likely that before the Spanish conquered the South American continent, aboriginal Indians such as the Incas used Cocos as a casual fishing camp, finding the land too rough to establish more permanent settlements.

However, that tough jungle growth may now harbor buried treasure of another era. Known to European navigators as early as 1541, Cocos in the seventeenth century reportedly served as a haven for buccaneers, including privateer and naturalist William Dampier and Dr. Lionel Wafer who, in their ship *Batchelor's Delight*, prowled the west coasts of North and South America, retreating to Cocos to rest, make repairs, and hide their loot. Other buccaneers also frequented Cocos, including Benito Bonito, one of whose capers was to waylay a gold-laden mule train enroute from Mexico City to Acapulco, the gold supposedly ending up on Cocos.

While Cocos might seem to have been a long way from the mainland to go — in the days of wooden sailing ships — to seek haven and stash a booty, for the buccaneers of the 1600s it was preferable to risking the time and dangers of a voyage around the Horn to return to Europe. Their victims were often Spanish ships carrying gold from Peru and Chile to the Isthmus of Panama, where it was taken by donkey train to the Caribbean for shipment to Spain. Cocos was off the beaten track, high enough for lookouts to spot approaching ships, and dense enough to make it impossible to find anyone who wished to remain hidden.

Legends of buried gold have thus lured many fortune hunters. Since the 1800s, more than 500 expeditions to the island have searched in vain for these treasures. One ill-gotten hoard in particular, however, has inspired more frustrated expeditions, "authentic" location maps, wild tales, and general "Cocos Hocus-Pocus" than any other: the $12,000,000 to $60,000,000 in bullion and gem-encrusted religious relics taken from Lima, Peru, during a revolt against Spanish rule in 1820. Fearing attack, Spanish viceroys and clerics stowed their considerable wealth in an English ship, but her captain fell prey to either temptation or mutiny, made off with the treasure, and reportedly buried it on Cocos. Accounts of his life and clues to the treasure's whereabouts have been so numerous and contradictory that no one knows what really happened. The captain was eventually hanged without giving his secret away, and the hunt has been on ever since.

Predictably, such tales have inspired an odd assortment of beachcombers, wealthy adventurers, con men, scientists, and metal-detector inventors to go digging on Cocos. The strangest of the lot was August Gissler, the "Cocos Hermit," who as a young German sailor met a man whose grandfather had reportedly sailed with Bonito and bequeathed him a treasure map. In the early 1800s, Gissler led an expedition, which failed, then another, and finally decided to live on the island. For 17 years he dug and grew vegetables, and in 1849 he was named governor of Cocos. Later he left to retire, ingloriously, in New York City.

The most tangled tale of fortune-hunting developed in the 1930s. A cagey British captain, Charles Arthur, sold stock in several intriguingly titled search companies, then disappeared when problems developed with government permits. He was found, however, and brought to trial, but returned home to convince more gullible investors, launch a secret movie deal, and double-cross everyone.

There is little excitement in the venture today, but every so often someone else gets the bug, seeks a search permit from the Costa Rican government, and heads for Cocos with axes, shovels, and the "real" treasure map.

When we had exhausted the possibilities of the beach and waterfalls, we moved *Palawan* around to Wafer Bay on the more protected north end of the island. Presumably, this was once the retreat of Dampier and Wafer's infamous *Batchelor's Delight*. It was a spectacular anchorage, open to the northwest, but sheltered from the prevailing easterlies, with a lovely waterfall tumbling from a vine-covered cliff. It appeared idyllic, until we went ashore and walked along the beach. Here someone had set up housekeeping and later abandoned the site, leaving a terrible mess. Strewn around the skeleton of a half-finished, cut-pole hut were piles of bottles, plastic containers, rotting clothes, slickers, rubber boots and shoes, food, bedding, and mattresses in a disgusting jumble.

Our company in Wafer Bay was a 32-foot sloop named the *Hugh Cabot*. Curious about her, we asked the couple aboard to join us for dinner before we weighed anchor and headed for the Galapagos. Long-distance voyagers never cease to intrigue me: I feel a bond with them, and I like to hear their stories.

This couple proved to be a young Canadian and his British girlfriend who had sailed from England in late 1974. They said that they planned to sail to the Marquesas, Hawaii, and back to British Columbia. Their 32-footer was rather sparsely equipped, and they had so little storage space for water, they told us matter-of-factly, that unless they could catch rain water on the way to the Marquesas — a distance of 3,500 miles — they would be desperately short by the time they got there. I wondered at their courage — if that's what you could call it. They seemed alternately defensive and apologetic about their minimal preparations, and even about their voyaging.

After dinner we wished our young guests luck and said goodbye, cleaned up the dishes, and quietly powered out of the bay on a heading for the Galapagos, 640 miles to the southwest.

CHAPTER 4

DARWIN'S LABORATORY:

The Galapagos and Wildlife

One day out of Cocos we found ourselves continually surrounded by rain squalls, but never a drop fell on deck. Our breezes were light as we watched the squalls in the distance and passed two large freighters, which were probably headed for California from South America. Except for some electrical charge-rate problems that developed shortly after our departure, and which Paul and I spent some time solving, the crew quickly settled into a passage routine. The next afternoon all was quiet aboard and those of us off watch were napping, when suddenly a raucous disturbance arose amidships. We rushed on deck to behold a seaweed-draped Father Neptune Riverdale clambering up a rope ladder and in booming tones inquiring whether this was the first crossing of the equator for anyone aboard. Several crew members owned up, and for the next hour all other activity ceased as they were properly initiated (in a ceremony of local origin) into the time-honored family of those who have crossed the equator.

Unbeknownst to me, and with the assistance of Paul, Robin had mixed up a bucket of flour paste, hot sauce, and salt water. Then, with a very stiff paint brush they proceeded to paint the faces of the men who were neophytes and the backs and hair of the women. They then tried to do some shaving — with a very dull razor — but that didn't work, and the women were modestly tortured in a variety of ways. Eventually everybody had a good washdown followed by a special dinner, and all felt quite appropriately initiated into the venerable society of seagoing veterans who have crossed the equator. The ceremony livened things up for a while.

Throughout the cruise, while such spontaneous shenanigans were going on, I joined in for a while but soon found my mind returning to shipboard responsibilities and, particularly in the early passages, often to problems of navigation.

Palawan is usually navigated using H.O. 229, a U.S. Hydrographic Office publication. For those not familiar with navigation systems, these tables in combination with the *Nautical Almanac* give a pre-computed position line for the sun for all areas of the globe and for all times. The navigator measures the sun's angle with a sextant, at the same moment noting the precise time of the sight by referring to the chronometer. Data for the day's date and time from the *Nautical Almanac*

LOG ENTRY: FEBRUARY 1, 1976

We have entered the broad Pacific in earnest. All the way to Cocos we had the security of knowing that a change of heart and a 90-degree turn to starboard would quickly put us back on the Central American coast. Now both continents are behind us. Our bow is pointed toward the Orient and the 15,000 miles of ocean in between. Our next landfall, the Galapagos, will be just a short stop on the way. We hope to reach there in just over three days, even with the cold Humboldt Current slowing us down as it flows west and north along the coast.

allows the navigator to make a few simple calculations using 229, and then to plot a line on a chart giving a line of position (LOP), which is always tangential to the sun's position. For instance, since the sun rises in the east, a morning sight will produce a north-south line.

At noon the navigator measures the sun at its highest angle (this is not possible when the sun is directly overhead, as it was for a period south of Galapagos). This highest point, called "Local Apparent Noon," or LAN, is translated by a simple formula into latitude, or an east-west line. By advancing the morning line along the compass course by the number of miles sailed between the two sight times, the two lines cross at the ship's position. Generally, the navigator also takes an afternoon sight, advancing both morning line and LAN to the afternoon line as a confirmation measure. During the entire Pacific cruise, this method seldom put us more than two miles from our actual position.

However, between Cocos and the Galapagos, Jimmy and I found our navigating a bit rusty and our efforts somewhat less than successful. We took our first sights the morning of 1 February, but out of carelessness we used the *Nautical Almanac*'s data for 31 January, and did not discover our error until nightfall. So, although we knew by dead reckoning (DR), that we'd gone about halfway, we had to drop all the sights for the day.

Jimmy's first sight the next morning put us almost exactly at the DR position. Then, despite my lack of recent practice, I decided to do a LAN fix. It placed us 40 miles closer to the Galapagos than the DR. Deciding to rely on the sight I had taken, we altered course slightly to the west after an afternoon sunline. With Jimmy working like a Trojan we waited confidently to spot San Cristobal, easternmost of the nine islands of the Galapagos archipelago, by nightfall.

When dinner time came and went with no sign of land on the radar, we realized my noon sight must have been off. However, by 2200 we were beginning see land shadows on the screen, and by midnight the whole contour of San Cristobal's northern end was clear. When we finally reached it, the log (a distance-registering device that works electrically from a 3/4-inch propeller under the hull) read within seven miles of what it should have read for the distance covered (about 600 miles) — amazing accuracy.

On a previous cruise Robin had taken his twin-keeled *Bluebird of Thorne* into San Cristobal's Wreck Bay so, when he wisely suggested that we lay to until daylight rather than risk a night entrance into the rock-bound harbor, we followed his advice. At dawn we motored in past Kicker Rock, a split boulder 100 feet high, through whose narrow cleft Robin told us with some pride that he had maneuvered *Bluebird*. Upon anchoring in the bay, we were soon boarded by four inscrutable ensigns of the Ecuadorian Navy. Apparently unable to speak English, they inspected our documents and cleared us, all within 30 minutes. However, to our dismay, the clearance was only for San Cristobal.

Several years ago, the Ecuadorian government wisely closed the Galapagos, one of the world's few remaining untouched natural habitats, to all unescorted visitors. Thus, it is illegal to cruise through the islands or go ashore unless one is aboard an Ecuadorian sightseeing boat, or one of the few vessels available for charter at Academy Bay, where the government has approved the captains as escorts.

Unaware of this new law when planning our itinerary, I had barraged the Ecuadorian government with letters from the World Wildlife Fund, the American Museum of Natural History in New York, and the Smithsonian Institution for permission to visit the islands — all to no avail. Cruising in the Galapagos was strictly forbidden. So I was about to give up the idea and plan instead to sail directly for Easter Island from Cocos, when Dr. David Challinor, Assistant Secretary of the Smithsonian, came through with a suggestion. If we would take on board two of their scientists who needed to collect some Galapagos coral, our visit would achieve the status of an official expedition. Overjoyed at this offer, we then arranged to meet the scientists here at Wreck Bay.

The Ecuadorian ensigns took me ashore to a small, Spanish-style building at the head of the town dock. I soon saw that Wreck Bay, site of many penal colonies from the 1830s on, merited its name in other ways as well. Beyond the government building spread a number of sorry-looking huts, a depressing sight after our built-up image of untouched terrain and wildlife. Furthermore, our scientists were nowhere to be found. As our official communications continued slowly in broken Spanish and English, we began to wonder whether red tape and misunderstandings would bring all our plans to nothing and leave us waiting at Wreck Bay indefinitely.

Finally, I was ushered into the office of an English-speaking official, who told me the scientists had gone to Hood Island, some miles south. Confused, I asked to use the crackling government radiophone to call Craig MacFarland, chief of the Smithsonian's Darwin Station on Santa Cruz Island. The call was made, and he told me that our permission to visit the islands had expired. Only then did I remember that we had originally planned to arrive two weeks earlier. I had forgotten to tell anyone of the change. Craig promised to wire the U.S. military attache in Guayaquil to ask that the permission be extended. While awaiting a reply, to ease our tension and frustration, several of us decided to take a walk through town.

Some of the village houses, we noticed, were built of wood, others of lava. Apparently the natives, searching for a bit of greenery, had lifted up huge pieces of lava to form walls, and this had left them small plots of rich soil, which they made into gardens. They seemed friendly, but we had trouble communicating with them, despite what the crew called "unusual humility" on my part. Craig had asked me to call on Antonio Belasco, local representative of the Darwin Station, so we asked directions to his house. On arrival, we found him sick but ready with an unusual and refreshing greeting. As each of us entered the house, hot and dusty, Antonio motioned for us to dash a bottle of highly scented toilet water over our faces and hands. We emerged refreshed and smelling considerably different from the rest of the crew.

Continuing our walk, we eventually heard *Palawan*'s foghorn — our prearranged recall signal — and rushed back to the dock to learn that we could be cleared as soon as the afternoon siesta was over. The government office opened again at 2:30; by 3:15 we were on our way, and had even been provided with a pleasant escort named Juan Serranasera, who would accompany us until we joined the scientists. The Galapagos Islands were now at our fingertips, and we were free to depart for our rendezvous at Hood Island.

Formed by a series of volcanic eruptions over the past million years, the Galapagos present a severe landscape of black lava plains, scrubby pampas, and dry, rocky hills. "Nothing could be less inviting in appearance," Darwin wrote in 1831. "A broken field of black, basaltic lava thrown into the most rugged waves and crossed by great fissures, is everywhere covered by stunted, sunburnt brushwood, which shows little signs of life. The dry and parched surfaces, being heated by the noonday sun, gave to the air a close and sultry feeling, like that from a stove, and we fancied even that the bushes smelt unpleasantly...." Later Darwin found that Chatham Island, with its "black, truncated cones" above a sieve-like stony plain, reminded him of "those parts of Staffordshire, where the great iron foundries are most numerous."

The first visitor to the Galapagos may have been the Inca king Tuopac Yupanqui, who sailed west to some "islands of flame" and reportedly brought back black-skinned slaves, gold, silver, and animal hides. The latter part of the story is sheer fantasy, but when anthropologist Thor Heyerdahl searched the Galapagos in 1953, he concluded from the aboriginal potsherds he found that well before the Spanish conquests the Indians used the islands as camps during fishing trips, although they never settled there.

After the Indians, the next known visitor was the Spanish Bishop of Panama, who searched here for water after drifting off course on a coastwise cruise of Central America in 1535. He described the islands as so rugged "it seemed as if God had showered stones" there.

During the next three centuries, the Galapagos became a haven for buccaneers and whalers seeking refuge and refreshment, and for successive waves of conquistadors, who named them the "Enchanted Isles" because they seemed to shift position in the tricky currents. In 1807 a British deserter named Patrick Watkins became the first permanent inhabitant, selling vegetables to passing ships and eventually going mad. Melville wrote of him in his story "Las Encantadas," describing a wild creature who lured sailors into his cave and made them his slaves.

In 1832 the islands were annexed to Ecuador, and General Jose Villamil founded the first penal colony on Charles Island. Other penal colonies followed on other islands, but all ended in either abandonment or revolt. Several agricultural colonies met better success, and during World War II the U.S. built an air base on tiny Baltra Island. Academy Bay, home of the Darwin Station, is now a small but thriving community. This, along with several other settlements, brings the archipelago's population to about 3,500.

The Galapagos are famous for their unique giant tortoises, and the islands were named after them by early Spanish visitors, who noticed that their backs were shaped like large saddles, or

Carter Christiansen greets one of the giant Galapagos tortoises, only one of the tame, intriguing species of animals we encountered on these islands.

"gallapigos." To the visiting whalers, the reptiles, weighing up to 700 pounds, were precious sources of food and oil. To Melville, they seemed embodiments of evil: "black as widows' weeds, heavy as chests of plate"; grim prisoners "writhing century after century through the shades." And even to such an objective observer as Darwin they seemed like "antediluvian animals" as they lumbered through the underbrush. It's interesting that much of America was covered with turtles of this same family 10,000 years ago. The mystery is how these reptiles got to the Galapagos, since they are not aquatic.

The islands have long been recognized as a unique natural environment, inspiring writers and scientists alike. It was here as a young man that Charles Darwin made studies of the isolated wildlife that would lead him, years later, to propose his startling theories of natural selection and evolution.

Since his visit in 1831, dozens of expeditions have visited this scientist's paradise. During the nineteenth century, visitors to the Galapagos included Harvard zoologist (and Darwin's foe) Louis Agassiz, two tortoise-collecting trips on behalf of British Lord Rothschild, and researchers trying to prove that the archipelago had once been part of a large, submerged land mass. In 1905 the California Academy of Sciences sent a team on the schooner *Academy* to spend a year in the Galapagos, and their surveys were the most comprehensive ever made there. This expedition has been memorialized by the name Academy Bay, on Santa Cruz.

During the 1920s, naturalist William Beebe made two visits to the islands aboard the yachts *Noma* and *Arcturus*. His two descriptive books about Galapagos wildlife make delightful reading. Finally, in 1955 a UNESCO expedition resulted in the founding of the Darwin Station — a permanent research outpost.

Unfortunately, not all those who have visited the Galapagos have had as much appreciation as Darwin and Melville for the uniqueness of their natural state. First the buccaneers and explorers, then later scores of whalers, captured hundreds of the tortoises at a time and took them out to their ships in longboats. Stacked on their backs and flushed down with water once a week, the hardy "Gallapigos mutton" could survive in a ship's hold for almost a year, providing the crew with fresh meat and oil. During one 37-year period in the nineteenthth century, 13,000 turtles were taken during visits by 97 ships. Later visitors killed or removed more, so that by 1977 the tortoise population, once numbering in the hundreds of thousands, had been eliminated on all but three islands, and the number of species had been reduced from about 20 to 11.

Another long-term threat to the turtle population resulted from human abuse of this delicate environment. Beginning with the era of Spanish exploration, ships left pigs and goats on the islands to provide emergency food for return trips or for later visitors. Over the years, the goat and pig populations skyrocketed, so that despite frequent hunting forays by the government and the Darwin Station, thousands of these animals remained, competing with the turtles for the scarce vegetation they needed to survive.

The goats in particular multiplied very rapidly. In 1957 several were left on Pinta Island, without permission, and by 1973 there were 35,000 roaming the island. Further problems were created by the introduction of dogs, cats, rats, and donkeys, which also roamed wild, multiplying rapidly and adding to the ecological imbalance.

Having read extensively about these problems in the Galapagos beforehand, and having finally won permission to visit them, once cleared, we headed over to Hood with great anticipation.

Our attempt to land on Hood the next morning taught us a lesson about surf that served us well for the rest of the cruise. Even though the beach was well protected, we soon discovered that any break in the waves caused surf to wash over the stern of our dinghy — a potential hazard to cameras and other sensitive gear. After one big splash, I powered down to the protected end of the beach, anchored close to shore, and had everyone walk the rest of the way in. This, I decided, would have to be our procedure from then on.

We spent the entire day on this lovely, deserted beach. Like other Galapagos beaches, it was a scene almost beyond description. Many good writers have written about these islands, and we

LOG ENTRY: FEBRUARY 4, 1976

Powered to Hood Island late yesterday afternoon, and entered the harbor just at sunset. A strange and beautiful sight — gold and sepia skies outlining the rugged hills. This island is one of the few in the archipelago that were formed by the folding and lifting of land from the sea floor, rather than by volcanic activity. As a result, its terrain is quite different. There is some greenery along the shore, but inland all the brush is burned dark brown.

When anchored, I called my wife Olive, who is vacationing in Colorado. The call went through Hi-Seas Radio Station KMI Oakland. Already the single sideband radio is proving a great help. It appears we will be able to make frequent shore contact all the way to Fiji.

had read a number of books about them, but none of us was quite prepared for what we found — a wide assortment of unique creatures mingling in natural harmony, hundreds of miles from civilization. There were no white hunters, no minibuses, and no campers. We realized that for the first, and perhaps the last, time we were totally alone with nature.

At our feet and brilliant against the black lava rocks, colonies of red Sally Lightfoot crabs moved in endless streams; wrinkled, ugly land iguanas — which Darwin called "little imps of darkness," — and their cousins, the gray marine iguanas, scampered about, ignoring us. Varieties of birds swarmed the beach: boobies, flightless cormorants, albatross, and Galapagos gulls, which William Beebe called "graceful bits of animate volcanic ash." Pelicans flapped by scouting for fish, and penguins — Melville as "grotesquely misshapen" — waddled about, at home neither on land or sea nor in the air, while rolling in the surf were hundreds of baby sea lions, which frolicked with their mothers as the chief of the herd swam to and fro offshore, bellowing fiercely.

I wandered off to sit alone on a rock overlooking the beach. Around me half a dozen finches — tiny birds that Darwin studied so closely to learn of differences in evolution from island to island — hopped and pecked a few inches from my feet. Suddenly, they all disappeared. Turning, I saw a Galapagos hawk newly perched on a nearby rock and, ten feet away, his mate. They were fearsome-looking, with sharp beaks and talons, but obviously meaning me no harm. I deduced they had come in search of a finch dinner. A few minutes later, I saw a finch fly out and land, unnoticed and unmolested, on the head of a pelican that had been fishing in the surf.

I rose and began walking back toward the others, musing on the intimate relationships that exist in nature. At that moment an incident occurred that might easily have triggered Darwin's revelation on the way species adapt for survival. An iguana sprang out in front of me, and I decided to chase it. It could run about as fast as I could, in a fashion that was highly comical. The front and back feet stuck out sharply from the body and then angled down, churning like paddle wheels as it ran, its tail flailing wildly. I'm sure anyone watching the two of us would have found it a ludicrous sight. When the iguana finally reached a black rock, he froze abruptly on its face and practically disap-

peared. Adapted through centuries to the exact color of the rock, he knew he was protected.

Darwin was only 32 and a college drop-out when he spent two months on the Galapagos as naturalist on the ship *Beagle* in 1831. With increasing awe, he noted that many of the plants and animals he found were unique to the archipelago and that many subspecies were also unique to separate islands within it. "We seem," he concluded, "to be brought somewhere near to that great fact — that mystery of mysteries — the first appearance of new beings on earth."

Returning to England, Darwin married and retired to a village in Kent, where he remained a recluse for years. Not until 1859 did he publish his views on evolution, which helped to shatter the traditional belief in a divinely ordered, unchanging species. Although scientists accepted his theories within a quarter century, they are still debating the origins of the Galapagos Islands and the creatures that inhabit them. How did the giant land tortoises get there? And when? Did they swim to populate the various islands, and, once there, lose their ability to swim? Were the islands once connected to the South American coast by a submerged ridge, or did all their inhabitants have to journey originally by wind and wave? Why didn't mammals ever reach the Galapagos on their own? These questions intrigued us increasingly the more we cruised from island to island.

Shortly after going ashore on Hood we met the scientists who would be with us for the rest of the tour: Peter Glynn, 42, a coral specialist from California, who had directed the Smithsonian Panama Station for eight years, and his assistant, Gerrord (Jerry) Wellington, 27, a graduate student in marine biology, who had been a Peace Corps volunteer and before that had spent two years studying the Galapagos's coastal marine environment for the Ecuadorian government.

Peter was warm and obviously capable; everyone on board came to respect him in the short time he was with us. Jerry possessed an enormous knowledge of and love for the islands and their wildlife and taught us a great deal. They both suggested that before leaving Hood we visit a special bird walk at the other end of the island. We set out immediately, and upon landing on the beach, following directions, began pushing our way through the bushes of the interior. Some distance from the sea we were aston-

Our navigator Jimmy Madden relaxes on the volcanic rocks of the Galapagos at far left. At near left is one of the Sally Lightfoot crabs that are everywhere alongshore in these islands. Below is an iguana taking the sun.

ished to come upon several large sea lions happily crawling about. To us they seemed out of place.

The walk took us through colonies of blue-footed boobies and the haunts of solid-tailed gulls, owls, Galapagos ducks, and nesting albatross. As we approached their nests, each booby defended its territory with squawks and threatening beak motions, although we never challenged any of them to see if they meant it. David, meanwhile, had remained behind to play with the sea lion pups. However, when an intolerant 800-pound bull charged him, he wisely retreated to the beach.

That night, in darkness we motored across to Floreana Island and anchored in Post Office Bay, named for the mail barrel set up on the beach in the late 1700s to enable passing whalers to deliver each other's mail. The barrel was still used — but it was now of plastic — and the mail was picked up by Margaret Wittmer, the unofficial mayor of Floreana. We left postcards with money for stamps there, and all reached their destinations.

Floreana has the most bizarre history of all the islands. In the 1930s two German families — Heinz Wittmer and his wife Margret, and Dr. Friedrich Ritter and his companion Dore Strauch — decided to retreat from civilization and find a purer life on this two-mile square of rock. But the refuge became a nightmare with the arrival of a certain "Baroness Wagner-Bosquet," an Austrian woman accompanied by two gigolos. The baroness proclaimed herself Empress of Floreana and began to wreak havoc in the little community. She stole supplies, tortured farm animals, and created bizarre scenes that led to international press accounts, a movie, and, finally, the mysterious death of the baroness and her two lovers.

While she was there, the Floreana families had little peace. However, although Ritter died and Strauch fled home, the hardy Wittmers remained, and in 1977 Mrs. Wittmer still lived on Black Beach, running a small hotel and acting as mayor.

We visited her clean, if ramshackle, establishment, and she showed us scrapbooks of visitors reaching back to the twenties, including Franklin Roosevelt and Vincent Astor. She had the inner strength that older, self-sufficient women often acquire, and a permeating radiance. "I know this doesn't look like much," she told us proudly, indicating with a sweep of her arm her small hotel and home, "but there are 50 years of blood and sweat in it."

We believed her.

The next day we sailed to Academy Bay to visit the Darwin Station, a modest group of buildings supported by several foundations and supervised by the Ecuadorian government. There, a few men and women, with the help of a $300,000 annual budget, were making inspired efforts to return the Galapagos as nearly as possible to their original state.

The young director, my contact Craig MacFarland — a dedicated man with a delightful wife and daughter — had approached this task in a number of ways. First, he used Ecuadorian Park Service hunters to shoot thousands of goats wherever they endangered the original wildlife. Second, he was helping to protect the islands against outside encroachment, an effort requiring severe government restrictions on visits to the outlying islands. When one is writing to Guayaquil, seeking permission for a visit, the attitude of the government may seem overly strict, but once a visitor has seen the devastation of this natural environment and the attempt being made to undo it, the government's position makes sense.

The Darwin Station has studied each of the islands where turtles originally existed and has been making an attempt to replenish the species, breeding tortoises under careful conditions and returning them to their natural environments. Although the tortoises mature slowly in captivity, the station has already managed to return several hundred to island homes; without these efforts, the eight scarce species would probably already have died out.

Here we visited the tropical compound of Carl Angemeyer and watched him demonstrate, rather startlingly, how tame the vicious-looking land iguanas are. Responding to his odd calls, they emerged from cellars and roofs, out of the woods and from under rocks, swarming fearlessly over his body to get at the rice he held aloft. Carl was one of two surviving brothers who, with a third brother, had left Germany in the early war years under sail. They planned to sail to a place where they could live their lives in peace and tranquility. Hitler was just beginning to emerge in their country, and their parents encouraged them to seek their fortunes abroad. After various adventures — including shipwreck — they arrived in the Galapagos. Here they built their lives very much as they had intended. Almost the first settlers of Academy Bay, they soon became influential citizens. One of the brothers died before our arrival, but the other two, in their 60s when we met at Academy Bay, were great fellows, still looking for fun and adventure. They had already found happiness.

Later that day, we drove to the higher parts of Santa Cruz Island, where we found the land transformed from volcanic desert to lush, fertile farmland and pastures supporting herds of cross-bred Holstein, Brown Swiss, and Black Angus cattle and a number of Brahma bulls. Another day we walked up into the hills to find the tortoises in their natural environment; luckily, we came across half a dozen of the mammoths ponderously pushing their way through the grass. Their strength was amazing; with Ellie perched comfortably on its back, one of them effortlessly lifted itself and stalked away. Because their shells are so rigid, they breath in by expanding their bodies in the neck area, which is unencumbered by the heavy carapace. They exhale by contraction, emitting an ominous hiss.   On the way back to the ship, our guide stopped at his mother's shack — a squalid, primitive hut on stilts. We were astonished to learn that she owned land and cattle and was a rich woman. Later, we heard that farmers often walk into the local Land Rover agency at Academy Bay and put down $10,000 cash for a car from their cattle earnings. To look at these people and their homes, one would think them all destitute — their sudden wealth has come ahead of their needs and tastes.

During that fascinating week in the Galapagos archipelago, we powered 468 miles and explored eight of the nine major islands, often going from one island to another at night to save daytime for exploration. As I look back, my most vivid memory is of Fernandina Island, a place that demonstrated the compatibility of Galapagos wildlife, but was nevertheless so desolate and so crawling with odd forms of life that a castaway might think he was in hell. Thousands of marine iguanas, harmless but grotesque — each three or four feet long — swarmed in piles atop one another between deep cracks in the black lava, and the sea around them boiled with thousands more, tumbling among dozens of sea lions. From overhead, pelicans streamlined themselves and dove on their marine victims as penguins and flightless cormorants waddled about, their useless wings protruding like some evolutionary punishment.

The lava was treacherous underfoot, and in trying to climb it I slipped and wound up with a badly twisted ankle and a bruised hand. "Caution, Tom," I thought, "take your own advice — an accident to one is an accident to all." Exploring the wild places of the world is risky, quite apart from the possibility of any natural disaster. Most of us live our daily lives within an hour of a hospital emergency ward and pursue our life style with that subconscious knowledge comfortingly stashed in the back of our mind. Put us in the wilderness, where adequate medical attention is days — if not weeks — away, and it takes a lot of discipline and a few minor accidents to make us focus on the vital importance of thinking "safety first" at every moment.

After five days of exploration and night passages between islands, I began to grow uneasy. Although Jimmy was a wonderful navigator and the radar precise, the charts noted repeatedly that one should "navigate with caution inside the 100-fathom curve." This curve is a dotted line drawn on some charts to delineate onshore from offshore navigation. We had been inside the curve ever since entering the archipelago, and I began to think how foolish it would be to run aground at night simply because we were in a hurry to finish up our "scientific" tour and reach Easter Island on schedule. So, although we had merely skimmed the surface of what there was to see and learn in the Galapagos, it was a relief to Jimmy and me when we could return to Academy Bay to prepare for sea once more.

As always, sailing day produced a frantic rush to lay in what supplies we needed. The Station generously filled our tanks with clean rain water, a relief from the chlorinated water taken on at the Panama Canal, and we combed the few primitive stores for additional provisions — looking in vain for fresh greens. Finally, with available stores all on board, we began to ready *Palawan* for 10 to 15 days at sea.

When starting out on a long passage such as this, I usually make a final check of the boat, walking from bow to stern, examining fittings. Starting with the fittings at the stem, I check the windlass and cleats. I inspect the mainmast thoroughly for signs of chafe or worn lines, and I usually have someone help pull me aloft in a bo'sun's chair to examine the spreaders and take a long look at the wind direction and speed instruments to be sure they are working properly. I also check to see that there is no unusual wear in the sheaves that lift all the sails aloft or in the fittings that

Paul Wolter paddles to the beach through the rocks and the seals on a southern island in the Galapagos.

hold the backstay and the forestay in place. These two fittings are vital, and the loss of either one of them would put the mast in great danger of going overboard.

Then I go aft, making sure that all the lifesaving gear is in place and the lashings on the dinghies are secure. Finally, I go below to check the accuracy of our chronometer and see that the sextants and other navigational gear are where they should be. I want to be sure that we have the landfall chart (in this case Easter Island) in the chart drawer and that the plotting sheets are readily available.

When all this is done, I go to my bunk and keep out of the way until I hear the dinghy being winched on board with the main halyard, and the anchor coming up. Then I go on deck, ready to enjoy the departure.

At such times I value in particular the judgment and assistance of Paul Wolter. Paul is a top professional seaman and a faithful friend. We met when I was looking for someone to help me supervise the final construction of *Palawan II*, at Abeking and Rasmussen in Germany in the spring of 1958. During the years since, he has greatly expanded my pleasure and knowledge of the sea. A genius when it comes to making mechanical repairs at sea, he will tackle any failed mechanism from a wristwatch to a 180-horsepower diesel engine, and nine times out of ten he will be able to fix it.

Paul can occasionally be difficult, like all of us, because he is not perceptive in his relationships with others. Still, he is quick to accept criticism and will make moderate adjustments in his conduct to conform.

Fortunately, Paul's assets far outweigh any shortcomings. Strong and capable, he sailed with me on numerous ocean races and was always willing to pile out of a bunk in the middle of the night, get on the foredeck regardless of the weather, change a sail, cook a meal, or lend a hand. During our years together, Paul has provided me with some of the happiest times in my life. I admire him greatly and consider him the finest professional captain in the game.

Paul and I spent our last afternoon in the Galapagos tending to the pre-departure chores. Finally, with the vessel in readiness, some of us went ashore for cocktails with the MacFarlands and dinner at the Station, a happy farewell celebration to send us on our way to Easter Island.

CHAPTER 5

POLYNESIA:

Myth and Mystery

I spent a good part of the year preceding our Pacific odyssey studying the history of this largest of oceans and reading about the European adventurers who had sailed it, especially Captain Cook. In a way, he inspired our voyage. He was among the first Europeans to arrive at many of the places we were headed for, but he had sailed with no knowledge of what islands, people, or weather lay ahead. For years I had dreamed of following his path, and at last the dream had come true. We were on our way. By the time we left Panama, most of the others aboard had read at least a smattering about the European sea adventurers and Pacific history. But oddly enough, it wasn't until we found ourselves some 200 miles from the Galapagos and approaching the vast triangle of Polynesia that we began to speculate about the most important Pacific seafarers of all — the Polynesians.

Suddenly we were all combing *Palawan*'s book shelves for more information on this fascinating ancient race. The more we learned about their primitive exploits, the more our European heroes paled in comparison, and by the time we reached Fiji the Polynesian navigators had emerged as the true heroes of our Pacific voyage. In the meantime, we had supplemented the ship's library with books on the Polynesians sent from home to Easter Island or brought by arriving crew or bought along the way.

While Cook remains in my mind the greatest modern navigator, the feats of the Polynesians who preceded him by at least a thousand years fascinate me still more.

Polynesia: what a lovely, romantic word! Derived from Greek, it translates, less euphoniously and somewhat vaguely, as "many islands." It is, in fact, a well-defined triangle of more than 12 million square miles bounded by Hawaii, New Zealand, and Easter Island. Scattered across this vast expanse of ocean, its hundreds of islands comprise only a few thousand square miles of land. The skill and courage of the ancient race that colonized this entire ocean in canoes between 2,000 B.C. and 1,000 A.D., guided only by the stars, the elements, and their own intuition, defy the imagination.

Who were the Polynesians? Where did they come from, and how did they learn to navigate? Unhappily for posterity, these ancient sailors had no written language and left few artifacts that can be accurately dated by their carbon content. The sciences of skeleton and blood type comparison are still quite primitive and inconclusive. Thus, although anthropologists have studied the Polynesians for years, and their descendants continue to populate the area today, we know relatively little about this greatest of all seafaring races. A few hints come from snatches of shadowy myth and memorized genealogy, or from remains of ancient temples, stone tools, and roads. But these discoveries give only a sketchy indication of how this primitive people colonized the Pacific. The one incontrovertible fact is that they did reach nearly every habitable island in the Pacific triangle, colonizing many and leaving traces on others, although the distances between many of the island groups range from 1,500 to 2,000 miles.

We are also certain that all Polynesian dialects are derived from an original Austronesian parent language. A Tahitian traveling with Cook in the 1770s was able to understand the Easter Islanders reasonably well; a pure Rarotongan could once have communicated with a Maori from New Zealand. We also know that, while the inhabitants tend to have darker skin, curlier hair, and more Negroid features in Western Polynesia (Tonga, Samoa, and Fiji), all Polynesians are roughly similar

Two Polynesian canoes are shown here with typical claw-shaped sails, one being rigged and the other being sailed. These are proas — double canoes with the mast stepped on the leeward hull. These examples from Tonga represent only one of many types of canoes for everything from lagoon fishing to voyaging thousands of miles.

in appearance. They are, in fact, one race spread over 12 million miles of ocean. Finally, radiocarbon dating has given experts a good idea of when the earliest settlers reached each group of Pacific islands, and the dates are impressive: Fiji, about 2,000 B.C., the Marquesas and Tahiti sometime before the birth of Christ, and a spreading in all directions during the centuries immediately following.

But the question of the Polynesians' origin has long sparked heated debate among anthropologists and intrigued Pacific scholars. Their racial characteristics include Caucasian, Mongoloid, Australian, and Negroid features. Because experts have had to rely primarily on similarities of language in determining possible homelands, they have arrived at a variety of conclusions using the same information. Some more adventurous theorists have even managed to connect the Polynesians with such diverse groups as the Twelve Tribes of Israel, the Peruvian Indians, and the Japanese.

During a visit to Tokyo, I saw a number of things that seemed to support the theory of at least a few early migrations from Japan to Polynesia. The ancient stonework of Tokyo's Imperial Palace bore a striking resemblance to stonework I had seen in the Pacific. The sennit (plaited coconut husk cord) used to bind Japanese bonsai trees was identical to the material with which the ancient Polynesians "sewed" their canoes together. And the music, facial expressions, and hand and foot motions of a traditiional women's

dance I watched in a village near Tokyo reminded me very much of the dances I had witnessed on various Pacific islands.

To make some sense of it all, I tried to supplement my uneven knowledge and vague speculations by reading widely on the subject of the Polynesians when I returned from the Pacific. The most helpful to me were Edward Dodd's *Ring of Fire* trilogy, Margaret Mead's writing on Pacific cultures, and the works of Sir Peter Buck (Te Rangi Hiroa), a Maori from New Zealand, who studied medicine in his home country and went on to become the world authority on Polynesia. He was knighted in 1946, became a professor of anthropology at Yale, and was eventually made director of the Bernice Bishop Museum in Honolulu, a center for Pacific research. From reading these and other experts, I arrived at what seems, to me at least, a believable theory of Polynesian origins and migrations.

We know that Java Man — who was among the first inhabitants of Indonesia — goes back more than 1,000,000 years. At the height of the Ice Age, when the Bering Strait was dry enough for North America's first settlers to walk to America from Asia, both Australia and New Guinea were also probably either connected to the Asian mainland or separated from it by short, shallow stretches of water. The first extended boat or raft voyages suggested by archaeological excavation probably crossed the Timor Straits at least 20,000 years ago, so that eons before the Polynesians had begun to emerge as a race, both Australia and

New Guinea, and the islands stretching to their northwest, became home to a dark, squat, primitive people, who had moved slowly down through Asia.

Sometime between 20,000 and 10,000 B.C., a separate race developed among the rivers and lowlands of south Asia, where the lush land was ripe for agricultural development. These people bred pigs, dogs, and chickens. Probably the world's first sophisticated farmers, they learned to hybridize and improve plants, including taro, bananas, and breadfruit. Most important, they learned the uses of the coconut. In the centuries to come, this meaty, well-protected fruit would become their staple food and beverage supplier on long voyages. Together with the adze — a unique stone Polynesian cutting tool — the coconut is a sort of atomic tracer by which one can follow the Polynesians' eastward path across the Pacific. Where there are coconut palms, there are or have once been Polynesians. Where there are none, the Polynesians either never arrived or else found the local conditions unwelcome and moved on.

Two other crucial skills these proto-Polynesians began developing along the rivers of China were boatbuilding and later very rudimentary navigating. At first they probably travelled along shore in rafts, then turned to riding astride single logs for greater speed and maneuverability. They soon discovered that logs could be hollowed out with their stone adzes and fire, but found at once that while this new device — the boat — could be paddled more easily, the finished product was dangerously unstable. Eventually, some prehistoric genius invented the light balancing pontoon, and the Polynesian magic carpet was created. By 5,000 B.C. outriggers were probably in widespread use for fishing and short voyages of exploration, and the Polynesians had laid a base for the sophisticated nautical culture they would become by the first millennium before Christ.

Toward the middle of the second millennium B.C., this quiet shoreline race on the East Asiatic Coast began to feel pressure from more warlike people to the west and from the great Aryan hordes that were sweeping across India. So the river people began moving seaward, first toward the inner islands of Indonesia. There they mingled with an older Caucasoid race from the Tigris-Euphrates valley, also forced east by Aryan invasion.

At this point, expert opinion divides on whether the Polynesians on their way east took a northern route through Micronesia or a southern one through Melanesia. Peter Buck supported the Micronesian theory, noting deep social and physical differences between the latter-day Melanesians and the Polynesians. A recent computer simulation found that it would have been easier to drift east through Micronesia than through Melanesia. But the prevailing current opinion, based on a trail of pottery and linguistic links, is that the seafarers followed a southern arc through the Solomon Islands, the Hebrides, and New Caledonia, picking up some features of the dark aboriginal inhabitants as they went, and possibly looping back to make contact with Micronesia later. How they ended up with relatively light skins after centuries of contact with the Negroid inhabitants of Melanesia is just one of many Polynesian mysteries.

Whichever route they took, the Polynesians moved on smoothly, propelled by the generally good weather, their continual need for more land to support simple subsistence economies, and their growing faith that there was always a new island waiting over the horizon. Between 5,000 and 2,000 B.C. they reached Fiji, with its arable land and abundant forests. It was probably here, during a centuries-long pause of stabilized existence on the two large Fiji islands, that the Polynesians finally stopped long enough to develop into a homogeneous race. It was here, too, that they found a perfect classroom for navigation in the hundreds of islands spinkled around Viti Levu and Vanua Levu. And as growing confidence in their nautical skills kept pace with their hunger for new lands, the Polynesians became truly amphibious.

Polynesians have long been characterized as a primitive people who could not possibly have conquered the Pacific by purposeful, systematic exploration. And it's easy to understand why. Our modern-day sail through Polynesia's vast spaces had the benefit of a diesel engine, food freezer, Dacron sails, single-sideband radio, depth sounder, two good sextants, a chronometer, and complete astronomical tables; yet navigating *Palawan* was no simple matter. It was even harder for Europeans of the seventeenth and eighteenth centuries, with their primitive astrolabes, their unreliable maps (if any), and their difficult living conditions at sea. So how could an ancient race have reached every habitable island between 20 degrees north and 20 degrees south in the Pacific without possessing even the ability to write down their calculations?

Many theorists (the foremost being English scholar Andrew Sharp, author of several books on the Pacific islands) believed that the Pacific must have been settled at random, by accidental drift voyages. Anthropologist Thor Heyerdahl's celebrated *Kon-Tiki* voyage established that ancient Peruvian Indians could have drifted to Tahiti on balsa rafts. But a number of facts do not jibe with this disparaging view of the Polynesian sailor. First, it's hard to believe that odd crews of fishermen, lost in their canoes, would just happen to bring enough food, animals, women, and seedlings to reach and establish colonies on hundreds of islands scattered across millions of miles. They had to have gone forth on purposeful, well-equipped voyages of exploration, and been able to return home and pick up the essentials for permanent settlements on new islands.

Second, why would the Polynesians have labored so over their beautiful canoes — let alone evolve a sacred ritual and mystique around the art of canoe-building — merely to take themselves fishing? The canoe was to the Polynesians what the horse became much later to Ghengis Khan and the camel was to the desert nomad; it was his means of long-distance travel, and thus the most important product of his society.

Just imagine a people with the drive and dedication to build a 50-foot canoe with stone tools; imagine hollowing out its giant hulls with adzes and fire, boring holes with sharks' teeth every three inches along its entire length, fitting planks accurately to its sides to raise the freeboard, and then sewing — yes, sewing — the planks to the hull. The perfect miro (rosewood) tree for one canoe might be chosen years in advance. Incantations were chanted at every stage of the canoe's construction. The artisans who chipped, lashed, and decorated canoes were highly respected, and the navigators who guided them were considered half-priest, half-royalty. So careful were Tahitian artisans of their "most perfect mechanical production," as Captain Cook observed, that the canoes were always built and preserved under long shaded bowers, or otherwise covered with "cocoa leaves...to prevent the sun hurting them."

As one gains understanding of these admirable people, certain strong characteristics emerge. They had used the water as a means of transport and communication for so long that they became "of the sea." Their gods were water gods; their holy places were usually at the edge of the sea. Despite the availability of large arable land areas inland on many of their islands, their homes were always near the water. Fish was predominant in their diet, and they were clever and resourceful fishermen.

The European navigators, on the other hand, out of necessity in colder climates designed ships that would protect and separate them from the sea, and thus they built vessels with high bows and sterns, and hatches that could be battened down to keep the sea out. The Polynesians had no urge to separate themselves from the sea other than to avoid drowning. The water was warm throughout their triangle, and their early rafts and logs were merely an extension of swimming. Later, they created low, easily driven vessels suitable for both sail and paddle power. If a wave overwhelmed them it wasn't the end; they hung on to the swamped canoe and kept their provisions together as best they could. When the storm ended, they bailed the canoe out, climbed aboard, and resumed the voyage. If many supplies had been lost, they could rely on their expertise with a hook and line; soon a fine catch would be on board and the ship would be restocked. Basic stocks of food and water were stored in bamboo containers and tied onto the canoe.

During his Pacific travels, Cook observed and admired many types of Polynesian canoes. On Atiu in the Cook Islands, he noted that the natives "seemed to have taken more pains" to decorate their canoes than they did in tattooing their own bodies. In Tahiti he saw a huge double canoe, "built to row with 144 paddles and...capable of carrying a far greater number of men." The Tongans especially impressed him with their "great dexterity in Naval Architecture." Using typical stone adzes, shark-tooth drills, and fish-skin rasps, they sewed the wooden hulls so tightly with sennit that it was impossible, "under any circumstances whatever," Cook wrote, "for them to sink so long as they hold together."

Several factors, including the great care the Polynesians gave to canoe-building, convinced Cook that they were not built only as "vessels of burden but for distant navigation." The Tongans, he said, could manage at least five-day, or 150-mile voyages, "directed by the fix'd stars," or in overcast, "guided by the swell of the sea and wind." One "proof of the distance or at least of the stay they make at some places," he continued, was that "they always carry a considerable quantity of cloth, matts and provisions....The number of people, amongst which there are always several women, being at least four times more than is sufficient to navigate the boat, implies some other kind of business."

Modern skeptics of ancient Polynesian seafaring abilities have often failed to account for another equally important, though less tangible, factor: the Polynesian character. Unlike the oft-praised Phoenicians, who probably never ventured more than 150 miles from shore, the Polynesians were deep-water sailors, completely comfortable on the high seas. Rather than using latitude and longitude or some equivalent for navigating, they relied on their memories, developed over generations, for hundreds of star positions and all of the environmental data necessary for successful landfalls.

Another facet of the Polynesian character that supports the theory of purposeful, long-distance voyages is the still-prevalent Polynesian tradition of emotional leave-taking. Often the ancient voyagers were motivated by sheer desire to conquer new lands, but in many cases they were physically forced to leave. Either their small islands had become intolerably overcrowded, or their tribes had lost local land feuds and had to choose between death, slavery, or permanent exile. In this case, to choose anything but departure was considered a disgrace, as illustrated by this chant of a Mangarevan mother whose son has balked at the idea of following his defeated father into the unknown:

> O Tupou, my king!
> The breakers roar on the outer reef,
> And fierce winds wail in company.
> They weep and wail for thee,
> O Tupou, my king!
> You sought the open sea
> With your seven rafts,
> But the double canoe of my son delays,
> What will he do, O Tupou, my king!

Since such risky voyages often meant that the sailors would never return, their approaching departure was always a time of anguish. Anthropologist Margaret Mead told me of Samoans who came to her in tears "because you are leaving," although she had another six months on the island. She also spoke of sobbing crowds gathered on piers to see off friends who were departing on interisland schooners to visit relatives 20 miles away for a few days. It's unlikely, Dr. Mead concluded, that leave-taking would have become such an emotional event in a culture unless purposeful, permanent goodbyes had once been a way of life.

In addition to these somewhat intuitive objections to the "drift" theory of Pacific settlement, three scientists cast doubt upon it several years ago when they conducted a painstaking computer simulation of thousands of possible drift and purposeful voyages among Polynesian islands. Accounting for wind, currents, storms, and human endurance, the researchers — Michael Levinson, R. Gerard Ward, and John W. Webb — concluded that it would have been impossible for the major islands to have been discovered merely by random drifting. They did not, however, rule out occasional discoveries by drift, even from South America, which would help account for the mysterious presence of the sweet potato in Polynesia.

If the Polynesian was, in fact, capable of celestial navigation, and thus of two-way voyages, how did he do it? His principal guides were the celestial bodies, and he chose the same seasons each year for his voyages, which placed the stars in approximately the same positions each time. Since he was usually heading east or west, the stars passed overhead roughly along his course. Without the ability to write down calculations of star positions, he logged the principal stars and at least a hundred others in his prodigious memory; he knew which stars related to particular islands for outbound voyages to known destinations; and he knew which star could be counted on when aiming for home in case his mission failed.

The Polynesian talent for memorizing is illustrated by Edward Dodd with a tale of a man who returned to his ancestral homeland after an absence of four generations. He arrived at a time when his family homestead was being disposed of because the family line had ended. He claimed the land as his by right of bloodline, and when the skeptical resident asked him for proof, he instantly and correctly recited his family's entire genealogy, all the way back to the original settlers.

Along with celestial guides, the Polynesian also used ocean indicators to chart his path. The visible dividing or joining points of ocean currents, the wind, wave patterns, weather, bird

At left is a yellow hibiscus
painted at Tahiti in 1769 by
Sydney Parkinson during
Cook's Endeavour voyage.
All the botanical and
zoological illustrations in color
in this book are from
Parkinson's cruise with Cook
as chief artist.

flights, floating feathers, driftwood, and smells — all went into the Polynesian's mental computer to give him his position and new course.

His unusual ability to detect the presence of land from up to 50 miles off, by cloud cover and other signs, enabled him to head for groups of islands, which greatly narrowed the distances he had to cover in the "unknown." Touching upon the outermost island in a group, he could move quickly to others. Returning, he could aim broadly for the center of his home group, easily finding his way to his particular island. Considering the advantages and limitations of his methods, it becomes obvious why he discovered out-of-the-way island clusters — like the Marquesas — long before groups like the Cook Islands, which fell along his migration paths but were much more widely scattered.

Along with all of the above navigation assists, the Polynesian also seemed to have an uncanny innate sense of direction. Just as migratory birds fly directly to a precise destination thousands of miles away, blind bats leave a cave to hunt and later return to the same cave, and a pet left by error at a gas station finds its way hundreds of miles home, the Polynesian navigator seems to have been able to find his way out and back again, no matter what the conditions or the distance.

Offering more modern proof of such ancient mystic powers, anthropologist Ben Finney and a mixed crew of Hawaiians and whites sailed the *Hokule'a*, a hand-built replica of a double- hulled Polynesian voyaging canoe, from Honolulu to Tahiti during the summer *Palawan* was cruising the Pacific. The crew carried only provisions prepared and stored as the ancient seafarers would have done, and they were guided only by the directions of Mau Piailug, an aging royal navigator from the Caroline Islands in Micronesia. Although a long way from home base and familiar stars, Piailug successfully steered the canoe to a Tuamotus landfall in 23 days, then on to Tahiti. At no time was his estimate of *Hokule'a*'s position more than 60 miles off the one calculated by modern navigating equipment on the escort ship following behind.

Like the long line of navigators before him, Piailug had begun his formal training at age six, was initiated as a star-path navigator at 18, and had since roamed Micronesia far and wide. In 1974 the *National Geographic* documented a 1,000-mile trip he took in the Marianas, from Satawal to Saipan and back, alone in a 30-foot

canoe without chart or compass. Such a feat recalls an anecdote repeated by Dodd in his book *Polynesian Seafaring*, about an American sea captain in 1860 who met a canoe-load of Micronesians far from land. After the captain had self-importantly shown the native chief how his modern compass and navigation instruments worked, the chief nodded casually toward his navigator and said, "His head all same your compass."

These are random observations about the Polynesians' seafaring abilities and how they may have developed, but from what we know of the Polynesian character and the indisputable evidence of their discoveries, there is no doubt that the theories of island discoveries resulting from haphazard landfalls or storm-lost canoes are wrong. The Polynesian wanted new worlds to conquer, and he knew that there was always another island beyond the horizon — if not in one direction then in another; if not in 100 miles, then in 1,000. Most important, he knew how to find his way home and try again in a different direction if he didn't find his new kingdom on the first try. No wonder his navigators were revered; no wonder his gods were aquatic.

During their centuries in the Fiji archipelago, the Polynesians improved their navigational skills by traveling among the many nearby islands, then reached farther east into the vast archipelago, until they were finally ready to begin serious long-distance voyages. By now they had been on the water for two or three thousand years; they had become deep-sea sailors, and voyaging was in their blood. They knew how to read the stars, the currents, and the wind. They knew how to preserve water in coconuts and bamboo sections; how to keep flour and fermented breadfruit in water-tight pandanus-leaf bundles. They had learned to ration provisions strictly, making sure the pigs and chickens were kept alive to breed in the new land and that the precious shoots and seedlings were not eaten in panic. Compelled by a spirit of adventure, they had learned to temper it with the control necessary to ensure survival on long voyages. Now they were ready to take the measure of the entire Pacific.

Heading east from Fiji, they reached Tonga, 300 miles away, and Samoa, 500 miles, at least 500 years before the time of Christ. Lively trade patterns soon built up within their familiar

125,000-square-mile triangle, from which there was no easy island path farther east. But to the sea-bred, thirtieth-generation voyager, the vast area separating his homeland from its eastern neighbors was no longer a permanent obstacle. It was only a matter of a few centuries, experts now think, before the voyager had worked his way 2,000 miles east to the Marquesas, which gave him easy access to the entire Tuamotus-Societies chain.

As the Polynesians slowly moved eastward from island to island, they carried with them many old customs and myths, along with tools, weapons, and skills. They were adept at spearing fish, at making tapa cloth from the bark of mulberry trees, at cultivating taro and coconut, and at raising livestock. As the Polynesians traveled, they slowly lost contact with their forebears to the west, and differences in language, customs, and religion developed.

Aboard *Palawan*, as we sailed westward through the islands retracing this cultural tide of several thousand years ago, we were intrigued to find striking variations among the people and cultures of different islands that shared a common heritage, a common tropical atmosphere, and the omnipresent graying effect of modernization. Yet our books and our questions to local people gave us so few satisfactory answers! The Fijians, for instance, are dark with kinky hair, while the Tahitians are much lighter. How did the Polynesians maintain their integrity as a race while passing through Fiji? Obviously some groups must have sailed directly to the Marquesas and Societies, but even the most informed scholars can only speculate as to how the rest arrived in the eastern Polynesian homeland with essentially Polynesian characteristics and skins lighter than the people inhabiting the islands whence they came.

When the Pacific settlers reached the area now called Central Polynesia around 2,000 years ago, the Society Islands, and particularly the lush isle of Raiatea, became the center from which numerous exploratory voyages radiated in all directions. Raiatea is often referred to as "Havaiki," the ancestral homeland of Polynesian myth, although other accounts have named a succession of islands from Java to Raratonga as the true Havaiki. Today, anthropologists are quick to discourage the once-popular idea of great fleets of canoes emigrating in waves from any of these Havaikis. The settlement of the Pacific, they emphasize, was a gradual, natural process that took thousands of years.

From Central Polynesia, the seafarers soon began making longer exploratory voyages. By 300 A.D. they had reached Easter Island, more than 2,000 miles from the closest Polynesian inhabited point — Mangareva, at the southeast tip of the Tuamotus. As we, in *Palawan*, sailed that distance from northeast to southwest, running before the brisk easterly trades, this particular Polynesian voyage seemed the most remarkable one of all. During the first few hundred miles of their eastward voyage, they might have encountered Oeno, Henderson, and Pitcairn Islands, and perhaps a few other isolated spots, but for the next 1,700 miles there was absolutely nothing to help a non-celestial navigator — just a waste of endless ocean, and a wind that blew unceasingly against them.

Night after night on that long ocean stretch between Easter Island and Mangareva, I dreamed of these great sailors, compared their canoes to Palawan or even to Cook's *Endeavour*, and wondered how they had ever done it. How much easier it all would be to explain if they had, in fact, been Incas, and had come downwind from South America. But when Captain Cook arrived at Easter with a Tahitian companion, he found that the inhabitants spoke a language very similar to his friend's. By 600 A.D. other Polynesian seafarers had also reached the Hawaiian Islands several thousand miles north of Raiatea, the center of Polynesia, and by the tenth century they had settled in New Zealand. The entire South Pacific was theirs.

Why then, when Cook visited Hawaii, did he not find the great canoes traveling frequently to Tahiti? How did the most highly developed seafaring society let its most valuable art fall into decay? One may speculate that once they had reached every habitable island in their triangle, and their endless efforts to find more had ended in frustration or death, the Polynesian voyaging canoes and navigators disappeared. In short, their abilities, their ambitions, and their existence had been dominated for more than 4,000 years by the drive to find more land, and they had found it all. They must have concluded that further voyaging was pointless.

Today, the Polynesians remain people of the water. The men are constantly fishing, surfing, and swimming, and in front of nearly every dwelling Polynesian families keep an outrigger canoe raised on racks. They are keeping alive the most important symbol of their heritage as the greatest seafaring race in history.

CHAPTER 6

WHERE PAST IS PRESENT:

Easter Island Rendezvous

Weather conditions were generally as forecast for this time of year in the Pacific — calm and hot sun — and we had been making steady use of the engine when, suddenly — only 40 minutes before Friday the thirteenth — the oil pressure warning light for the gearbox lit up. We're not superstitious, but this seemed an ominous beginning to our first long ocean passage. We immediately shut down the engine and tested the oil in the gearbox. It looked milky and tasted salty. Warm Galapagos water had apparently slowly worn the soldering in the oil gear cooler and seeped into the gearbox. Hoping to maintain way while we worked on the problem, we quickly hoisted sail, but there was hardly a breath of air. Paul and Dave resolutely went to work, using compressed air to isolate two leaking cores in the small radiator, then inserting epoxy and wooden plugs to fill them. To my amazement, that worked. We changed the oil several times until the last trace of salt was gone, and by 2000 were powering on as before. Without their superb ingenuity and teamwork, this passage could have taken far longer.

During the next two days we slowly worked our way into the southeast trade winds, and the crew's spirits rose accordingly. There is nothing more pleasant than sailing in these steady, moderate winds with fleecy clouds overhead and a blessedly cool temperature on deck. Pacific voyagers, from the Polynesians in their canoes to Ferdinand Magellan in his primitive, 110-ton ship, *Trinidad*, must have felt similar relief as they entered the trades after sweltering, motionless, for weeks in the doldrums.

I had asked Jimmy to let me take over the navigation between the Galapagos and Easter. His brother was very ill, and there was a strong chance that Jim would have to return home. Because it had been several years since I had taken full responsibility for the navigation on a long offshore passage, I wanted to get in some practice while his tutorial assistance was still available. At this point we were almost directly under the sun. Four days south of Academy Bay the sun's angle of declination would equal the latitude. Since the sun would be directly overhead at midday, noon sights would be impossible. But for the first two days I was able to take fairly accurate morning, noon, and evening sights as I relearned this art under Jimmy's watchful eye.

As we left the Galapagos and its teeming wildlife for the mysteries of Polynesia, Craig MacFarland and his daughter, Bennet, joined us for the passage through the coral heads to the open ocean, their Zodiac tied alongside. During dinner at the Station this evening, I spent some time talking with Craig and other scientists about the work being done in the Galapagos, trying to discover ways to be helpful. There was much to talk about; it's been a stimulating evening.

We came back aboard about 9:00 P.M., and got underway immediately under power. There is no wind and the sea is glassy under a lovely moon and a cover of stars. After a short time, the MacFarlands slipped over the side into the Zodiac to make their way back to the Station, leaving us to settle into our 2,000-mile, possibly two-week, westward passage to Easter Island.

LOG ENTRY: FEBRUARY 14, 1976

When we look back, I think we'll all agree that this was the happiest and most carefree part of the voyage. The crew is getting along exceptionally well, and the cooks are increasingly creative with the fresh meat and vegetables we have left. The three girls seem to bicker constantly and goodnaturedly with Paul, although Ellie, who got to know him well on the Greenland passage, keeps her feelings largely to herself. The differences between them are heightened by the fact that Ellie has never developed a real interest in the nautical aspects of the cruise. In the past few days she has complained, in fact, that the preoccupation of Robin, Jim and me with navigational tasks has substantially reduced the pleasure of the sail. I disagree. Missing our Easter Island landfall might be more serious than she could possibly imagine.

The wind has picked up and we're averaging nine knots with the boat moving easily.

Jim Madden is a remarkable man. He is a fine navigator, shipmate, and friend, and is patient to a fault; I've never seen him lose his temper. I admire him above most men. I have sailed many hundreds of miles in competition with — and usually behind — him as he raced his lovely 57-foot sloop *Gesture* in countless ocean races. At the 1936 Olympics in Germany, Jimmy and his sister represented the U.S. in pairs skating, a sport that takes great physical and mental agility. Much of this has remained with him ever since, and on this cruise, as during our Greenland passage, Jim's nautical skills, humor, and companionship had contributed tremendously to the ship's morale. I knew I would miss him greatly if he were to leave.

Just after sunset two days out, we came upon one of the half-dozen vessels we were to encounter at sea along the entire route. At first it appeared to be a small freighter with a steadying sail, but as we got closer it turned out to be a sparkling, modern tuna boat out of San Diego. As we circled to watch, the crew, aided by two large workboats, floodlights, and clanking equipment, were hauling in an immense netful of flopping tuna with a hydraulically powered sheave. The bull wheel must have been six feet in diameter. The work looked highly efficient but hazardous; the decks were slippery and the boats were pitching and rolling considerably.

Shouts rang out between the mother ship and the workboats, which we first attributed to our female crew members, but it soon dawned on us that the men had hardly noticed us. Their attenion was riveted on $20,000 worth of tuna wriggling in a $10,000 net. As the sun sank, the machinery clanked and whirred, the crew struggled with their treasure, and we sailed off into the soft night.

Anticipating possible engine or electrical problems, I decided to take Paul off watch so he could give full attention to our mechanical and electrical equipment. I, too, stood down as skipper-navigator, and the other three men each took one watch with one of the women. The single-sideband radio was proving to be a great morale builder. Each crew member was able to get a message to his or her family at least once a week; I spoke with Olive in Vail, Colorado, frequently, and we arranged with our shipyard in Maine to have a spare oil cooler sent with the crew joining us at Easter Island.

The trade-wind clouds climbed every day from the southeast,

moved in stately parade across the sky, and receded to the northwest. The sea was an intense blue, and from the foredeck I could see flying fish spraying out from under the bow. Depending on the sun's angle, their translucent wings reflected green, purple, or yellow during their brief moment of flight. In these tranquil seas, I found I enjoyed spending long periods alone on the foredeck, feeling the ship's motion and watching the fish, while lost in thought about the Polynesians who settled Easter Island.

Palawan was comfortable and easy to handle as the wind increased, and we had many sail options to use. One night we furled the mizzen, which eased the helm and slowed the boat down; a few hours later the motion became uncomfortable again, so we reduced sail further, changing to a small jib and single-reefed main. The sail changes went well; we ran off in the process to ease the motion, but the women needed more practice in handling sail.

All seemed to be going well, but as time went on and our destination neared, I, as navigator, began to get nervous. One night I dreamt that my calculations had been wrong and we arrived at the spot where Easter Island should have been to find no land at all. Embarrassed, and imagining the notoriety this would bring me among my nautical friends, I sailed in a square pattern, then finally had to request radio assistance for an ignominious landfall. When I awoke from this nightmare, it took me a few minutes to shake it off and realize that *Palawan* was actually making good progress and my navigation so far was apparently accurate. In my dream I had forgotten that Jim Madden was aboard, backing me up.

The wind continued steady, and on the seventeenth we ran 212 miles by dead reckoning, with the sun still too high to take a noon sight. Well and good, but Easter was still but a tiny five-mile-by-eight-mile speck rising perhaps 1,800 feet on that vast ocean, and still some distance away.

Not quite a week on our way, I noticed that the first water tank was running dry. I calculated that each person must be using about 2-1/2 gallons a day — far too much. Hoping to scare some sense into the crew, I posted a dramatic notice saying that if consumption did not immediately drop to a gallon and a half per day, I would turn off all the water except the galley pump. This produced results. Everyone now monitored pump use, par-

Squalls at midnight with winds 18-25 knots. We reached 10 knots at times. The course was 215 magnetic; longitude at noon — 96 degrees, 6 minutes west; latitude — 9 degrees, 25 minutes south. 622 miles from Academy Bay and we have been at sea 88 hours. Our average, including the time down with a bad engine, is 7.3 knots. Not bad.

ticularly of the pump in the main head, which was audible in the two forward cabins where the four women were sleeping. There were immediate loud protests whenever Carter pumped the handle too many times in the process of becoming her immaculate self. As an additional conservation measure, I hooked up the saltwater pump and hose on deck and offered the crew daily deck baths after lunch. The conservation efforts worked well, and, as it turned out, we had plenty of water all the way to Tahiti.

The wind quieted down early on the morning of the eighteenth, and Paul took three morning star sights, which I later confirmed by an 0830 sun line. The next day, with winds steady at 20 knots, we logged 207 miles, again through occasional squalls and rain. But by 1800 on the twentieth we were only 503 miles from Easter.

That night I belatedly discovered that I had been using a base compass course with a nine-degree error, putting us 60 miles to windward of the rhumb line. The mistake, immediately corrected, caused us no real problem, although if it had been to leeward we could have had some difficulty. Then, the fitting on the exhaust of the auxiliary charging engine broke; a minor mishap, but combined with my navigation error, it was enough to give me insomnia. My stomach was already in a knot, suffering from the typical navigator's "I'm not sure where I am" syndrome.

Perhaps one reason for my making the voyage was to experience, at least in part, the thrill that the Phoenicians, Vikings, Portuguese and, of course, the Polynesians, must have known when they made new landfalls. The world's oceans have now been thoroughly explored, but one can still come a little closer to the feeling of the ancient mariners by sailing into remote regions in small boats. So, there I was, equipped with the latest in mechanical and navigational devices as well as creature comforts, searching for new nautical challenges with a very nervous stomach proving I had found them.

Yet, already there were rewards for the worry and effort. During long sea passages, sailors enter a world of their own. For those 12 days from Galapagos to Easter, *Palawan*'s crew was free from civilization and its problems, and we experienced — for a time — the isolation that must have been felt by Cook, Magellan, and Hotu Matu'a. Our concerns were with food, wind, sails, weather, and little else. We even stopped listening to short-wave news broadcasts. Only *Palawan* mattered; so much so that it took

a little time to adjust to new faces, new companions, and new conversation when we greeted new crew members at Easter.

On the morning of the twenty-first, as I was fumbling through the radio frequencies, I picked up, loud and clear, a signal identified as IPA — Isla de Pascua (Spanish for Easter Island) — dead ahead. When Jimmy heard it, he turned in and slept for eight hours. Had he, too, doubted my navigational abilities? That night, to celebrate, Carter prepared a marvelous Quiche Lorraine. While the rest of us had long since reduced our culinary efforts to the simplest fare, she was still doing her exotic cooking, leaving innumerable pots to clean, but a very satisfied crew. As long as the clean-up squad didn't object, her creations were great morale boosters.

By early Sunday, we had only about 150 miles to go. At 2030 that evening shadows appeared on the radar, and shortly after 2300 Dave and Paul spotted land lights. We then hove to ten miles offshore, set up single-man watches for the night, and broke out the champagne. Once corrected, our course had taken us right to the center of the island. I had made a number of other small errors, which I listed for future reference: mismeasuring the mileage on the plotting sheets, failing to adjust the course each day to a new rhumb line, and making numerous math mistakes in working out the sights. But since this was my first major celestial navigation effort in 30 years, I wasn't altogether unhappy with the results.

At dawn we were motoring around the island, staring at its several volcanoes, grassy hills, and the black lava coastline rising from white pounding surf. As we rounded the southern tip of land, we recognized the cliffs of Orongo, the "Bird Rocks," site of the traditional birdman rites. According to legend, each spring servants of the chiefs dove from the cliffs and raced out to Moto Nui, the nesting rock of the sooty tern. The first man to swim back with an intact tern egg was the winner, and his chief was named the new "Bird Man," an annually rotating position of half-mystical, half-political island leadership. We're told this rite of ruler selection was practiced until less than 100 years ago.

We dropped anchor at 0930 off the village of Hanga Roa in Cook Bay — actually just a bight in the shoreline and a very uneasy anchorage — where we rolled for the entire five-day visit. Fortunately, the resourceful Paul had built a plywood "flopper

The coastline of Easter Island is a generally steep-to shore of black lava rock with only a few harbors or anchorages.

Here settlers arrived about 2000 years ago and built a sophisticated civilization that has left remarkable artifacts and many mysteries.

stopper," a hexagonal piece of wood pierced with many holes and weighted with lead. When suspended out from the side of the ship on a spinnaker pole with a bridle and dropped about 10 feet into the water, it acted as a counterweight to reduce the boat's uncomfortable rolling motion.

In such restless waters I felt we also had to establish some basic rules for the use of the dinghy. We agreed that only Paul, David, or I would operate the outboard and that no shore trips would take place unless one of us was observing from *Palawan* to make sure that the prevailing winds didn't carry a stalled dinghy and its helpless occupants off toward the Marquesas. Landing was an equal challenge: one had to steer between two reefs, then turn suddenly inland, and the water near the landing place was full of rocks washed by a constant surge. It required tricky maneuvering and a firm hand.

With safety procedures now established, we were all eager to get ashore and to see some of the artifacts we'd read about: the huge "moai" statues with their one-ton topknots of red "hair"; the carved figurines of mythical hybrid creatures; and the caves that honeycomb the island.

No one is sure whence Easter Island's first settlers came. One theory holds that the island was once part of the lost continent of Atlantis. Carbon-dating has shown that the island was populated shortly after the birth of Christ. Anthropologist Thor Heyerdahl believed it was settled by South American Indians, and the presence of both the sweet potato and stonework that resembles Inca ruins as much as Marquesan stonework tends to support his claim. However, most anthropologists agree that the settlers followed Polynesian paths, with an early group arriving from the Marquesas, and perhaps a later one from central Polynesia.

Whoever they were, the inhabitants managed to build — completely isolated from the rest of the world — a sophisticated society of up to 6,000 souls, whose craftsmen erected huge stone figures and whose wise men developed a script that has yet to be deciphered. Yes, at one time it was a balanced, artistic, and adequately governed society. Then something inexplicable happened. It must have evolved slowly, but the result was that the ruling members became obsessed with the notion that very large statues could add to their earthly influence, give them immortality, or both. So more and more workers were diverted from the fields or fishing to statue-making until, about 1600 A.D., they were literally starving themselves to death.

Tensions mounted, the once-united population became fragmented, and finally the Golden Age crumbled. According to legend, the enslaved race overthrew its masters in 1680, toppling the statues it had been forced to erect, and the people quickly deteriorated into a rabble of terrified cave-dwellers and disorganized savages. The present-day inhabitants of preponderantly Tahitian and Chilean blood show the effects of this revolution and other blows even today, some 300 years later.

Easter Island has been given many names. The Spaniards who visited there in 1770 called it San Carlos. The early natives named it variously Whyhu, Tamareki, Teapy, and Ti Pito or Te Henua, or "Navel of the World." Modern Polynesians call their home Rapa Nui, or "Great Rapa," because it resembles the slightly smaller Rapa Island in the Austral chain. The name "Easter" came from Dutchman Jacob Roggeveen's chance discovery of the island on 6 April 1722, which was Easter Sunday. Roggeveen thought the island to be "Davis" Land, an island previously spotted by buccaneer Edward Davis. (Subsequent analysis suggests that Davis either mistook a cloud for land or was a poor navigator, for the location of his "island" was at least 1,000 miles from Easter.) Following Roggeveen's discovery, the island came to be called "Easter," or "Isla de Pascua."

Disappointed that he had not discovered the great southern continent, Roggeveen evinced only a cursory interest in the several hundred tall natives with strange hats and stretched earlobes, who lived in rude huts and cooked in the ground, and whose women seemed to be hidden or dead. Moreover, the strangely incurious Roggeveen barely bothered to mention "certain remarkably tall figures," which he assumed were "formed out of clay or some kind of rich earth."

A somewhat more detailed account came from Captain Cook, who paid an equally brief visit in 1774, recording similar evidence of poverty and noting that many of the statues had fallen down. "The present inhabitants," he concluded, "have more certainly had no hand in them, as they do not even repair the foundations of those which are going to decay." Among other traits, Cook noted the islanders' now-famous penchant for petty thievery. So daring were these chronic, if good-natured, thieves, he reported, that "it was with some difficulty we could keep the hats on our head."

Only one other explorer, Frenchman La Perouse, called on Easter during the late 1700s, finding during a casual stopover in 1768 that the natives seemed to be in greater number and better spirits. Soon afterward, however, a different opportunist — the slave trader — began to visit Easter, opening another sad chapter in its ravaged history. Ships raided the island throughout the nineteenth century, and one particularly poignant account from 1805 tells of a group of captives, who, released on the deck of a New London slaver many miles from land, instantly dove overboard in a vain attempt to swim home.

In 1862, a Peruvian slaver took some 1,000 natives (virtually the entire useful population), including the last island king and many of the wise men with memorized knowledge of island ritual, to work in the Peruvian guano mines. Protests eventually forced Peru to return the captives, but by then 900 had died of disease and demoralization, and the few who came home disastrously infected the rest of the populace with smallpox.

It was a miserable, menacing horde that confronted Father Eugene Eyraud, Easter's first missionary, when he arrived in 1864. His Christian zeal, however, proved a mixed blessing, for he ordered many of the "rongo-rongo" script tablets burned, thus cutting a few more links with the past that war, raids, and leprosy hadn't destroyed. Luckily, later missionaries saw the need to preserve these links. Father Sebastian Englert, a gentle, white-bearded Capuchin, who lived

Helen and I pose on one of the pedestal-shaped stones to be found on Easter Island. They, along with the ring of stones at right, are among the many enigmatic works of the civilization that built the famous statues.

on the island from 1935 to 1969, spent years interviewing elderly natives, recording bits of legend and genealogy, and painstakingly collecting material to give the world a fuller account of Easter's past. He wrote a number of books on the island, some of them rather technical and others for the casual reader. We felt that his information was the most dependable we had found.

At the turn of the century, the world had finally become aware of this rare ethnological test tube. In 1886 an American ship's paymaster, William Thomson, spent 11 days there and, with help from a half-caste sheep rancher, compiled an extensive report on the island's customs and myths. In 1914 a determined and resourceful Englishwoman, Katherine Scoresby Routledge, built a ship, organized an expedition, and spent several months on Easter living among the natives. When trying to coax once-memorized lore and myth from the minds of aging inhabitants, she found that the younger ones had no interest in the great statues, which they considered an "everyday fact of life, like stones or banana trees."

From the Franco-Belgian Expedition of 1934, Alfred Metraux produced a wealth of research on island habits and lore, and during his 1956 visit, Thor Heyerdahl cataloged an amazing array of ancient ornaments and artifacts — grotesque petroglyphs of double-headed male figurines with protruding ribs, and more rongo-rongo hieroglyphics. Although the ancient island culture had disintegrated long before any serious studies were made of it, the painfully gathered, remaining fragments are priceless aids to learning more about both the Polynesians and the development

of a unique society with 15 centuries of total isolation. The statues, of course, are the island's most unforgettable feature, but the typical skeleton-like figurines carved recently and available for sale impressed me profoundly. I couldn't help but feel that their source lay in that first canoe of brave Polynesian seamen who must have been very close to starvation when they arrived at Easter nearly two thousand years ago.

My youngest daughter Helen, my wife Olive, and my sister Helen Buckner were joining us at Easter. About an hour after we anchored, a jet bringing the three of them appeared overhead, circled us, and vanished ominously into the hills. We were relieved

moments later to hear the familiar sound of jet engines reversing on a landing strip. Soon after this we were boarded by three slight, Latin-looking men, who shared a beer with us, stamped our passports, and told us in broken English that we could not go ashore until we had been cleared by the local doctor. David immediately took the dinghy in to shore and returned with the doctor and with the weary but smiling new arrivals. It was a wonderful but strangely nervous reunion after our long passage.

I had been anticipating, in particular, the arrival of daughter Helen — to whom this book is dedicated — one of the loveliest, kindest, most unpredictable, most maddening, and most lovable people I know. Each of our six children has great strengths, and each is very different from the others. Helen loves adventure and often plunges into new situations without a great deal of thought. Since I am very direct in criticizing, we occasionally clash. But she also has the tremendous asset of a great and warm heart, so our differences are quickly settled.

Now I looked at her with real concern. Always a thin, lanky girl, she looked to my worried eyes like a walking skeleton. Was it college, a boy friend, or something deeper? Unable to define the problem, I fretted silently about who or what could have done this to my beloved flesh and blood.

Helen was born in July of 1956, just a few weeks after the death of my father. Dad was a very strong man, whose influence and absence I feel deeply even to this day. And so in many ways, Helen is what the Lord gave as he took away. She was a lovely baby but kept us constantly on the alert, first because of intermittent fevers, and later with a vexing hip problem.

She was two when we made our family junket to Scandinavia in 1958, and one bleak night at the Goteborg Yacht Club we called home to find out that she had a fever of 104 degrees. We decided to wait 24 hours, and if it wasn't better by then, one of us would return home. Later that night, we heard on the radio that the U.S. had landed troops in Lebanon to quell an incipient revolution. Still later, our 14-year-old son was taken to the local hospital with what proved to be pneumonia. It was a long evening for Olive and me. About 1:00 A.M., with heavy hearts, we walked back to the boat in the rain, figuring things could only improve from here. And so they did. By the next day Helen's fever was down, Tom was recovering, and the Russians had not entered the Middle-Eastern fray.

One day several years later, Helen came in from skiing with a slight limp, and my ever-alert wife took her to a doctor. A week later we were faced with these alternatives: dig into her hip socket with a large needle to examine the bone, or wait several months while her problem was followed by X-ray. It was a hard decision, for had the biopsy proven positive, Helen would have had to lose her leg. We opted to wait and pray. Fortunately, that proved to be the right decision, and eventually everything worked out happily. However, those were anxious days for us.

I also have many happy memories of Helen as a child; and these must be the greatest blessings of parenthood. She loved to ride behind me on a motorcycle, and later there were many weekends in Vermont or Maine with Helen and a pal sharing a weekend in the woods with Pop. Happy memories.

Helen radiated happiness all around her, and she had a talent for making good friends, whom I usually liked as much as she did, in the end. But what a spectrum they ran — from nice or conventional to way out. I couldn't argue too much over the assortment of men — boys — creatures, because we had a common bond: we loved Helen. At boarding school, she had a facility for getting into minor — and, occasionally major — trouble, but she usually managed to talk and charm her way out of any crisis.

In fact, while she was filled with adventurous spirit, she had more than her share of luck, and could usually land on her feet. One evening in 1972, as Olive and I sat on the deck of *Palawan* in the Hardanger Fjord in Norway, worrying and waiting for an overdue Helen to return to the ship from a hiking expedition, her friend Carter said, "Mr. Watson, don't worry about Helen. She does lots of crazy things, but she always manages to come out all right." Just at sunset Helen and her friend returned, having reached the snow line as planned, reassuring us there was nothing to get excited about.

In 1974 she went off to Pitzer College in California, where it all began to come together for her. She had always been artistic, and now she channeled her activities and improved her talents. She also grew fond of her art teacher, who was a steadying and helpful influence. She had grown into a lovely young woman, still maddening enough to make her real, but increasingly an adult who was a lovely friend as well as a beloved daughter. Small wonder that, when she asked to go voyaging with me in the Pacific, I was flattered and delighted.

It was a while before I learned what was bothering Helen at Easter Island, but eventually the story unfolded. She was sad at leaving an unnamed someone in California, and worried about whether to enter this nautical microcosm, from which there would be no escape for extended periods, or to tell Daddy no thanks and accept the storm and lecture that might follow. Those first five days together were difficult, but before we left Easter Island, Olive had smoothed everything out and Helen and I began the nicest three-month period I have ever spent with a young adult. Without my wife's great patience and tact, however, the conclusion might have been less happy.

Once ashore on Easter, we lived in three rooms in the small Hanga Roa hotel. Olive and I had one room, my sister Helen Buckner a second, and the crew rotated turns in the third. The first impression that penetrated our sea-numbed consciousness was that the island, despite its modern airstrip and government efforts to make it a tourist attraction, could barely support its 3,000 residents. Dozens of wood carvers hovered around the docks, with not one tourist to buy their wares. Yams, taro, and other vegetables were on sale at the local market, but the farming efforts seemed limited, the methods primitive. In addition, the island was overrun with horses. Kept for sentimental reasons, they are slowly consuming the great pastures of the island, which in the late nineteenth century supported thousands of English sheep.

In the recent past there have been several unusual attempts to organize island agriculture. One group of enterprising natives built a series of citrus plantations on the understanding that a Chilean fruit-processing plant was to be set up on the island. When no factory arrived, one very industrious native began buying the fruit instead and feeding it to his expanding pig herd. From this start, he moved on to other projects and eventually became a wealthy man and an island leader.

During the late 1960s, the son of former Defense Secretary Robert McNamara spent considerable time on Easter. Quickly accepted by the islanders, he later persuaded them to participate in a constructive agricultural plan. Rounding up all the untended cows, he organized them for milking, giving the owners half of the income and putting the rest back into the project. During *Palawan's* visit, young McNamara was at college in California, and the islanders were anxiously hoping for his return.

These and occasional other ventures have unfortunately had little effect on the overall poverty of Easter Island life, and we found it hard to blame the natives for trying to take advantage of wealthy-looking tourists who arrived on planes and yachts. On her arrival, Helen's camera vanished, then mysteriously reappeared after she offered a $40 reward. Another evening, while returning to the hotel I was pursued by, of all things, a procurer. Although I couldn't help feeling complimented that he considered me, with receding hairline and wrinkled face, a potential customer, I was

eager to lose him. He was insistent, offering me marijuana, girls, boys, and whiskey, and only as we reached the front steps of the hotel did he retreat; a thoroughly unpleasant fellow.

The next morning we found an excellent Chilean guide, Charlie Wilkins, with whom we toured the island. Although the residents were now clustered in just a few settlements, the land had once been widely settled. Evidence of a former civilization was everywhere on the grassy plains: a cluster of round stones, an ancient segment of road, the bow-shaped foundations of a small stone house. The most overwhelming sights, of course, were the statues. Until you stand in the shadow of an immense, solemn stone face half-buried in centuries of earth, you cannot fully comprehend what the adventurous Mrs. Routledge meant when, after six months there, she wrote:

> *In Easter Island the past is present; the inhabitants of today are less real than the men who have gone; the shadows of departed builders still possess the land...the whole air vibrates with a vast purpose and energy which has been and is no more.*

As we drove around the island, we passed dozens of moai statues — there are 245 in all, representing about 75 tribal burying grounds. The figures range up to 55 feet tall and weigh as much as 75 tons. Underneath the statues are platforms called ahus, in which dead chieftains were buried; common folk rested beneath the squared stones laid on a platform in front of each moai. Although stylized, each huge face seemed to have some distinguishing features, and must have corresponded, at least impressionistically, with the noble buried beneath. Gazing with infinite dignity across the plains, or toppled to odd, randomly intimate angles, the great heads seemed, as one writer put it, "to be talking among themselves."

Most of the statues now standing have been painstakingly re-erected by Prof. William Mulloy of the University of Wyoming. Having returned many times since he first came to Easter with Heyerdahl, he probably knows more about the island than anyone else. The professor is a legend so beloved by the natives for giving them back their heritage that the Chilean government has given him a home here, to which he intends to retire.

For years anthropologists puzzled over how the early inhabitants could have carried and raised the giant statues, and the legend that the moais "walked" wasn't much help. Under Mulloy's dedicated efforts, the mystery appears to have been solved. To move the stones, he determined, the natives probably hung them between two large beams fastened together like scissors. They pulled this cradle along step by step, first the lower ends of the legs — then the hard pull of the apex from which the statue was suspended — levering the huge stone figures ahead a few feet at a time and making the statues almost seem to "walk."

To place the statues in an erect position on their platforms, the ancient builders probably used levers that raised them a few inches at a time, piling up more and more rocks underneath and slowly bringing the heavy figures upright. Curiously enough, although the Easter natives Mulloy encountered seemed entirely ignorant of these methods at first, they eventually proved not only willing to help him work but also seemed instinctively familiar with how to go about it.

The professor's most important project, completed in 1960, was the resurrection of a line of seven statues called Ahu Skivi, north of Hanga Roa. Native legend says that they were built first in memory of the first seven settlers. Unlike any other moai, they face directly towards Tahiti.

There was so much more to see! First, the ruins of the stone houses at Anakena on the north shore, where it was said Hotu Matu'a first landed. Then the Poike ditch, a long, grassy depression cutting off the northeast corner of the island. Local legend says that in 1680 the Long Ears, the ruling family, fearing a rebellion by the enslaved Short Ears, fled to Poike and dug the trench behind them, planning to fill it with brush and set it afire if they were attacked. But the plan failed when the Short Ear wife of a Long Ear warned her tribe, which enabled them to quietly surround the peninsula. In the surprise attack, most of the Long Ears perished in their own ditch. Thus began the long period of warfare that led to the mass destruction of the moais and the disintegration of early Easter culture.

On our last day Olive and I drove to the quarry where the moais had been cut out of the volcanic slopes. At a distance, the grassy slope of Rano Raraku seemed to be covered with lumps of black earth, but we soon saw these were giant heads, tilted in the soil just as they were left centuries ago. The workers had formed

Above is one of the moais shown prone in the quarry where it was shaped, ready to "walk" to its place among the 245 such statues on the island. At right and at the top of this page are lesser but equally fascinating works in stone, including my old-man-with-goatee.

a primitive production line. At the bottom of the quarry were clefts from which many statues had been removed. Halfway up were partly carved figures, some barely outlined, others almost finished and held to the rock by slim keels. All were carved so close together that not a square foot of rock was wasted. It was staggering to think of the millions of man-hours needed to carve all these figures. Imagine the extraordinary feats of engineering required to move each one, weighing at least a dozen tons, down the steep slopes uninjured. No wonder farming was neglected.

At the very bottom of the slope was a lone, very old, and haunting statue, dating from the fifth or sixth century. It was an eroded figure of an old man with a goatee, who hunched there, musing, it may be, at the folly of the efforts being made on the slope above him. He looked simultaneously enduring, pathetic, and mysterious — in short, he looked like Easter Island.

From the quarry an ancient road meandered across the plain, with statues strewn alongside. It was as if that one moment of terror — the sudden holocaust of rebellion — had frozen the scene. One felt that the workers only a few moments before had dropped their tools and hurried away to fight.

From the statue quarry we drove to Punapau, a smaller quarry site where the natives had once carved out red tuff stone to make "top knots" for many of the statues. These head ornaments weigh as much as a ton each, and again scientists had no clue as to how they were placed atop the statues until Heyerdahl and Mulloy managed to lash one in place on a prone statue and prop it up with levers. Finally, we returned to the southern end of the island to inspect more closely Orongo, with its intricately sculpted cliffs. We then hurried back to Hanga Roa just as night was falling.

We had been at Easter for five days, and had managed to visit everything of interest except the caves that wind among the cliffs or underground, and where the natives are said to have hidden their family treasures during periods of war and vandalism. Actually, I was just as glad to avoid this aspect of Easter history after reading of Mulloy's perilous descent down sheer cliffs to find cave entrances, and of Heyerdahl's harrowing experiences as he wriggled through winding tunnels to enter the caves. He wrote:

It is a horrible feeling to lie closely walled-in down underground with rock right in your face and your arms forced back over your head so that you cannot use them...You ought to think of nothing and only shove yourself along feet first by twisting the shoulder blades and dragging the heels until you notice that you can bend your knees and kick about in empty space — or that you cannot get any further along the shaft because the soles of your feet have met solid rock.

Someone once called Easter "a mystery wrapped in an enigma," and no matter how much research is done, for me it will always remain just that. In my hotel at Hanga Roa, I sometimes lay awake, awed by the remnants of an ancient culture whose secrets lie buried there. As reluctant as we were to leave this fascinating island and cast off for Pitcairn, the vast expanse of ocean stretching before us seemed comforting in comparison.

Our last day at Easter was especially sad. Not only was my wife leaving for home, but Jimmy Madden received a message that his brother was mortally ill in Boston, so he decided to return to the mainland with Olive. Since we now had an extra bunk, I asked my sister — who was no stranger to sailing, having raced boats with me in Maine when we were youngsters — to join the crew. She was surprised, as she had expected to return with Olive, but she was game as usual, and accepted. Short of sailing attire, she quickly preempted some of Jimmy's shirts and pants for the voyage.

As we started west once more, our crew make-up had shifted slightly: we had lost our gentle, capable navigator and gained two Helens. What would the next leg bring?

Olive and I stand with the seven statues said to memorialize Easter Island's first seven settlers. Aboard Palawan, *above, Lord Riverdale and my sister,* Helen Buckner, *inspect a more recent island artifact — one of the thin, fierce-looking figures carved today for the tourist trade.*

PITCAIRN:

Climax of the *Bounty* Saga

As we left Easter, wind and seas increased, making *Palawan*'s motion choppy and at times violent. It was dangerous to move about the ship unless you went from handhold to handhold, and the rolling gave us all queasy stomachs. My sister had her sea legs back within 48 hours, however, and she soon fell comfortably into the ship's routine, standing galley duty, wielding the deck mop, and participating in the daily hosing down on the stern. Both Helens were beginning to fit well into the crew, bringing fresh ideas to both the galley fare and the dinner conversation.

For most of the 1,700-mile run to Pitcairn, we expected smooth sailing, with a course clear of dangers and the prevailing wind generally abaft the beam. The Onan battery charger with the faulty exhaust repaired on Easter was working well. Although exhaust smoke had blackened part of the engine room, we were relieved that we no longer had to rely on the main engine to charge the batteries.

A period of flat calm four days out necessitated using the engine, but we kept a close watch on the gearbox oil temperature; Tahiti, location of the closest repair facility, was still a good 3,000 miles away. Although we were experiencing no other operating problems, persistent calm got on our nerves. The relentless sun on deck, unrelieved by cooling trade winds, the engine noise, the continuous rolling of the ship, and the warmth of our sleeping quarters as the aluminum hull absorbed heat from the 80-degree water combined to lower morale. A calm is one of the sea's more unkindly tests of endurance; there's nothing to do but wait it out.

Fortunately, this one did not last too long. The moment the new wind filled in, we killed the engine and our spirits lifted as the ship began to sail once more, with cooling breezes flooding below to ventilate the cabins. My confidence as navigator had returned; the crew settled into the happy routine of long after-dinner conversations, reading, games, and general relaxation; and the rest of the run was delightful.

We were all excited with the idea of visiting the island settled by the *Bounty* mutineers 200 years ago. During the run from Easter we reread the ship's paperback copies of the *Bounty* Trilogy by Charles Nordhoff and James Norman Hall, which first familiarized the world with the story of Fletcher Christian and

LOG ENTRY: MARCH 3, 1976

We continue to be amazed by Lord Riverdale. Although he sometimes forgets that he's not captain of this boat, he is certainly the most experienced cruising man aboard. He has been sailing for 60 years. He has endeared himself to all of us, and the other night we had a special dinner in his honor. He seemed quite touched. We've found several of his peculiarities amusing, especially his aversion to helping with the cooking or dishes. He more than makes up for this, however, with his eagerness to undertake any other seagoing task.

Lately I've noticed that in the leveling environment of shipboard life, the gaps between young and old tend to disappear, and the deference normally due to a man of Riverdale's age and dignity is casually forgotten. One night when His Lordship was reading at the dinner table in violation of ship rules, shy Carter stepped into the breach and loudly admonished, "Come on, Riverdale, bag it!" He complied with a chuckle, and I was glad to see the enigmatic Carter handle the situation with humor.

William Bligh, and with the existence of a tiny, mid-ocean colony of mutineers' descendants. Although fictionalized by Nordhoff and Hall, the stories were based on considerable fact.

Two days before Christmas in 1787, a small ship, HMS *Bounty*, commanded by 34-year-old Lieutenant William Bligh, sailed from England for Tahiti to gather breadfruit trees, which were considered a potential cheap source of food for slaves on British West Indian plantations. Bligh was an able navigator who had sailed with Captain Cook aboard *Resolution*; but, according to some accounts, his temper was violent and his conduct brutal, even for those days of generally harsh sea discipline.

The ship reached Tahiti in October 1788, and during the six-month sojourn there discipline deteriorated and a number of men, including a moody master's mate, Fletcher Christian, fell in love with native women. All were reluctant to leave. Bligh made some wrong decisions in attempting to bring discipline back to normal, and morale was further lowered when individual food gifts from natives were expropriated for the officers. Relations between officers and crew gradually worsened, and as the *Bounty* left Tahiti they were rapidly reaching a flash point. Less than three weeks out of Tahiti, matters came to a head. Bligh accused Christian of stealing his coconuts. Two mornings later, on 28 April 1790, a bitter and desperate master's mate seized the ship in what was to become the most famous mutiny in history.

Cast adrift with 18 loyal men in a dangerously overloaded ship's longboat near uninhabited Tofua in the Tongan Islands, Bligh piloted the craft more than 3,600 miles to the Dutch settlement on Timor, an Indonesian island north of Eastern Australia. During this astounding six-week journey, the men were sometimes reduced to 1/4 pint of water and 1/25 pound of bread per day; once they divided a captured bird into 18 pieces, "with salt water for a sauce." Hailed as a hero upon returning to London, Bligh was immediately promoted, and he continued a successful, although turbulent, naval career. Even today, his voyage is considered to have been the most remarkable open-boat voyage in history.

Of the 26 men remaining on the *Bounty*, 14 chose to return to Tahiti to await rescue. A year and a half later, a search vessel, HMS *Pandora*, hove into sight, and all 14 men, even those who had taken no part in the mutiny, were surprised to find themselves manacled and confined to a hot "Pandora's box" on deck.

After searching unsuccessfully for the remaining mutineers (and discovering several islands between the Tuamotus and Solomons in the process), *Pandora* was wrecked on the Great Barrier Reef off the Australian coast. Four prisoners drowned in their chains, but 10 were eventually returned to England for court martial. Three were acquitted, four were found guilty but later pardoned, and three were hanged.

Meanwhile, after resting in Tahiti and Tubuai in the the Austral Islands, the mutineers who had stayed with Christian accompanied him aboard *Bounty* to search for a permanent hiding place. With them were a number of Tahitians — men and women of both royal and common blood. Christian had vague hopes of reaching Pitcairn Island, which explorer Philip Carteret had discovered and named for the seaman aboard who first sighted it during a voyage in 1766. After several weeks they spotted the tiny island, landed, and began building a community under Christian's leadership.

Peaceful island life was short-lived, however, for the combination of ignorant seamen, lovely Tahitian women, and proud Tahitian men proved volatile. As a last insult to their "inferiors," the mutineers discussed dividing up the island without including the Tahitians; finally, in a week of bloody vengenace, seven men, including Christian, were murdered. Meanwhile, two other crew members began spending more time at a secret still they had built, with tragic consequences. One threw himself off a cliff during an attack of delirium tremens, while the other slowly degenerated into a crazed animal and eventually had to be killed.

By the year 1800, Seaman Alexander Smith, who changed his name from John Adams, was the last of the mutineers left alive. He found himself the leader of a community of numerous Tahitian women and 23 children of mixed parentage. Finally freed from the violence of drunken, desperate men, the island thrived undiscovered until 1808, when Captain Mayhew Folger in the American sealing vessel *Topaz* happened by and listened with astonishment to Smith's story. Here Nordhoff and Hall's tale ends, but the continuing island history is far from dull.

During the next few years several more British ships visited the colony, including Frederick Beechey's *Blossom* in 1825, and several seafarers took up residence in this quiet refuge from the world. When Smith/Adams died in 1829, settler George Nobbs, a minister, was appointed to succeed him as island leader. By now the community numbered 87 people, and it was feared that the crops they planted on the tiny island would not be able to support them much longer. In 1831 the entire colony left to go to Tahiti, but many soon trickled back, unbearably homesick.

The island's quiet was soon shattered once again by the arrival of Joshua Hill, who persuaded the islanders he had been sent by the Crown to govern them. This despot began a reign of terror, and succeeded in driving all other Englishmen from the island. He was removed by the British in 1838. During the next 20 years the island thrived again, and passersby reported that its dwellers were hospitable and hardworking. On Sundays they could be found in church singing the Pitcairn National Anthem composed by Reverend Nobbs.

By this time the English government and people had begun taking a serious interest in the welfare of the Pitcairners. Visiting ships often brought gifts of food and supplies, and when fear of overcrowding arose again, the Crown helped the entire colony to move once more. In 1895, they sailed to Norfolk Island, a recently abandoned penal colony 4,800 miles to the west. Here the Pitcairners took up whaling and began to fare better economically, but again homesickness struck. Several families returned to Pitcairn, and their descendants have inhabited the island ever since.

After eight days of good sailing in steady winds, we sighted Pitcairn early on the afternoon of March sixth. Bounty Bay, where the mutineers once anchored and later sank their haunted ship, provided an extremely rough anchorage with little protection from the wind. Instead of anchoring, therefore, we decided to heave to for the night with a watch on deck. We would visit the island in shifts the next day, leaving a skeleton crew to tend ship. As we looked shoreward now, the island seemed wild and unsettled with a pounding surf surging over black rocks against a backdrop of restless bright green foliage. Our imaginations were colored, perhaps, by the island's romantic, adventurous past, but we wondered with what anticipation or misgivings the mutineers had approached these shores.

At nine the next morning, a motor longboat put out from the beach and headed toward us. We marveled at the rugged, homemade vessel as it maneuvered in the surf; at times these boats will carry as many as 50 people on this precarious passage. This one tied up alongside, bringing the island administrator to greet us. He was a well-groomed professional named Ivan Christian, the eighth or ninth generation in direct descent from Fletcher. With him was Stephen Christian, a likable young man who reassured us in a clipped British accent, "He'll get all that bloody passport business out of the way directly and we can go ashore."

Shortly, everyone except the watch boarded the longboat, which was a delicate operation. Both the longboat and *Palawan* were rolling and pitching, making balance difficult. One toe misplaced between our hull and the longboat gunwale would have been removed instantly.

There was a moderate sea running, and as the heavy boat headed for shore, I could see several boathouses, but no place for a safe landing. Stephen, at the helm, made occasional remarks to Brian Young, the engineer — a 350-pound, very shy man who later proved to be a delightful fellow. Suddenly, we seemed to be running aground in the surf on a shallow, rocky beach and boathouses and people on shore became a blur to the left. The engine roared, we swung hard to port, and within seconds we stopped just short of a log skidway, tied up to a 50-foot pier still in quite a surge. Our arrival had been as dramatic as the island's appearance.

However, local land transportation was somewhat more sophisticated; the island was abuzz with motorbikes. Stephen, who was to be our host for the visit, immediately invited me on the back of his Honda for the ride up the dirt trail to Adamstown and his home.

His house was rambling and wood-framed, the largest dwelling on the island. It was comfortably equipped with a freezer, refrigerator, electric lighting, and a hand-cranked telephone. In addition to Stephen Christian, his wife, and their children, the house was home to assorted others: Ivan Christian and his wife, Verna; Stephen's aunt and uncle; 73-year-old Andrew Young (whose ancestor was *Bounty* midshipman Edward Young, and who resembled a retired English businessman); and an elderly Polynesian-looking grandmother, who cared for the youngest child.

As we were greeted with coffee and cake, Stephen started cranking the phone, explaining in the thickest of British accents, "I'm calling foh moh tronspoht." This obviously meant motor-

bikes; shortly a number of them were rumbling around outside awaiting us. When we had finished the refreshments, we were off on a rapid, dusty, sometimes reckless and often dangerous tour of the island. We visited the courthouse, church, and post office, in front of which rests the huge, rusted *Bounty* anchor that the crew of one of Irving Johnson's *Yankee* cruises had raised from the bay a number of years before. From 1946 to the mid-1960s, Johnson and his wife, Electa — "Exxy" — made several two-year, round-the-world voyages with selected crews of teenagers. Their vessel — *Yankee* — was a 92-foot schooner. Pitcairn was a regular stop, and the Johnsons are still remembered with affection by the islanders.

For our sightseeing tour, I rode on Brian Young's motorcycle. Although his great bulk made him somewhat retiring, all his shyness seemed to drop away as soon as he mounted the heavy Yamaha. I began the ride holding on to the taillight, and ended up hanging on for dear life, grabbing for handholds of Brian's ample flesh as we careened down hills and across shortcuts in his determination to be first to arrive at the next tourist attraction. Many of the paths were covered with slippery leaves or loose clay dust, but there were no spills or missed turns, and although we seemed to be going too fast it was never quite fast enough to bring disaster.

One of the Pitcairn families, the Youngs, had adopted my sister on arrival, and while the rest of us were high-tailing it around the island, she spent the day with them at Sunday school and church. Helen is a religious woman, and the devout Seventh Day Adventists seemed drawn to her, inviting her to their service. Noting their Sunday-best garb, she at first protested that her borrowed pants, frayed shirt, and Panama hat were hardly suitable for the occasion — actually they made her look like a down-at-the-heels missionary — but the Pitcairners insisted that she was welcome anyhow.

When she emerged from the service and met us three hours later, Helen had much to report. All the worshippers had been immaculately dressed, she said, although many had slipped their shoes off as soon as they arrived. The sermon was in pidgin English, but the kindly Mrs. Young had translated for Helen. Her overall impression was that the minister was for motherhood and against sin, and the singing was beautiful. Throughout our four-month voyage, as we moved deeper into Polynesia, we realized more and more that all Polynesians seemed to sing well and to incorporate joyous singing as much as possible into their spiritual activities.

After the service, the Youngs invited us to visit their home, and soon the entire party roared up to the bungalow. On being introduced I had the strange feeling that we hadn't come so many generations from the *Bounty* after all. Every face had a Polynesian cast, but while the men were mostly thin, light-skinned, and European-looking, and spoke English fluently, the women were generally overweight, darker, and probably not too different from the women who left Tahiti 200 years ago with the *Bounty*. All were kind to us, pressing upon us gifts of native watermelons, peaches, and lemons; I can't remember ever having spent an afternoon in a more warm and welcoming atmosphere.

Pitcairn, with no harbor, receives supplies from ships standing off, bringing loads ashore in a motor longboat.

Later we returned to the Christians' home and gorged ourselves on a huge buffet supper that included bully beef, jelly of almost solid banana, and a variety of hot and cold Pitcairn dishes, all cooked in the outdoor cookhouse ovens that are a Pitcairn legacy from its original Tahitian women. When leaving, we presented them with two boxes of gifts that we hoped would help replenish the dent we had made in the spare Pitcairn larder.

Like most of the island men, Steve carves wooden curios for the tourists who arrive on steamers, and for people aboard the occasional visiting yacht such as ours. To boost this income and replenish the meager supply of wood that grows on the island, the Pitcairners traditionally make an annual trek to Henderson Island, more than 100 miles to the northeast, where they have cutting rights in the miro wood groves. Stephen's carving specialty was sharks, and he showed us some specimens, two of which I bought and now see hanging above me as I write these words in my study.

If the story of Pitcairn Island is fascinating, the story of the writing team that made it famous is equally so. Although both were born in 1887, the romantic, Iowa-raised Hall and the austere Harvard-educated Nordhoff could hardly have been less likely collaborators. Both had done some writing and had flown for France and America in World War I. They met in 1918, jointly commissioned to write the official history of the famous American all-volunteer French flying unit, the Lafayette Escadrille.

Although they took an instant dislike to each other, they found that collaborating came quite naturally. While working on the history, they planned a trip to the South Seas, with a tentative promise from *Harper's Magazine* to publish a collection of stories they would send back. Moving to Tahiti in 1920, they traveled separately among the Polynesian islands, published *Faery Lands of the South Seas*, and then separated again for several years to write and publish independently.

One day in 1928 Hall was rearranging some bookshelves in his dusty Tahitian study when he came across a slim volume he had bought in a Paris bookshop during the war. It was *The Mutiny and Piratical Seizure of H.M.S. Bounty*, written by Sir John Barrow, Secretary of the British Admiralty, in 1831. Glancing through it, Hall was struck by the dramatic potential of the dry official account and rushed over to see Nordhoff.

The usually reserved man quickly agreed that the tale was a

"natural." Neither writer could quite believe that someone like Stevenson, Melville, or Conrad hadn't discovered the story first, so they feverishly set about locating all known accounts of the mutiny. They discovered only Bligh's emotionless report of the voyage to Timor, several brief works by seamen who had visited Pitcairn, and three sympathetic accounts by mutineers' descendants, including one called *Aleck, The Last of the Mutineers*, published by J.S. and C. Adams at Amherst, Massachusetts, in 1845.

Hall quickly interested his old old friend and Atlantic Monthly editor Ellery Sedgwick in the project, and the authors went to work, poring over transcripts of the court martial, examining a replica of the ship and charts of the area, and writing alternate chapters. They soon saw that the tale would make an ideal trilogy, but they were unsure that the general public would take the same interest they had taken. Initially, therefore, they wrote only one book, which they called *Mutiny on the Bounty.*

First published in serial form, the mutiny story was so successful that Nordhoff and Hall were encouraged. The tale of Bligh's voyage, called *Men Against the Sea*, came quickly, but the bloody island history proved harder to deal with. Sedgwick's helpful assistant, Edward Weeks, advised them to tone down the goriest parts, which they managed to do by telling the tale of Pitcairn through the blurred lens of seaman Smith's fading memory. After five years of work, the trilogy was complete.

All three books received tremendous public acclaim, and Metro-Goldwyn-Mayer bought motion-picture rights to both the mutiny and island tales. In 1935 MGM made a movie based on the mutiny, starring Clark Gable and Charles Laughton, which won several Academy Awards. In 1962 the studio produced a remake with Marlon Brando and Trevor Howard, but never did film the story of Pitcairn, which Hall felt would have made a better picture.

Although they were never to hit the literary jackpot again, Nordhoff and Hall continued writing adventure stories for the rest of their lives, producing a total of 36 books between them. Hall remained happily married on Tahiti, and when we got there one of the most interesting of our Pacific experiences was to sit in his study near Papeete, talking with his daughter, Nancy Rutgers, and his charming French-Tahitian widow. The latter described some of the trials and tribulations Hall went through

wiritng his many books, and of his relationship with Nordhoff. I found her stories fascinating.

Nordhoff's married life was not as happy; he eventually took to drink and died in despair in 1947. Hall died four years later. The two authors and the whole *Bounty* saga seemed very real to us as we ended our Pitcairn visit, enjoying the hospitality of Fletcher Christian's descendants.

Finally, at 4:00 P.M. we reluctantly headed back toward the longboat to be ferried out to *Palawan*. We could easily have stayed here for a week, visiting Fletcher Christian's cliff-top hideaway (to which Helen and Carter had climbed) and looking at the various symbolic wall-scratchings and artifacts that had provided visiting scientists with evidence that Polynesians — probably from the Tuamotus or Marquesas — had lived on the island as early as 500 A.D. We also speculated about the difficulty modern native sons would have returning to the pace and routine of life here once they had tasted life on the mainland.

As the longboat headed toward *Palawan*, we learned from Brian and Stephen that their gracious hospitality had not been accidental. As soon as a ship is sighted, they told us, the islanders draw lots to decide which families will entertain the new visitors. We had been lucky, we agreed later, that the luck of the draw had placed us in the care of the Youngs and Christians.

After depositing us safely on board, the boatsman lay ahull to await the imminent arrival of a New Zealand freighter bringing supplies and several homeward-bound islanders. It arrived a short time later, as we were storing gear and readying *Palawan* once more for sea. Eventually we got underway, circling the freighter to watch as the men unloaded her cargo. They unloaded three oil drums at a time, and we were fascinated by the sight of huge Brian Young standing with fantastic barefoot grace on the rising and falling foredeck of the longboat, steadying each load in his great arms and guiding it aboard. One misstep and he would have sheared a foot, a hand, or an arm.

As we departed, for the sake of good-fellowship and with perhaps pardonable pride, we hoisted the main and spinnaker at a distance to windward of the freighter and then sailed by in what we hoped was eye-catching splendor, waving farewells as we headed out for the Gambier archipelago and the island of Mangareva.

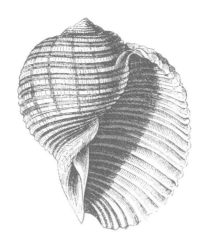

CHAPTER 8

LES ISLES OUBLIEES:
The Gambiers and Mangareva

Mangareva means "floating island" in Polynesian, and when you've made a landfall there, you understand the name. From its shores, Mount Duff rises 2,000 feet to tower over all of the other islands of the archipelago. Consequently, when you approach, Mangareva is the first land to be seen, and it does indeed seem to be floating over the water. The closer you get, other islands appear until the whole beautiful, mysterious island group spreads out across the sea.

Now called by the Tahitians "Les Isles Oubliees" — the Forgotten Islands — because of a declining population and because they are off the beaten track and not frequently visited, the Gambiers were referred to by the early navigators as "the Dangerous Archipelago." The slow, unwieldy ships and poor compasses of those days were no match for the currents and concealed reefs of the area.

We sailed into the center of the archipelago through the western pass, leaving the island of Taravai, with its village church and cluster of houses and piers nestled under the bluffs, to starboard, and circled around the southern end of Mangareva. As we neared Mount Duff, the islands of Akamaru and Aukena were visible to the east. Preoccupied as we were with our landfall, and looking forward to our first peaceful anchorage in weeks, we didn't at first notice the strange lack of any sign of life. But as we passed more villages, we fell silent under the spell of the eerie emptiness on shore. There were no sounds of children playing, no fishing boats in the lagoons, no canoes pulled up on the sand, and no one standing on the pier observing the arrival of a foreign sailing yacht; there can't be too many dropping by. The entire island group appeared to be deserted.

Our curiosity now fully aroused, we headed in toward the anchorage. As we passed over the outer reefs, the coral was closer to the surface and the deep purple-blue water changed to light green, so clear that the coral and sea-fan gardens seemed only inches under the surface, although our depth sounder indicated 15 to 30 feet of water under the keel. The coral grew in huge profusions of green, pink, and yellow, and multicolored seaweed swayed with the ocean surge. Towering to port as we closed with the land were the steep cliffs of Mount Duff.

The chart indicated a well-marked passage to Rikitea Harbor.

It is noon, and Carter, ever the sharp-eyed lookout, has just sighted the steep hills of Mangareva, largest of the Gambiers, dead ahead. I am greatly relieved. The voyage here from Pitcairn has been a tough one for me. As we started out, I had just finished reading Hall's "Tale of Shipwreck," in which he vividly described how one stormy night in 1933 his small schooner struck a reef off Timoe Island, which lies 40 miles southwest of the Gambiers, directly on our route from Pitcairn to Mangareva.

I remained on watch throughout the night to be sure we gave Timoe and its off-lying reefs an ample 30-mile berth; currents are tricky here and careful steering is vitally important. In this area there is little, if any, aid for a vessel in distress. Hall was lucky;

although lashed by wind and rain, his schooner remained pinned on the reef until dawn, when his crew made their way to shore. I want no similar surprise grounding.

This morning, reasonably sure that we were beyond the reefs, my confidence has been returning, but I haven't yet slept; I could not give up my vigil until we sighted the Gambiers.

Even though the sun was setting and the course was directly into it, making it difficult to eyeball the passage, I still made the unwise decision to try to thread our way through the coral. Fortunately, we were proceeding very slowly, with David up the mast directing our progress, when suddenly he shouted, "Full reverse!" A solid barrier of coral blocked our way. Stopping to survey the situation, we noticed about 100 yards to the south a channel marker that had been broken off just above the water and replaced with an obscure flag affixed to a short pole. Easing over to it, we continued at a crawl into the inner harbor, where at last we dropped the anchor.

Only then did it dawn on us that this was the first time since Panama that *Palawan* had been motionless at anchor. All through the Galapagos the anchorages were in open water; we had rolled at Easter; and at Pitcairn we hove to and never anchored at all. Here, after six weeks, crew and ship were finally at rest, but it was almost too quiet. Too fatigued for after-dinner games or even to talk much over dinner, we turned in soon after anchoring.

In the morning, after a good night's sleep, I gathered up the ship's papers and crew passports and rowed ashore in search of an official to inform of our arrival. With no one in sight still, I tied up to a very well-built pier and set off on a dirt road to the village center — a hamlet of several shops and a few dozen small houses — where I was suddenly startled to find myself in front of a huge stone cathedral — an astonishing construction in this primitive setting. It rose incongruously from the brush to tower over the tallest palms; I was to learn later the unhappy story of the building of this 2,000-seat house of worship.

Still seeking an official, I continued inland, fascinated by the scents, colors, and sounds surrounding me. The road tunnelled through an archway of mango trees walled by grapefruit and banana trees and bordered with luxurious clusters of bougainvillea, hibiscus, orange blossoms, frangipani, and small red orchids. Through this abundance, finally a sign of life — the smell of strong coffee being brewed. Then I began to notice people and shy smiles as I passed flower-smothered shacks set back in the brush. Shortly, I had an escort of several giggling children, and now I could see several light-skinned men and women working in the gardens. The island was not as deserted as we had thought.

I finally arrived at a house marked "Gendarmerie," and here I was greeted by Jacques Bazin, the island's only civil officer. Formal in tone, but very courteous, he explained in French that the Gambiers were restricted French territory, being less than 200 miles southeast of Mururoa, the atomic testing site of Charles de Gaulle's "force de frappe." Eventually, however, he accepted our passports and extended a welcome, asking only that no firearms or alcohol be brought ashore. I reassured him, thanked him, and returned to the ship to release the crew to do as they wished.

Man is essentially a gregarious animal, but my solitary walks ashore — I made several during the week we were at Mangareva — reminded me how much we all need moments of solitude and, on a cruise, how important it is for the crew to jump ship and scatter for a time on their own when you get into port. Shore leave lessens the personality tensions and petty irritation with annoying habits of others that are inevitable when people unused to each other are thrown in contact for extended periods. Some people adjust to it better than others; a good shipmate will find a cocoon of solitude when needed.

However, in addition to overall boat and safety responsibility, a skipper often faces special problems and tensions: how to handle a budding shipboard romance; how to reprimand a lazy dishwasher without hurting feelings; how to silence the constant talker; and how to deal with temperament and moods. It's a tremendous challenge to keep boat and crew operating smoothly. For me, it's a little like returning to the management of a business. Perhaps that's one more reason I like going to sea. But it does take its toll; hence my need for time alone and a chance to regain perspective.

As I expected, the crew returned from shore leave each with a story to tell of the day's sights and activities. However, we were all mystified by the empty cathedral and the remnants of European architecture in the deserted towns. At one end of Rikitea stood the priests' abandoned residence and beyond it a complex of stone buildings, once as impressive as the grand chateaux of France and now a maze of ruins — collapsed towers and huge blocks of cracked stone overrun with jungle vines. It seemed like the work of a giant madman.

Although some of us had read a little about the Gambiers before coming here, our knowledge was much too scanty to

LOG ENTRY: MARCH 9, 1976

After a long quiet afternoon ashore, as I relax on deck, many thoughts crowd my mind. When I returned from the gendarmerie, I was very tired and out of sorts with the world around me. I was still feeling the effects of having the full responsibility for both ship and navigation ever since Jimmy had left us at Easter to visit his ill brother. I was also aware that because of my preoccupation with the ship and navigation there had been long periods when I had been withdrawn and not as good a companion to the others as I should have been. Finally, with the crew on their own and the ship in a secure anchorage, I needed some time by myself. So I put on heavy shoes and a protective straw hat and went ashore once more, this time walking down the dirt road toward the north end of the island. The village houses ended in a scattering of huts and then there was just the heavily scented foliage. Deep

This watchtower is one of many European-style structures put up in the middle of the last century by Mangareva's Father Laval. The largest of all is the cathedral in the jungle shown on pages 98-99.

in thought, striding comfortably and feeling the confinement of shipboard living falling away, I hardly noticed my surroundings.

Three hours, five miles of walking and a swim later, I am back aboard. Now, as I bask in the sun on deck recovering from my walk, I'm physically exhausted — which I'll remedy with another good night's sleep — but I'm mentally refreshed and eagerly awaiting the return of the others.

explain what we were seeing. We did know that the first Polynesian settlers had come from the Tuamotus or Marquesas around the first century A.D., and thereafter their culture had been marked by bloody internal wars and cannibalism. Later, through reading the research of experts on Polynesia, we learned the true story — as far as it is known — of these islands and their troubled past.

"The oral history of Mangareva," wrote Polynesia expert Peter Buck in his *Ethnology of Mangareva*, published by the Bishop Museum in 1938, "consists of the struggles between different families and districts in their attempts to gain power or avenge defeats." Underlying all the unrest was a basic mismatch between the growing population and a limited amount of land. There just wasn't enough food to go around.

After Capt. James Wilson first sighted the Gambiers in 1797, no westerners, except random whalers and one British explorer, visited there until 1834, when an extraordinary French priest named Honore Laval arrived at Rikitea. We anchored there 140 years after Laval, and at first the huge deserted cathedral seemed the only evidence of his 30-year stay. During the following week, however, we were to see an exceptionally shocking example of the havoc wrought by the forceful imposition of Christianity throughout Polynesia.

Stationed at a monastery near Valparaiso, Chile, Laval was inspired to visit Mangareva by sailors' tales of beautiful pearls of great value being exchanged for trinkets, and of a cannibal kingdom where grisly religious rites were performed at maraes (altars), and where it was even said the people had to guard their dead from the scavenging flesh-eaters. Apparently, the lonely monk had a vision that he must go to Mangareva and save these sinful souls.

When Laval and a companion priest arrived, they found a society that was typically Polynesian in many respects and had changed little for hundreds of years. Noble chiefs handed down control over a dozen or so tribes to their first-born sons; common men set traps for fish and casually cultivated taro and breadfruit; artisans built canoes for tatooed warriors; priests

made sacrifices to Tu or lesser gods on open-air maraes; children climbed coconut palms and memorized their family's genealogy; and the routine of the subsistence economy was broken by frequent feasts and celebrations.

But the constant scarcity of arable land on the five tiny islands of the group, coupled with a haphazard approach to agriculture, had made the Mangarevans a hungry people, practicing strange customs. Boundary disputes could easily escalate into war, and captives were often eaten. The underfed islanders so admired obesity that they force-fed noble children until, Laval reported, "they stumbled under their own weight."

Impoverished and ripe for a new religion, the natives fell easy prey to Laval's stern authority and to his dream of establishing a tropical bastion of Catholicism. Convincing King Ma-Puteota that the new Christian God was superior to Tu, Laval systematically set about destroying the islanders' religious heritage, smashing their idols and maraes, and substituting a rigid Christianity. Having gained complete control of a race that looked to him for salvation, Laval next ordered the people to begin building a great cathedral, churches, and other structures. Driven to unceasing labor by the fanatical priest, and thrown into Laval's dungeon if they disobeyed, the people grew weak and demoralized. They became prone to the white man's diseases and their numbers dwindled. By the end of Laval's reign, the population had dropped from 5,000 in the 1600s to under 1,000.

In the 1860s, French officials from Tahiti, who had heard of Laval's empire from passers-by, began to visit Mangareva. To one of them, who accused Laval of killing the natives off with forced labor, the priest is said to have replied, "True, Monsieur, they are dead, but they have only gone to heaven the more quickly." Although a horrified French tribunal in Tahiti forced Laval to leave in 1864, the islands never fully recovered and the population continued to dwindle.

Ironically, the man responsible for the Gambiers' cultural demise also gave the world an admirable account of the society he was destroying. Laval's book on Mangarevan myth and custom has been praised as a thorough, unbiased work of anthropology. One of its many grisly tales concerns a "kaia," or flesh-eater, who in a time of famine went looking for a meal and found a young woman alone. "He tied her to a tree, cut off one thigh

and took it home," Laval wrote. "The next day he returned and cut off the other one. When her parents arrived, they found only a torso, which was still breathing."

Actually, Laval noted, cannibalism was confined usually to times of war or famine. But the people were vengeful, and the theft of even one breadfruit could precipitate "attacks, massacres, assassinations....Peace was rare, and if truces existed they were to better deceive and surprise the enemy."

Although Laval could neither understand nor accept the natives' moral and religious practices, he objectively described their infanticides, "informal" marriages, and "vaudeville-like" funerals. One can imagine this sober man taking notes in a boisterous island ceremony: "It is a melee, with all sorts of cries, leaps, contortions, spears in the air; a frightening spectacle."

Not surprisingly, the care Laval used in documenting the Mangarevans' daily life vanished when he came to describing the heavy labors he forced on them. "The heathens are capable of prodigious momentary effort, but they dislike long periods of work," he noted cryptically. "If you want to put them to the same task for more than two weeks, you must vary their activity." Even in his later, more detailed memoirs, he avoided mentioning his own role in such projects:

Without any machines, our people had to carry on their shoulders...not only foundation stones, which were sometimes enormous, but also the column stones and those used for windows, doors and corners....It was painful for those so unused to work.

Only in a second book written years later did he casually mention the dungeons in which visitors reported he locked adulterers, unwed mothers, and young boys who giggled in church.

Laval's stern brand of Christian discipline was certainly inappropriate to nineteenth-century Polynesia and much more extreme than any other missionaries' efforts to impose white man's religion on various Pacific islands. Yet, by sheer will he made it succeed for 30 years. He was a misdirected fanatic, perhaps a lunatic, but there can be no doubt as to his dedication. His undoing came when he began subjecting foreign visitors to the moral code of his island autocracy, finally imprisoning a

French sea captain for adultery. After an inquiry, the Tahitian tribunal decided to remove him from his post, saying,

With his tyrannical spirit and hot-headed character, isolated from the world and swept up by his exaggerated religious ideas, this man wants to save souls at any price, and to that end (he) sees all methods are good.

It is evident from his memoirs that Laval was deeply hurt by the criticism he received during his last years in the Gambiers, but his impassioned self-defense in numerous letters to French officials has a half-mad ring. In one letter he even quoted from the *Bible* in Latin, charging that his detractors were trying to "crucify" him.

On the second day of our stay at Mangareva, Ellie and I climbed a trail leading from the cathedral over Mount Duff to a village and church buildings on the other side. We reached the top of the hill and stood on a stone platform imagining that lookouts once perched there blowing conch-shell horns to warn of invasion. To the east lay the houses of Rikitea, the cathedral, and *Palawan* peacefully at anchor. To the north and west was a clear view of the beach, the outer reef, and the blue Pacific beyond, unchanged over thousands of years. In the words of author Robert Lee Eskridge, this was Polynesia as it had been before "Laval came trying to slip a Catholic soul into a Polynesian body with a shoehorn of fanaticism."

A painter and writer whose adventurous spirit drew him to odd places, Eskridge made his way to Mangareva in 1931 by steamer, freighter, interisland schooner, and canoe. His lyrical book, *Mangareva, The Forgotten Islands*, describes a number of strange, mystical experiences among the same empty and silent stone buildings we had found 45 years later.

Another unusual visitor was sailor Alain Gerbault, a French tennis champion of the 1920s, who left civilization for the sea, finally settling in Polynesia, where he died. During a 1925 cruise he spent three months in the Gambiers, where his initial delight in the dazzling color and tropical atmosphere soon gave way to disillusionment over the effects of European influence on the island. He described this in his travelogue, *In Quest of the Sun.* "Imported pine planking and corrugated iron constituted the

village huts," he wrote. Native dances had been replaced by the "latest European steps...straight from Tahiti." Mangarevan school children, educated under the French administration, "knew the history of France, and all about its sub-prefectures, but were totally ignorant of where Polynesia lay in the world."

As we wandered across the island half a century later, we looked in vain for signs of traditional Polynesian culture. Pushing through some pretty berry bushes, we found coffee beans growing wild where once the islanders had cultivated them. And where were the familiar canoes? Although we saw a few plywood outriggers with outboard motors, the Mangarevans apparently no longer made the traditional lagoon canoes we later saw on most of the other islands. It seemed as if this demoralized people had lost interest in passing on any of the skills that once helped them thrive.

While we were on Mangareva, and as we moved deeper into Polynesia, I found I was spending more and more time with Ellie. There were several reasons: first, she had a very inquisitive mind, and she and Anne had done more research on the Pacific Islands than anyone else in the crew, and she was always eager to explore and discuss the places we visited. Also, I admired her perceptiveness and judgment, so whenever I had a crew problem I discussed it with her. I had known Ellie a long time — her parents are old friends — and I considered her one of the most powerful personalities I had ever known. On this cruise she was willing to undertake any task no matter how unpleasant, and at night around the cabin table she was a clever conversationalist — informed, enthusiastic, and refreshingly frank.

As I began spending more time with her, there were complaints that I was showing favoritism. They weren't altogether unjust, but because of the above, I felt willing to accept the complaints and weather them as best I could.

During our week of exploring, we returned often to the cathedral Eskridge called "a Notre Dame lost in the jungle." Its rows of wooden benches were empty. Memorials to various priests lined the walls, and religious ornaments of shell strings and mother of pearl added a Polynesian touch. In front of the altar was Laval's tomb. The atmosphere was so peaceful that during our stay here we often sat in the pews writing letters or working on our diaries.

Laval's exploitation of the natives had been all-encompassing.

Children of Mangareva stand by a plywood version of the essential creation of their ancient seafaring culture — an outrigger canoe.

Even the pearls they found were given to the church, and the piers and pens he had them build were used as oyster storage areas. Before the priest arrived, the native kings had never understood the commercial value of the pearls they gathered from the lagoons, but used them as ornaments and gave many away to the early passing traders. Maputeota gave Laval a huge blue pearl, which eventually found its way to the Vatican and became a prized part of its collection. There is no evidence, however, that Laval ever used these island riches for his own gain; it was all for the glory of God.

One day David, Ann, and I took a picnic to the island of Aukena. On the island's southern tip we found a carved stone guardhouse that could have graced Versailles. A well- preserved road of coral blocks ran along the shore, and through the thick growth we glimpsed another large stone building, but had trouble making our way to it through the tangled vines that clogged the path.

Reaching a stone archway, we peered into the deserted church and saw enough pews to seat 300 and a crucifix hung with strings of shells. Walking forward we saw, in one corner, a large iron-bound chest. Filled with fantasies of Mangarevan pearls, we came closer, then quickly stopped. A swarm of black, fierce-looking bees buzzed ominously around the chest. We beat a hasty retreat. The pearls, if they exist, will long remain safety hidden in the chapel at Aukena.

After a week's sojourn on Mangareva, I reluctantly returned to the gendarmerie to pick up our passports. Again M. Bazin warned me about the atomic test area. He had, however, received a reassuring telegram from Tahiti about us. He warmed up a little, and helped me plot a course that would take us well clear of the Mururoa test area as we left. As a final gesture, he came aboard for a look at the boat and a final farewell. Then we cast off for the Tuamotus.

Our course is northwest under stars and a good breeze; the ship's motion is restful. As we leave Les Isles Oubliees, my mind is filled with questions about them: Just how were the Gambiers settled 19 centuries ago? Did an expedition from Rarotonga paddle directly 1,500 miles to land at Rikitea, or did the Marquesans island-hop through the Tuamotus until they reached the archipelago's southern tip? Was Pitcairn settled by Mangarevans, and when its original inhabitants left — long before the Bounty *arrived — did they find their way back to the Gambiers or did they go on to Easter? If Laval had never set foot in Rikitea, would an ancient society still exist, or would it have been torn apart by internal wars and corrupted by commercial exploitation?*

Tahiti and the Societies lie ahead; I never expect to see Mangareva again, but I will never forget this beautiful, fertile island, where a towering cathedral now stands with no one to pray at its altar.

CHAPTER 9

TUAMOTUS:

The "Dangerous" Archipelago

Noting that tensions cropped up among the crew on the way to Easter, it occurred to me that perhaps we all needed something to take our minds off ourselves, and that some kind of stimulating mental activity might do the trick. So, after dinner each night, instead of splitting up to find our own diversions, I initiated a routine of putting one person on the helm — assuming mild weather — while the rest of us gathered around the cabin table to deal with some mind ticklers. These sessions were an immediate hit.

Sometimes we played The Game, an idiomatic charade that all enjoyed, but which both Paul and Lord Riverdale found difficult, for different reasons. A native of Hamburg, Germany, Paul had become quite facile with American colloquialisms and loved to talk in nearly any language. Despite his impressive miming powers, he found it extremely trying to express himself silently, because acting out a foreign language is much more difficult than speaking it. Robin, on the other hand, was usually a brilliant conversationalist, but when deprived of the use of his vocal cords he was often stumped by relatively simple words. He would stand before us with a perplexed look on his face, making small, tentative motions. Frustrating as this was to him, it made him seem rather more human to the rest of us. Among the others, Carter and Helen were a little too inhibited to do too well; Anne, my sister, and I were adequate; and clever Ellie won consistently.

As an alternative to The Game, we tried a number of other intellectual exercises, introducing a variety of leading questions such as: What would you expect in the ideal mate? Such sessions were often very revealing. As I listened, there was much that I wanted to say, but for the most part I remained silent and thoughtful. Occasionally during these discussions, as they became more and more philosophical, I was jolted back to reality with the thought that here were eight of us, comfortably contained within a cozy, well-provisioned-and-appointed cabin, discussing abstracts and listening to Chopin, while just two feet under the cabin sole was a vast, deep ocean — its bottom perhaps two or three miles straight down. Strange creatures prowled the dark, pressurized depths beneath us, and only a quarter-inch of aluminum formed the protective shell that prevented *Palawan* from plunging into those depths and disappearing forever.

LOG ENTRY: MARCH 13, 1976

After we left Easter Island, as usually happens when several people are thrown together during an extended cruise, the crew has been pairing off: Paul and Robin are getting chummier; Anne and Ellie have become fast friends, and Carter and Helen frequently have their heads together, usually plotting a mutiny. Although our stateroom is only 15 feet from the main cabin, my sister and I have started to feel insulated from the rest of the crew as we settle in and reminisce, getting reacquainted with each other.

David — diplomat par excellence — has been doing his best to divide his time among the four girls, all of whom seem to have fallen a little in love with him at various times. Often I see him sitting at the bow with Helen, deep in conversation; at other times he's doing the same with Carter or Anne. Fortunately, he hasn't concentrated on one to the exclusion of the others, and

I'll be surprised if that happens. For a 22-year-old, Dave is remarkably adroit at keeping things on an even keel with all ages, and everyone likes him.

Several factors seem to have contributed to Paul's and Robin's growing friendship. Both are experienced seamen and they are much closer in age to each other than to the younger crew. Also, lately, both have found a common adversary in "The Game."

This was a sobering, chilling thought, and although I could stack up a hundred practical reasons why such a disaster was improbable, the possibility of it remained in my subconscious throughout the voyage to surface periodically and plague me.

Dusk comes with sudden finality in this part of the tropics, and Helen and I were often in our bunks as the last rays of the sun disappeared and myriad stars filled the heavens. For a while, we watched the stars through the hatch, or if the ship's motion was vigorous, watched them rock up and down through the portholes. Often childhood memories flooded our thoughts at such times, and we reminded each other of activities and events that neither of us had thought of in years. Some were recalled with a chuckle; others brought a lump to the throat.

Helen and I had had unusual childhoods. There are always cliques in families, and from earliest memory I had always felt a particular closeness to Helen, who was my second sister. Now, both our younger brother, Arthur, and our other sister, Jane Irwin, were dead, and Helen and I had only each other. As we looked back, those "dreadful crises" of youth seemed more clinically interesting than important, but reliving those times with her added a new dimension to the cruise for me, one rarely afforded a brother and sister in the latter part of their lives.

We left Rikitea on March twelfth and headed northwest for four days, avoiding the southern Tuamotu atolls. Their name, "Islands Out In The Sea," seemed apt, for the myriad small atolls stretched over almost 1,000 miles, and we soon saw why the early European navigators had named them the "Low" or "Dangerous" archipelago. None of the atolls we passed — Turiea, Nengonengo, Manuhangi, Reitor, Hao — was more than 15 feet above sea level, although the fringe of palms made them somewhat more visible. My method of navigating the Tuamotus was calculated to produce the greatest amount of safety and permit a substantial margin of error without disaster. We sailed through the islands only for three nights, but the standing orders were to check the surrounding ocean with the radar — which clearly showed the outlying reefs — every two hours, and for most of the time during the nights I was awake and watching.

When trying to find an island during the day, we discovered that a crew member at the spreaders with binoculars could spot the palm trees from as far as eight miles away. At first the fronds seemed to be growing out of the sea; as we approached they acquired mushroom-like stems; and finally the beach and surf appeared. There were no shoals at all, and each atoll reef dropped abruptly to 1,000 fathoms all the way around.

However, the farther north we cruised, the less formidable the dangers seemed; also, we had lovely weather, unlike the normal Tuamotu overcast and squalls.

The Tuamotus were called the Paumotus, or "Conquered Islands," until the French colonized them late in the nineteenth century. They were probably first settled about the time of Christ. Little was known about their early inhabitants until the 1930s, when the Bernice P. Bishop Museum of Honolulu, then and now a renowned center for Polynesian study, sent two expeditions there headed by Dr. Peter Buck and another eminent Polynesian ethnologist, Kenneth Emory. Among other things, they found a number of maraes very similar to others found in Tahiti and Hawaii — thus helping to demonstrate the homogeneity of this widely scattered culture.

They also learned a great deal about the remarkable Tuamotuan canoes. The Tuamotuans found few sources of strong wood on their tiny atolls, and therefore became especially expert at "sewing" together bits of driftwood with braided sennit cord, as did the Easter Islanders. Some of the fishing canoes photographed in 1934 contained up to 50 small pieces of wood. Imagine sewing together a double-hulled voyaging canoe large enough to seat 60! With only stone adzes, stingray-tail or shark-tooth drills, and coconut-fiber caulking to work with, the islanders must have been expert at piecing the wood together, but each canoe would have taken years to construct.

Soon after the Polynesians arrived in the Tuamotus, they struck up a brisk trade with Tahiti, exchanging pearl shell for adze stone. But their primary need for canoes was for emigrating in search of food in times of scarcity. The tiny atolls could support life for only so long, and offshore supplies of fish, tridacna clams, and octopus would be exhausted after a few years. Buck and Emory found huge piles of shells from the ritual feasts of turtle meat, which the Tuamotuans considered sacred. For some reason, moreover, the chicken and the pig, both food staples in other parts of ancient Polynesia, never found their way to the Tuamotus. But with more than 75 atolls, none farther than 100

LOG ENTRY, MARCH 14, 1976

Complacency is the mother of trouble if not disaster. My sun plots have been perfect for several days, and today, for no good reason, I plotted LAN incorrectly. Some mental detective work and follow-up mechanism reminded me of my error before we strayed far, but the incident has put me back "on guard." At noon I plotted the morning sun line, crossed it with LAN and discovered that we had apparently been set westward about 13 miles in 12 hours. We assumed that this was partly due to leeway while sailing and partly to the strong current. I estimated the island of Reitoru to be about two hours ahead. Less than an hour later, while I was trying to nap, it suddenly struck me that I had plotted the LAN incorrectly. Rushing to the navigation table, I replotted it and yelled to the lookout to scan the horizon off the port bow. There was Reitoru, an hour ahead of schedule. Not in the least a disaster, but any mistake comes as a shock when you're cruising waters that can change from hundreds of fathoms to hard coral in a split second.

miles from its neighbor, the archipelago's inhabitants could hop from one to the next whenever food ran out.

Although their canoes were among the most delicately made in all Polynesia, the Tuamotuans lived in unusually primitive conditions until the nineteenth century. Early European explorers reported conditions of abject poverty on many atolls, and after an 1832 visit to Hao, J.A. Moerenhout had this to say of their huts: "It is difficult to conceive how they can construct such miserable habitations...they are so low that one cannot enter them except on one's knees, not standing up except in a bent-over crouching position, and if I had not seen natives go in and out, I would never have imagined them human dwelling places." Buck and Emery found the Tuamotuans using crude utensils for cooking and working the land almost 100 years later. But visitors to the Tuamotus have also found the islanders to be self-reliant and creative. According to Buck, their music, which they called "Gushing-murmur-of-the-waters," was extraordinarily lyrical, and the islanders joined in singing the ancient chants and myths on every possible occasion.

We were amused to learn that reputedly the Tuamotus had the highest population in the world of babies born in treetops. The statistic stems from the violent hurricanes that sweep these low islands. With atolls sometimes wholly underwater during a storm, the natives learned to lash themselves in the tops of coconut palms for protection. The pregnant women among the refuge seekers sometimes gave birth at the height of the storm, so the image of arboreal obstetrics was not quite as far-fetched as it sounds, nor is the statistic likely to be challenged.

Although we found the archipelago far less hazardous to navigate than we expected, we were still awed to read of the numerous European explorers who repeatedly scouted the vast, thousand-mile chain for new islands. Magellan narrowly missed the Tuamotus while searching for a new passage to the East in 1519, but no fewer than 25 Spanish, Dutch, English, Russian, and American explorers wound their way through the Tuamotus over the next 350 years.

With such a vast array of islands to choose from, we decided we had to limit our visit to two — one populated and one deserted. Soon after leaving Mangareva, Paul, Robin, and I had spent an evening reading in detail about each of the Tuamotus to find suitable anchorages. Among the inhabited isles, the most important was Hoa, a copra collection center; we noted a dozen smaller ones as well. We hoped to find islands with relatively easy access, preferably on the leeward side where the passes were safer. Surprisingly few seemed to fit this description. The coast pilot carried such warnings as, "pass filled with coral heads," or "pass takes sharp left and sharp right just before entering lagoon." Our final choices were Makemo and deserted Tahanea in the north central part of the chain.

When we reached Makemo the night of the fifteenth I gave Robin a start by announcing I was going to head almost directly for the island through a four-mile-wide passage in darkness. His Lordship had marveled at radar for nearly two months now, but he had not really accepted it as a dependable small-boat navigational device. I intended to shorten sail when we reached the entrance of the reef, and lay off until morning. Everything went smoothly, much to Riverdale's surprise. We made radar plots on the chart every half-hour, and we had a clear retreat downwind in case the radar failed.

In many of these lagoons the entrance is on the leeward side, and if the outlying reef to windward is low — as it is at Makemo — the wind can easily build up a sea that constantly washes across the reef and into the lagoon. As the lagoon fills with more water than it can hold, the overflow rushes out in violent streams through breaks in the reef. That morning the tide was running out through the pass at about six knots. As it was our first entrance into a lagoon, I was as nervous as a cat. But Robin skillfully conducted *Palawan* through safely, and we followed a small native copra freighter across the lagoon, anchoring off Makemo village at 0900.

An hour later we were on our way in two dinghies to the small concrete pier just vacated by the freighter. The first natives to greet us, as we were to find everywhere in Polynesia, were the children — always polite, and always laughing and chattering, though their broken French was hard for us to understand. They led us to a paunchy gentleman I assumed was the local gendarme but who was, in fact, merely the closest person who spoke French. He was a gracious Tahitian named Alex, who immediately bought us welcoming soft drinks at the local store. Knowing the general poverty of the islands, we were touched by the gesture. Then he offered to show us around.

We stopped first at a boarding school run by the French administration for Polynesian children from a number of nearby islands. The school was impressive. It was well-built and had a staff of able young teachers from France, several of whom later visited us on board. We walked through at lunch time, and in the dining room the children were eating with great gusto, using only their fingers. The food was roughly prepared but nourishing, consisting of bread, fish, and vegetables.

A few days later Ellie sat in on some classes. She reported that the children seemed alert and the teachers dedicated in their efforts to combat illiteracy. When we talked with the teachers who visited *Palawan*, they seemed discouraged by the high drop-out rate once the students had reached elementary reading and writing levels. "The future has so little promise for them here, with nothing to do but fish and make copra," they told us, "The kids say, 'why bother to stay in school?'"

The village consisted of some 40 small coral blockhouses with corrugated roofs. The paths between them were neat, and the huts were wreathed in flowers and decorated with shell arrangements. There were fish nets, outboard motors, and half-built boats in the backyards. When Alex stopped at one house and called out, an attractive woman of 60 beckoned us inside. The house had but one room, and the bedding had been stowed away for the day. The woman and her granddaughter, Catherine, greeted us with a traditional kiss and a small gift of a shell. Like all Polynesians, they exuded a faint aroma of scented coconut oil, were scrupulously clean, and were dressed in bright pareus. When not working to help build the new island airport, they made shell necklaces, and we later bought several lovely pieces from them.

Catherine really took our breath away. At 18, she was an exceptional beauty. Tall and slim, she had the long, lustrous tresses typical of Polynesian women, but her light complexion, high cheekbones, and delicate nose made us suspect she had some Chinese ancestry. We all took pictures of her, and Helen and Carter made some tentative arrangements to go to work at the airport with the two women the next day. But the women either misunderstood or were embarrassed at the menial nature of their work, for the next morning, when the boat went by laden with shovels, picks, and wheelbarrows, they waved but did not stop. A month later, when *Palawan* was in Tahiti, Catherine visited aboard while on her way to attend hotel school there. I was not aboard at the time, so did not have a chance to talk with her, but I was glad to hear that at least one child of the Tuamotus was destined for a future beyond fishing and copra-farming.

During our three days at Makemo, we saw firsthand how painful the transition of Polynesia from subsistence-level to "civilized" economy had been, and how the coconut has played a double-edged role in this transformation. Until 150 years ago, the Tuamotu native lived off the land. He fished in his outrigger. His few clothes could be woven from palm fronds or tapa. And he used the coconut for everything; its milk and meat were delicious and nourishing; its husk, shell, and wood material provided him with utensils and shelter. Everything was at his fingertips, and a few hours of work each day produced his needs. Life was filled with leisure.

Then came the white man, the natives' discovery of such gadgets as outboard motors and gas lamps, and the interest of foreign companies in copra. Copra is the dried meat of the coconut, from which oil can be extracted for use in cosmetics, cooking, and soap. Once their pearl-shell beds were exhausted by traders' increasing demands, the Tuamotuans found that laboring on the copra plantations — some owned by absentee companies, others owned by local traders or natives — was the only way one could make the money necessary to buy the new-found amenities.

But what hard labor it was, and for so little reward! Because of the coconut palm's great abundance throughout the Pacific, the historical fluctuation of copra prices, and the absence of labor legislation in these isolated islands, a man's pay for copra-making seldom rose to $60 a ton, or about a third of the price of the smallest outboard motor. One ton of copra, we guessed, would take at least 10 days to prepare.

Fascinated by this primitive industry, we spent a day wandering among the Makemo groves watching the natives at work. First, an agile young man shinnies up a palm tree, by means of ankle ropes or notches cut in the trunk, to knock off coconuts that haven't fallen naturally. On the ground, he smashes each one down on a pointed stick, splitting off the husk without damaging the shell. Then he carefully breaks the shell into several pieces and leaves the glistening sections to dry on a wooden platform, raised as protection from the rats that overrun these islands. For

the next few days, the man watches his precious source of income shrivel. Finally, he bags the copra in burlap sacks and carries it down to the waterfront, where it is weighed, sold through the local agent, and carried off in a freighter.

Throughout the archipelago, the government is working hard to promote tourism, which will improve an island's economy, and from the small size of Tuamotu families, I suspect that birth control is promoted there as well. Yet, during the slow transition to a modern society, the natives have actually become poorer; an irony that was illustrated poignantly to me by a young Tuamotu wife I met one evening as I walked through the village.

"Ia orana," she called out softly as I passed, using the traditional Polynesian greeting that means literally, "May You Live." She spoke excellent French, so I sat down to talk as we watched her husband building a boat in the backyard. Hesitantly she explained that the villagers were embarrassed that they couldn't welcome us in their traditional way. "When the foreign ships used to come 10 and 20 years ago, the chief always put on a feast," she said. "Now we are so poor we can scarcely feed ourselves."

This woman lived in a concrete house; her parents had lived in a thatched hut. Her husband had an outboard motor; her grandfather had paddled an outrigger. She cooked on a kerosene stove; her mother had used an open fire. Yet, she meant what she said. "Civilization" had not yet proved profitable. Giving a feast is easy when sharing is a way of life and food comes out of the sea and treetops. But once the knowledge of profit, tinned meat, and transistor radios is acquired, a feast becomes an unaffordable luxury.

Feast or no feast, for me the village of Makemo was a source of peace and comfort. Each night I walked along the dark village paths — only the school had electrical power — chatting with the villagers in my barely adequate French, smelling the aroma of flowers and of dinner cooking, and always followed by children and dogs.

One evening I wandered into the Catholic village chapel and sat down in a back pew. An old priest was saying mass at the rough altar, reading by the light of a single kerosene lamp, his sunbrowned pate shining above a fringe of snowy hair. Half a dozen elderly forms were scattered among the dim pews. As the priest's voice droned on monotonously in the near-empty church, the scene seemed eerie and unreal. Did he really feel he

LOG ENTRY: MARCH 18, 1976

I am relieved to be back aboard after just having made probably the most stupid seamanship mistake of my life. Late this afternoon, I asked Carter and my sister to join me in a trip in the 10' Delquay dinghy to the other side of the lagoon. I had made sure that we had enough fuel for the 16-mile roundtrip passage, and should have made sure that we had a walkie-talkie with us, but in the confusion of leaving I forgot it. As we crossed the lagoon, coral heads popped into our path continually; at first they were easy to spot just below the surface, but they became progressively less visible as the light faded.

Eventually, we anchored on the outer reef and were walking along enjoying the sea life in the shallows, when, glancing back, I was suddenly stabbed with the thought that I had forgotten the walkie-talkie, and that remote, tiny, bobbing boat was all there was to assure our safe return to Palawan. *If by chance the anchor pulled out or the shackle pin loosened and the dinghy floated off, we would be faced with spending a terrifying night on the reef in considerable danger. The sky was darkening, and the other side of the atoll was out of sight. No one would know where to look for us in the darkness. What could I have been thinking of?*

Trying not to sound too concerned, I suggested we return to the dinghy and start back, hoping fervently that the dinghy anchor would remain secure until we got to it. It did, but once we were aboard and underway, I worried about the shear pin. If our propeller struck a coral head, we would have to anchor and pray that someone would come looking for us — but in the darkness that would be dangerous for them as well. I felt helpless and irritated with myself.

Now back aboard Palawan, *and hoping the girls had not realized my uneasiness, I've made a solemn vow never to leave the ship again on such a venture without a walkie-talkie in hand and an alert crew on the other end of it.*

David Flanagan and Helen share conversation and a book during one of their off-watch interludes at Palawan's *bow. David the diplomat successfully divided his time between our vessel's four young women.*

was communicating with God and helping these poor Polynesians in their present or future lives? Or was he so accustomed to the litany that his performance was perfunctory? Feeling uneasy, and still unnoticed, I quietly slipped out into the moonlight and continued on my way.

During our stay, the natives became quite friendly and often stopped on *Palawan* on their way out to fish. One pair of young men came by several times and in return for the beer we served them brought us some drinking coconuts. The Polynesians have become so adept at using machetes that with four or five strokes they can strip a coconut half-way down, make the tops of the husks into neat handles, lock them to the handles of other nuts in pairs of four, and so provide an attractive gift. We were given a number of them, and some crew members developed a liking for coconut milk. To me it tasted thin and sour so I drank it only out of politeness.

As our evenings at anchor became more relaxed, the evening's galley crews tried to outdo each other in producing exotic dishes. Inspired by this imaginative fare, we took advantage of our quiet anchorages for leisurely meals, good conversation, and word games. Occasionally we broke out a bottle of wine, or someone decorated the cabin, and when a crew member's morale seemed particularly low — as sometimes happens on long cruises — we had an "aku" party honoring that crew member. His or her name was carefully carved in the grotesque handmade wooden figure I brought from Easter Island, and we recited poems of praise to the honoree, who immediately felt better.

One night I put on a grass skirt and presided over an aku party for Carter, who had been working hard on her seamanship ever since we left the Galapagos and was well on her way to becoming the most knowledgeable seawoman on board. Most of us — even Paul — grew to love Carter. She was original, amusing, and delightful to be with — as long, that is, as she was not being directed in any way.

As our camera operator, she sometimes left the camera on the vessel during visits to interesting spots ashore, only to get angry if asked why she wasn't taking pictures. Eventually, I gave up on the private lectures and let her have her own way except when necessary for safety. Privately I called her "Old Flint Head." Someday she will realize that only friends give directions and

advice; others just don't give a damn.

One evening's after-dinner entertainment included playing the question game, with younger crew asking an older member to describe his greatest mistake or character flaw. I broke the ice by saying that my occasionally ungovernable temper has caused me the most serious problems of my life. Paul followed, saying he thought he made decisions too hastily and acted without thinking, sometimes with disastrous results. Robin's answer was particularly interesting. He said he wished he was more sensitive to other people's feelings; his self-analysis was right on the mark.

After dinner and conversation, we usually sat in the cockpit drinking Sanka and watching the stars, becoming familiar enough with the evening sky in the southern hemisphere to recognize at least a few constellations — the Southern Cross, Scorpio to the east, and Orion in the west. Before setting out, I had heard that twilights were quite long in the tropics, but we found that darkness falls quickly — so quickly, in fact, that our star navigators had considerable difficulty identifying a star in time to measure its angle above the fast-disappearing horizon. A nice aspect of those evenings was that our sun-baked aluminum hull cooled down sufficiently to make our cabins comfortable for sleeping. Usually, by 2200 most of the crew had turned in.

On the afternoon of the nineteenth, we decided we'd seen enough of Tuamotu civilization and motored slowly over to Tahanea, which the *Pilot Book* said would be deserted except during certain copra-cutting periods. On the charts, two dotted lines indicated passes through the reefs, and we chose the easier one, but even there several coral heads awaited us just inside the entrance. We sent David up the mast with a walkie-talkie. At the wheel, I watched the channel and the depth sounder, and listened for David's firm directions from the spreaders.

Managing the pass safely, we conned our way a mile or two down the lagoon and anchored opposite a cluster of thatched huts. Safe anchoring was easier said than done because of the coral heads, so we adopted a technique suggested by Lord Riverdale: select a spot and then circle it to check for coral heads that could entangle our anchor chain. Ashore, we found the huts empty but well-scrubbed. A shiny outboard rested in a corner of one, apparently waiting for someone who planned to do some isolated fishing. Nearby was a lovely little cemetery, where a number of graves were marked with tenderly arranged strings of shells. In keeping with traditional Polynesian attitudes toward death, it was a happy, picturesque place.

On this pleasant, deserted atoll we found a chance for the rest — physical and mental — that we all needed after two months at sea and only a handful of days ashore. With little to do, we went our separate ways, spending time on personal chores, thoughts, diaries, swims, and walks. The feeling of primitive peace and undisturbed nature swept us all.

Carter, who had been filming the voyage from time to time, had also put together a short comedy script, in which she had made use of each crew member's particular attribute: Helen's seductive beauty, Anne's morale-building manner, Ellie's and Helen Buckner's protectiveness, and Robin's talent for emulating New Guinea war chieftain cries — with appropriate gestures. Deserted Tahanea provided the ideal setting for filming her script, so we spent all one day perfecting scenes until Carter deemed them ready for filming

The script featured Helen and Carter, dressed as natives, attacked by cannibals: Paul, David, and me. We captured Helen and dragged her off screaming. Then, Carter wriggled out of the bush in a lovely grass skirt with matching bra and headdress to divert the men long enough to allow Helen to escape. Suddenly, Chief Riverdale descended on Carter with wild whoops and dragged her into one of the shacks. Immediately the tiny window of the shack jerked open and out came headdress, bra, and grass skirt in rapid succession. The window was then closed, with a decisive bang. The End.

While the script left much to the imagination of the viewers, its filming provided an entire day of giddy diversion for the participants — a welcome safety valve of laughter and nonsense that brought us all together and dispensed any lingering tensions. The final result, viewed months later, wasn't nearly as amusing as the making of it, but we all were grateful to Carter for her inventiveness.

During our last day on Tahanea, as I devoted myself to reading, I stumbled across a story that, more than anything else I've read, illustrates the enigmatic nature of this remote archipelago. The author, James Norman Hall, while cruising these islands in a native schooner in 1920, met an Englishman named Ronald Crichton. Crichton was on his way to settle on the tiny atoll of Tanao with an old Polynesian woman and a Chinese cook. Hall stopped briefly ashore when the trio reached Tanae, but left still puzzled by this enigmatic man and his self-imposed exile.

Several years later Hall met the captain of a schooner that brought supplies to Tanao. To his surprise, the captain told him that Crichton wished Hall to pay him a visit. When he arrived at Tanao, his host greeted him coolly and disappeared. At 2:00 A.M., Hall was awakened by the crowing of a cock. Walking out on his porch, he saw Crichton in the moonlight, gently calling to the noisy rooster nearby. Seizing it, the man tore the bird to pieces, blood cascading over his clothes while he addressed the bird in endearing terms. Then he melted back into the shadows. Shaken, Hall left the next morning. Twenty years later he received the following letter:

Dear Sir: The service I am about to ask of you is one I would hesitate to ask even of an old friend, but you are the only white man I know in this part of the Pacific, and I must appeal to you however reluctantly.

I am ill, and as I have grave doubt as to my recovery, I must try to put my affairs in order. I have no one with me but an old Chinese servant, whom you may remember. Could you come and see me? I have chartered a Paumotu cutter for the purpose of carrying this letter, and if you find it possible to come, this same cutter will bring you to the island. I realize that you may not be able to leave at once and I have, therefore, instructed the man who brings this letter — he is the owner of the vessel — to await your orders.

Yours very truly, Ronald Crichton

Struck by either pity or curiosity, Hall decided to comply, and two weeks later he reached Tanao. As Hall approached Chrichton in his bed, the old man thanked him profusely, taking great comfort in his presence. Later he blurted out a cryptic explanation of his exile. Many years before, he said, he had realized he was "one of those men who are mistakes of nature," and had therefore decided to remove himself from civilization. He then told Hall what he wanted done with his fortune, his house, and the Chinese servant. He then sank back into reverie. That night he died in his sleep.

CHAPTER 10

SOCIETY ISLANDS:

Tahiti at Last

No one who has longed to sail the oceans of the world can fail to be deeply moved by a landfall at Tahiti. Ours was on a beautiful, clear day. The 300-mile sail here from Tahanea — once we were free of the last of the Tuamotus and in deep water — was a peaceful, rapid, and cool nighttime passage with a fair breeze. With the dawn we could make out Tahiti's high mountains. Later, we rounded the northern tip of the island, sailed by Pointe Venus in Matavai Bay, and finally entered Papeete Harbor, an easy approach with two fine range markers. We continued on to the yacht anchorage — a stone wall at least a mile long, which formed a quay. About 60 cruising boats of all descriptions were moored stern-to along the quay. Under the guidance of the harbor master, at a designated spot we joined them, dropping the anchor well out and backing in to a perfect landing. I had never moored that way before, but found the boats on either side very helpful in guiding us in, to protect both their topsides and ours.

During the previous ten years I had read a great deal about this inspiring place: James Norman Hall, in his autobiography, described his home on Tahiti as carpeted with grass ferns, walled with "blossoming things" and roofed with mango and frangipani trees "to catch and scatter the sunlight"; Herman Melville, whose novels *Omoo* and *Typee* tell of South Sea wanderings, said, "Push not off from that island; thou can'st never return"; and to Sir Joseph Banks, naturalist and patron to Captain Cook, it was the "truest picture of an Arcadia the imagination can form."

Some of the most eloquent descriptions of Tahiti came from someone who wasn't a writer at all: Paul Gauguin. Deserting his middle-class Parisian life for the sensuousness of the South Seas, Gauguin kept a notebook of his thoughts and impressions for his daughter during his years in Tahiti. At times he seemed happy to be sleeping with "nothing between me and the sky but the green roof...of pandanus leaves where the lizards live." At other times he seemed melancholy in his self-imposed exile. "The silence of the night in Tahiti is the strangest thing of all," he wrote. "It only exists here, without even the cry of a bird to disturb one's repose. Always this silence. I can understand why these people can sit for hours for days without saying a word, looking sadly at the sky."

During his ten years in Tahiti, Gauguin produced his finest

LOG ENTRY: MARCH 26, 1976

Tahiti at last. I have dreamed of this island, this landfall, this docking, for nearly 40 years. First, it was only a vague place where Joshua Slocum found friendly natives. Then, in Peking, China, in the summer of 1937, I met Bruce and Sheridan Fahnestock and their navigator Dennis Puleston, who had recently visited Tahiti while sailing from New York to Manila, and who described it with great enthusiasm. Later I learned about William Albert Robinson, who tired of New York's advertising world in the '30s and took off in a small ketch, Svaap, *to sail around the world with a Polynesian companion. His book about that voyage,* Twenty-Thousand Leagues Over the Sea, *became a classic, and I have read all of Robbie's wonderful books on the sea written since then. Unfortunately, Robbie had a*

stroke and we have not been able to see him. We did, however, come across his famous bark — Varua — in Papeete. It was sad to see her in disrepair, but she was on loan to oceanographers who planned to repair her and take her to sea again.

work. But, although his soul contained so much potential for finding and describing beauty, he seemed bent on self-destruction, and in this he was successful. When he died in 1903, his paintings were sold for pennies in Papeete.

When planning our voyage, I had built in a three-week pause here in the Society Islands to permit me to return home to tend to some business. Helen Buckner had decided to fly to New York with me, as had Robin en route to England. When we moored in Tahiti, we had only four days before our flight to New York, and the three of us had much to see in those four days.

By this time Helen had been on board *Palawan* for about a month and had gained the affection and respect of all. Her enthusiasm for everything from swabbing the deck to parlor games had been tremendous; if anything, she had been too eager to help. For her, the cruise had been triply enjoyable — a chance for brother and sister to spend time together, a change of pace from life in New York, and a visit to a part of the world she had read a great deal about. If we had pressed her more, she might have continued on to Tonga with us. When the cruise resumed, I missed her and wished she had.

In Papeete, she and I moved to the Bora Bora Hotel, into rooms that looked westward to the jagged peaks of Moorea starkly outlined against the setting sun. After settling in, we rented a car and with Robin began our tour of the island.

Tahiti is almost two islands — or two discrete clusters of volcanic hills connected by a low neck of land called the Isthmus of Taravao. Papeete is on the larger, more developed portion known as Tahiti; the southern, more rural peninsula is called "Presqu'ile," — or "Almost Island" — "Tiairapu" in Tahitian. According to legend the entire island was once part of a larger land mass, which turned into a fish during a dispute among the gods and broke apart to form the six islands and seven atolls now known as the Societies.

We crossed the isthmus and drove up among the hills of Tiairapu. From the top of the southeast hill we could look northwest and see the beaches, reefs, and all the charm of this island, with almost no sign of habitation. Nearby were trees with beauti-

ful white blossoms, others with clusters of red berries, with the island panorama spreading beyond. Even the usually talkative Robin was awed to silence by the view.

Continuing clockwise around the island, we came to Matavai Bay, which we had passed on our approach to Papeete. This was once the anchorage of Pacific explorers and traders, and it was on Pointe Venus that the *Bounty*'s crew passed the six idyllic months that made returning to the harshness of sea life difficult and which ultimately brought about the mutiny. Pointe Venus is also renowned as the spot where Captain Cook pitched his camp to record the astronomical phenomenon of the passage of the planet Venus between the sun and earth on 3 June 1769. He had been sent to observe this rare event by the Royal Society of London, which hoped that the observation would help advance the study of celestial navigation.

Cook's observation of Venus was relatively successful although dark shadows covered the planet during its six-hour crossing. But a more important result of the visit — and of Cook's subsequent stops at Tahiti during the next decade — was his detailed account of island life. He described the natives, who called him "Tootee," as an "obliging and benevolent" race, giving little mention to the fact that they happily filched every object in sight. He also explored several nearby islands and later named them the "Societies" after his sponsoring organization. Actually, the islands had been discovered two years before by the British explorer Samuel Wallis, who named them the "Georgian Islands" after the king.

Cook dined with various chiefs — or jui arii — and sampled roast dog and fermented breadfruit with aplomb, and after dinner sat through strange entertainments — confusing charades, wrestling matches, and lewd dances by the Arioi Society of priestly strolling players. In return for their friendship, the sailors found the Tahitians eager to trade much-needed vegetables, fruit, and meat for a few nails, beads, and red feathers. Many of the women, in addition, were happy to provide nocturnal company for the crew, although the austere Cook undoubtedly refrained.

Tahitian legend had long predicted that one day a ship with no outrigger would arrive and cause the sacred seabirds to

In the evening, a womens' outrigger-canoe racing team practices in the harbor at Bora Bora.

A bit of Tahitian culture, perhaps modified for the tourists, is this hula performed during a luncheon buffet at a large hotel in Tahiti.

mourn. Certainly the intentions of Cook, Wallis, Louis de Bougainville, and other early explorers were innocent enough. But they opened the way for a parade of other visitors — sailors bringing influenza and venereal disease, missionaries preaching severe Christianity, and traders eager to exploit the ignorant islanders. In 1773, Cook may have overestimated the population, which he thought numbered about 200,000. By 1850 the population had dwindled to less than 10,000, and historian Henry Adams, who visited that year, described a "sense of hopelessness and premature decay" among the "silent, bored, rather sad" people. Now forbidden to dance or pursue their traditional amusements, he added, "they do not even move with spirit."

What had caused this depopulation and demoralization in paradise? The bloody native wars and the ravages of white men's diseases were partly responsible. But the main cause was the well-meaning Protestant missionary, who managed to wipe out all traces of traditional island religion and custom. When the missionaries first arrived in 1797 aboard the ship *Duff*, under charter to the London Missionary Society, they were shocked at the moral state of their new flock. To missionary William Ellis, who wrote four volumes on Polynesia, the natives seemed hopelessly devoted to idol-worship, addicted to war, and "prone to indolent debauchery of the lowest kind." Moreover, he wrote, they practiced such "abominable" acts as infanticide and human sacrifice. Actually, these primitive forms of population control were not without a useful place in pre-Christian island life.

Whether because the traditional Tahitian gods had lost their magic, or because the missionaries were so persuasive, the islanders' conversion to Christianity was quite rapid. Soon, Ellis

Helen Watson, Anne Madden, Ellie Lazarus and my sister Helen try their hand at weaving palm-frond mats on an island beach.

noted, the ministers had won over the reigning Pomare dynasty, and within a few decades most native women were wearing bonnets instead of flowers in their hair, men had given up tapa loincloths in favor of trousers, and children were learning their ABCs in mission schools instead of memorizing their family histories. In 1820, with the king's approval, the missionaries instituted a code of laws punishing every "crime" from dancing to adultery. One Sunday, Ellis wrote proudly, a native sat and watched two canoes drift toward some sharp rocks without lifting a finger. To rescue them would have meant working on the Sabbath.

In the 1830s, French Catholic missionaries invaded the Protestants' island turf, and 12 years later the Societies were annexed to France. For several decades, westernization was partly checked by the power of the flamboyant and firm but benevolent Pomares. But when Pierre Loti visited Queen Pomare IV in 1872, he found an imperious old woman with a drunken husband who wept because "her kingdom, invaded by civilization, was falling into disorder." When her son Pomare V died five years later, Paul Gauguin mourned, "Maori history died with him."

The French colonial administration of Tahiti was criticized almost from the beginning. "The white population consists of businessmen and officials," Alain Gerbault wrote in 1929. "The first have brought thither their love of money, the others all the prejudices of European civilization." Forty years earlier, Gauguin found Papeete just like the Europe he had left, "only aggravated by colonial snobbism, and the grotesque imitation of our customs, fashions and vices." In his political newsletter, he jeered at the "pompous, parasitical" French bureaucrats, and bitterly denounced the gendarmes who spied on bathing girls and then arrested them for indecency, or swore in French at native men and jailed those who innocently returned the foreign "greeting." But Gauguin's protests were ignored by both local and Parisian authorities, and when he died the Tahitian officials sighed with relief.

During the twentieth century the Tahitians have become more sophisticated, a large middle class of half-Polynesian, half-French "demis" has developed, and the uglier side of colonial rule has gradually vanished. But anti-French feelings have continued to flare up from time to time; during the 1940s they were aroused by cult hero Pouvaana a Oopa, and 20 years later Charles de Gaulle's plans for nuclear testing in the Tuamotus drew huge protests. But the Tahitians realize how dependent they are economically upon France, and in 1957 they voted overwhelmingly to remain under French control.

As early legend had forecast, the seabirds had much to mourn during the first centuries of white influence in Tahiti, and its lovely people were misused in various ways by many Europeans. Two hundred years later, there cannot be said to be much mourning in Papeete. It is a vibrant, pulsating metropolis, with few visible reminders of the periods of utter hell it has been through. Over the years, the Polynesian inhabitants gradually mixed with European, Asian, and African visitors until the town of 30,000 has produced some of the most breathtakingly beautiful young women in the world. Once copra was the only major source of income here, but since 1960, when an international airport was built, tourism has become the major industry. There is money to be made in hotels, gift shops, and bars; motorbikes and cars crowd the narrow streets; and along the stone quay yachts of all sizes and types and crews of all ages and nationalities form a restless, ever-changing nautical community.

Helen and Carter, inseparable pals, pose for my camera in the lush landscape of Moorea.

The general impression one got from the various cruisers along the quay was that they were basically wasting time, and Papeete was a wonderful place to waste time in. The streets behind the waterfront contained everything from Chinese greasy spoons to expensive French restaurants; the open markets offered many fruits and vegetables; and there were new people to meet, lessons to learn, and experiences to be had. It didn't take me long to realize that these young people were going through the same indecision and reflection about their lives that I had gone through 40 years earlier. Would that I could have done it on the Papeete waterfront rather than behind a desk in New York.

However, this modern island haven is far from innocent. Crime and juvenile delinquency rates are high. Families from hill villages are crowded into downtown slums, and in the town's bistros a seedy assortment of prostitutes and hustlers prey on tourists who come in search of Gauguin's paradise. What the tourists find is a far cry from Gauguin's Tahiti.

We spent two days in Papeete, touring the cafes and shops, eating in good restaurants, and listening to beautiful singing in the churches. In one outstanding art and antique shop I found an obsidian adze — not such an uncommon object in these islands, but a deep thrill for me. To the ancient Polynesian, the adze was a mainstay of everyday life. With a variety of these stone implements he could chop down a tree to build a canoe, hollow out a log, bore holes along the top of the gunwale, and put on a plank or two to add freeboard. He also used the adze to clear land, build foundations for his house, and form utensils and bowls for his food. Holding this stone-age artifact in my hand, I could travel back to the time when Polynesian man needed only the adze to survive.

The third day of our visit, Ellie and I drove up into the hills and

I am anxious to keep Paul as happy as possible on this voyage. His role as a professional in a group of amateurs has been difficult from the beginning. During our ocean-racing years together, his responsibilities were specific, our relationship well-defined and the results successful. Here in the Pacific, we are in a different environment. After commanding Palawan *on the long passage from Maine to Panama, he suddenly had to revert to being my subordinate, although our knowledge of seamanship was equal and his ability in the engine room unquestionably superior. Now, after another three-week taste of being in charge of* Palawan *as she cruised the islands with Olive and Nancy aboard, he must once more turn the command over to me, and I'm afraid it's a difficult transition for him.*

up the Vallee de Papenoo, where we then hiked up the bed of a stream. The slope was steep at first, but it eventually widened into a broad, fertile valley, perfect for farming. Our path led us by many taro fields and breadfruit trees, but they were a relatively recent addition. For almost 1,000 years before the white man came, the Tahitians had lived on fish and the coconuts at hand in and on the edge of the sea, and had rarely ventured inland. We found few farms, but the increasingly booming tourist industry was a new market for produce and promised prosperity for the new farmers.

On our last evening there was a gala farewell party on board *Palawan* for Helen B., Robin, and me, with songs to each of us composed by the crew. It was a sad leave-taking for Robin and Helen, who were leaving for good, but I was looking forward to the break at home followed by my return three weeks hence. The next morning we flew to New York, and Robin continued on to London.

After Olive and I had spent some time together socializing with family and friends at home, she and a friend, Nancy Coleman, flew off to Tahiti to join *Palawan* for a leisurely cruise through the Society Islands under Paul's command. During this time I remained at home tending to various projects and business. When I returned to Tahiti to rejoin the ship on 19 April, the crew gave me a huge welcome, no doubt in large part because I had brought along 100 pounds of frozen meat and vegetables to restock the larder. I had also brought with me Paul's wife, Barbara, to surprise him. After almost four months apart, they would now have several days to spend together before she returned and we continued our cruise.

A highlight of our stay on Tahiti occurred shortly before Olive and Nancy Coleman took off again for home. Nancy Rutgers (Norman Hall's daughter) and her husband Nick had invited all of us aboard *Palawan* to a Polynesian party in honor of her mother's birthday in their home, a hilltop showplace with magnificent tropical gardens. It was built on the hill above the Norman Halls' home, and after the sumptuous lunch, native songs played on the hi-fi, and much dancing, Mrs. Hall led us down the path to see the house she had shared with her famous husband. Invited into his study, I sat at the desk where he had done much of his writing, noting his vast library and reflecting on his odd but fruitful collaboration with Charles Nordhoff. Mrs. Hall, meanwhile, told us many amusing and affectionate anecdotes about him and their life together. It had obviously been a happy marriage, and she admired him greatly. This was a memorable afternoon and a great thrill for me.

When the cruise got underway again, Jimmy had rejoined us following the death of his brother, and we had said our farewells to Olive, Nancy, and Paul's wife, who took off for home. Moorea was to be our next port of call. *Palawan* had visited there in my absence, but Jimmy and I had missed that. After observing its peak in the distance for so long from our anchorage in Tahiti, we were anxious to go there, so *Palawan* returned, powering the 30 miles to Papetoai Bay. It was now very hot with little breeze, so we dropped the hook in the middle of the bay to swing with the wind and keep the boat as well ventilated as possible.

Here I had the pleasure of meeting Edward Dodd and his wife. Olive had met them on *Palawan*'s previous visit and had told me about them. They now divided their time between a home in Vermont and Raiatea when not traveling, but previously they had combed the archives of the world for material for Dodd's *Ring of Fire* trilogy, which is probably one of the best works on Polynesia available. With their obvious love of the area, their intimate familiarity with it and years of study, they were for me a fund of fascinating information on the riddle of Polynesia. Tall and thoughtful-looking, with an excellent sense of humor, Edward Dodd was obviously flattered that we had read so widely in his works, and he modestly autographed one of my copies, "With thanks for actually having read it." For several hours we sat and talked, reflecting upon — among other things — how different Moorea was from Tahiti. A small air service now connects the islands, but Moorea remains relatively aloof and unchanged.

While there, I also rode a motorbike up into the mountains to visit the vast 10,000-acre tropical plantation which its developer, Medford Kellum, had operated for 50 years and then sold in part to the government. Some of it had been made into an experimental plantation, and I had read that the ancient Tahitian system of terracing and irrigating fields was as sophisticated as that of the early Chinese, and remnants of that system could still be seen there. Interested in seeing this if possible, I climbed up though the plantation for some time, noting the carefully planted and meticulously labeled fields of tropical crops. The plantation offered one more unique, interesting variation in island his-

---

LOG ENTRY: APRIL 26, 1976

My re-entry into the crew on return from home has not been as smooth as I would have liked. People living together at sea tend to create their own world — perhaps that's one of the things I like so much about going to sea — but once the bond is broken by separation, it's often difficult to recapture it. Jimmy's sorrow over his brother's death has added to the unhappy undercurrents. Also, for some reason, a feeling of hostility has developed between the crew and myself and I'm afraid it will take some time and some doing before we become a warm, working team again. Lying awake in my cabin these nights, I am sometimes filled with foreboding, knowing how many sailing expeditions to the South Seas have stalled in confusion or ennui at Tahiti.

tory and development.

Eventually, I started back down the rough road. Jimmy, who had started out on a moped with me, had returned to the boat earlier to rest. Once I was back aboard, I learned that the crew favored a return to Tahiti to obtain medications, motorbike and outboard repairs, and other incidentals needing attention before continuing westward. It troubled me that we found it necessary to return to Tahiti for these rather mundane purchases and repairs, but I saw that I was overruled and soon consented to the crew's desire.

Once back in Papeete, however, we solved all current medical problems, made the required repairs, and finally departed Tahiti for good at 1700 on 26 April, bedecked in shell necklaces and waving farewells to the girls' new friends aboard yachts moored along the quay. As we left the dock, I began to feel that my fears had been groundless after all.

During our stay, Helen and Carter had taken to "trolling" the quay in the evenings, and if anything started to follow, they brought "it" back to *Palawan*. Helen, tall and alluring at 21, seemed to be the best troller of all, and she brought back every kind of fish from a 19-year-old world sailor to a 45-year-old computer programmer. She and I had a few disagreements about this type of entertainment, but I was determined not to upset her on this cruise, especially if the fish kept coming in variety and without repetition. However, our departure solved the problem and no more needed to be said.

On 27 April we arrived at Huahine, the fertile island where Captain Cook took aboard the young native, Omai, who was his interpreter on his second world voyage. Once we were anchored, I went ashore alone once again for a long walk to work out the kinks from confinement aboard and to think. The crew problems were fading but still on my mind, and I wanted time to sort them out privately. Settling into a stride, I walked for some miles through villages of small, clean, and orderly homes, with fragrant flowers blooming everywhere and dozens of seemingly happy, carefree children playing along the streets, and my thoughts turned to them.

Western visitors in Polynesia often have trouble understanding the casual Pacific traditions of child rearing and adoption. In ancient times, parents gave children away for a variety of reasons — to lighten their own economic burdens, cement a political alliance, bring cheer to a childless couple, or simply because the child preferred to live elsewhere. The child was not automatically cut off from its natural home, and often its family was a group of adults with both natural and adopted children.

This custom led the missionary Ellis to write disapprovingly that the native children "pass their childhood in indolence, irregularity and the unrestrained indulgence in whatever affords them gratification." A British visitor to Pitcairn in 1849 saw the situation more positively. "The children...are not swaddled or tormented as they are in England, in consequence of which they are strong, independent imps." Despite the introduction of public schools, western clothing, and Christianity, children still play half-clothed throughout Polynesia, and Levy estimates that a full quarter of all Tahitian children are adopted.

Later, when Jimmy and I explored Huahine on mopeds, we found it less hilly than the other Societies, with many lagoons and many villages along the shores. Also, everyone seemed to have conveyances — scooters, motorcycles, bikes, and cars. The villagers displayed a mixture of customs — French bread is delivered to the breadbox in front of each house; each village had its tin-roofed Chinese store, a reminder of the enterprising Chinese workers who worked their way up to become wealthy traders on many Pacific islands. Each village also had its pier and copra-weighing station, symbols of its only visible means of income. Some men fished, but most seemed to be doing nothing productive in particular, and we wondered how they could maintain such an apparently high standard of living. Perhaps it had to do with the ease with which fish and coconuts — the essentials of life — were so readily available.

As we toured this island, I felt that at last I was beginning to really understand the ancient Polynesians. Our route led us along the shore of a particularly beautiful lagoon where there were four maraes in a row. They were hull-shaped and faced the sea like those on Easter, but more crude, with ill-fitting stones, roughly carved petroglyphs and, of course, no moais on top. It was a pleasant surprise to find that the missionaries had left so many undisturbed here. As we rode by them and the ancient rock walkways and men fishing in canoes, the entire historical panorama suddenly came into focus for me: This entire civiliza-

tion had been built with the adze and canoe. Arriving Polynesians had found the climate so temperate, the food so abundant, and the living so easy that they quickly returned home to bring back families and friends, colonizing each of the islands in progression. No wonder the islanders had developed an easy-going life of catching a fish when they were hungry and letting tomorrow take care of itself.

Our last night here we had a memorable breadfruit picnic ashore around a campfire. I was the cook, using an uncomplicated recipe from Nancy Rutgers that consisted of throwing the breadfruit on hot coals to cook for about an hour, and accompanying that with fried corned beef hash. It was hardly gourmet, but the crew ate it up, and despite the bugs we had a happy evening.

The next day we moved on to Raiatea, the legendary "mother of the islands," whence the great Polynesian voyages to Hawaii and New Zealand are said to have embarked. Again, setting out on mopeds, Jimmy and I passed many small inlets on the edge of the great lagoon, with spectacular ragged mountains rising into the clouds beyond. Small houses lined the inlets, and behind each one canoes perched on stilts in the water, covered with palm fronds to protect them from the sun. Although buses, motor scooters, and even an air service offered swift transportation, the canoe was still very visible. In fact, most Polynesians would feel uncomfortable without one nearby.

The charms of Tahitian women have been notorious ever since Bougainville christened the island "La Nouvelle Cythere" after the place Aphrodite first appeared. Early European visitors were greeted by throngs of girls eager to please the sailors and willing, as Wallis put it bluntly, "to prostitute themselves for a nail." Forster, Cook's naturalist, described Tahitian women swarming over the ships, performing lewd dances and pairing off with crewmen. But Cook, a sensitive observer, noted that many of the better-bred women "would admit of no such familiarities," and added that one could "with equal justice draw the characters of the women" in any British seaport. Forster suggested that the "simplicity of Polynesian culture makes many actions perfectly

Fishing nets are strung to dry in a tree alongshore in Raiatea. This island was supposed to be the cradle of Polynesian civilization and has many holy places.

innocent which according to our customs, would be blameable."

He was not far from the mark. Traditionally, the Tahitians saw sex as a casual, natural function. They allowed their teengers to explore it discreetly; in the accepted "motoro" ritual a young man crept into a girl's bedroom and stayed until dawn. Marriage bonds were flexible and, according to Ellis, "Neither party felt bound to abide by them any longer than it suited their inclinations." More often, a man and his "vahine" would live together for years and raise a family without marrying. Such practices horrified the missionaries, but delighted a libertine like Gauguin, who lived with a series of vahines and felt that relationships between Tahitian men and women were far more honest than any he had known elsewhere. There is little evidence that the Tahitians' casual attitude toward sex harmed their society, although the ravages of venereal disease were considerable during the early decades of visiting European ships.

During our stay here we also visited the mouth of the Fahaa River, the legendary location of Raiatea's first settlement, and the exact point from which many of the great canoe voyages were believed to have left, the last one for Hawaii in 1275 A.D. We found no maraes or other traces of early Polynesian occupation here, but later Ann and I came upon impressive proof of Raiatea's mythical status as an ancient religious center for all Polynesia. It was at a marae hidden behind a Catholic church on the island's west coast, but more massive than any others we had seen. About 70 feet long, it was paved along the bottom with rounded stones, and the sides were lined with upright flat rocks about four feet high, forming a giant boat shape. Obviously a great deal of preparation and devotion had gone into building this holy place.

Throughout the less populous Societies, there are maraes every three or four miles. Some are even marked on the tourist maps, and they are as inspiring to a layman as they are technically meaningful to an anthropologist. One in particular was the marae of Queen Purea, which Cook visited in 1769 and reported finding a stone pyramid more than 260 feet long, 80 feet wide and 40 feet high — "a wonderful piece of Indian architecture." This marae survived until 1865, when the French governor ordered it dismantled and the stones used for a bridge — which, soon after, washed away. Colonialism had failed once more.

Ellie and I went ashore on Tahaa and wandered into town for the afternoon, finding Hamene to be another sleepy Polynesian town, with the usual Chinese store and copra sacks on the pier. As we stood there, the interisland ferry from Raiatea tied up, with several passengers passing a wine bottle around, refusing to disembark until it was finished. The scene was not unusual. Before the arrival of the white man, Tahitians had known of no alcoholic beverages, although the kava — or pepper plant juice — which they drank ceremonially was widely believed to have intoxicating powers. But as visiting sailors gave the natives a taste for rum and taught them to distill the ti plant root, excessive drinking became a habit among island men and alcoholism is now a problem in the islands — another of the white man's gifts to Polynesia.

On May second we sailed across to Bora Bora, known for its easily recognizable, majestic mountain profile. It was once the site of bloody battles among the ancient islanders, and in World War II it was the site of a naval base. We sailed around the western side of the island and beat into the harbor — to me always so much more satisfying than motoring into an anchorage — and tied up at the town pier. Helen and I spent the afternoon riding mopeds around the perimeter of the island, exploring a marae, taking photos, and enjoying being together. It has occurred to me again and again that the most satisfying moments I have had during the cruise were spent sightseeing or walking with one other person. Somehow communication between the generations seems easier and more direct that way than when in a group, and this afternoon with Helen was especially rewarding.

For my last night in Bora Bora I rented accommodations ashore. I had a number of log entries to make and letters to write, and I wanted a quiet night before undertaking the 500-mile passage to the Cook Islands. Although anxious to get on with the cruise, I felt as did James Cook, who, when leaving the Society Islands in 1773, wrote:

Tis with some reluctance that I bid adieu to these happy isles, where I've spent many happy days. First, they abound with the very best of pork, fruits and vegetables...second, the women are very handsome and very kind...and the men are civil and to the last degree benevolent...In short, in my opinion, they are as pleasant and happy spots as the world contains.

Palawan's *crew at Tahiti —*
(l. to r.) David Flanagan, Anne
Madden, Ellie Lazarus, Helen
Buckner, Tom Watson, Jr.,
Robin Balfour (Lord Riverdale),
Helen Watson, Paul Wolter,
Carter Christiansen.

Bay Hamene, Tahaa. We sailed here from Raiatea yesterday, a delightful short passage northward through the reefs in water so clear and sun so high that we didn't need anyone in the spreaders to guide us. Also, the reefs are well marked with beacons and you find the navigation is not as complicated as it appears on the chart. We are spending the night here.

At Tahaa, Society Islands, six men and a boatload of copra. Copra-making, very tedious and ill-paid, is a principal industry in the South Pacific.

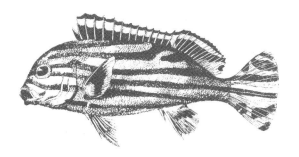

CHAPTER 11

THE COOK ISLANDS:

Atolls and Reefs

The Cook Islands lie roughly north and south, but they are so widely scattered they do not form a natural archipelago. Without modern navigation tactics, locating individual islands of the group is difficult, although the fact that some of the islands are very high and the weather is generally good in the area helps considerably. For want of any other designation, these disparate islands were arbitrarily lumped together in the course of nineteenth-century European politics. With less than 100 square miles of land among them, the 15 atolls and volcanic islands that make up the Cooks spread over 750,000 square miles of ocean between Samoa and Tahiti, with more than 800 miles between northernmost Penrhyn and southernmost Mangaia.

During our last days in the Societies, we studied the chart of the Cooks, trying to decide which islands to visit. The northern atolls would take us miles out of our way, but their histories were fascinating. There was Penrhyn, or Tongareva, where slave ships took captives in 1862, and where a mysterious flame is sometimes seen in the middle of the lagoon. Rakahanga and Manikihi are famous for pearl-diving, and their inhabitants once migrated each year from one atoll to the other to allow the fish and coconuts to replenish. Pirates stored treasures on Pukapuka and Suwarrow, legend has it, and in more recent times hermits made their homes there.

But these islands were too far off our course, so we concentrated instead on finding something in the central Cooks to visit beside the capital of Rarotonga. If we chose Palmerston, we would meet some of the 600 descendants of William Marsters, the Englishman who moved to this deserted island in 1862 with three native wives and a scheme for growing and exporting copra. We could also call at Mauke, where the taro groves are so swampy that the natives are said to dive for the fruit, or at Mangaia, whose history follows the bloody power struggles of the Ngariki tribe. Atiu Island seemed particularly appealing. Once the home of the Cooks' fiercest warriors, it now houses many of the islands' finest citrus plantations.

Finally, however, we settled on Aitutaki, a large atoll at the top of the lower Cook islands. It was discovered by William Bligh only a few days before the infamous mutiny on the

---

LOG ENTRY: MAY 8, 1976

It's about 500 miles from Bora Bora to Aitutaki in the Cook Islands, where we are heading. Winds have been light, and it has taken us about three and a half days to reach our destination. It's been a pleasant sail, but nostalgic. All the way across it has been in my heart that daughter Helen — along with Jimmy Madden — will depart for home from Rarotonga, capital of the Cooks, breaking up these happy, thoroughly enjoyable companionships.

If you ever plan to go to sea with one of your maturing children, give it a lot of thought beforehand. I've cruised long distances with most of my six children individually, and have usually found toward the end of the cruise that we were either much closer or much farther apart; the relationship never remained static. With Helen, although there have been times when I have been exasperated — as at times has she — I think we are now closer than ever. The cruise has been a great adventure for both of us.

Helen steers Palawan *during the 500-mile leg from the Society Islands to the Cook Islands, where she and Jimmy Madden, the sunniest friend I ever had, would leave us.*

Bounty. When the stern captain was rowed ashore, to his surprise he found he was required to rub noses with each island chief in an ancient Maori custom. One surmises that he complied. In 1821 the first missionaries brought drastic changes to Aitutaki, and the presence of American troops there during World War II hastened its modernization. Today the island has a thriving population, its copra and citrus plantations are booming, and its tamura dancers are known throughout Polynesia.

After a five-day sail we raised Aitutaki the morning of 8 May and circled the northern end, looking for the "reasonable" anchorage described in the pilot book. The island, with its high wooded hills and wide beaches, looked inviting, and we were eager to get ashore. But the trade wind had shifted from southeast to northwest, and we could see the surf breaking just at the point where the pilot book recommended anchoring. I was afraid that if we moved in close enough to anchor, we would be right on top of the surf, and to try landing on the beach in the small outboard with the wind and surf behind us would be courting disaster. So, after sailing back and forth for a while trying to figure out how to get ashore, we decided not to risk anchoring here at all.

As we were leaving, we watched a native trading vessel steam in right through the surf to the anchorage, drop a hook, and send a surfboat ashore. It didn't look that difficult from where we were, but the men in the boat obviously had a lot of local knowledge we didn't have. Also, I remembered reading tales of other visitors' terrifying rides in the surf over Cook reefs. At Manihiki in 1967, Maurice Shadbolt, a writer for the *National Geographic*, found himself in a slim longboat at the edge of a reef, surrounded by waiting oarsmen. Suddenly, "oars flashed as we hurtled forward on a high breaking wave, over perilous coral, to the safety of the pale shore."

Undergoing a similar experience in 1929, Peter Buck noted that if the waves were too shallow, the boat would ground on the reef, leaving the crew to "gaze fearfully down the vertical outer side" of the high makatea reef, and "into the yawning, gurgling chasm below. The newcomer," he added, "is not reassured by tales of people who have been sucked down into coral caverns from which they have never reappeared."

For us, Aitutaki would have to wait. We headed for Rarotonga,

140 miles to the south.

Looking at a map, one would suspect that ancient Polynesians settled the Cooks during eastward migrations from Tonga, stopping midway at Niue Island. However, many experts now believe that the early travelers split in Micronesia, with one group heading south to colonize Fiji, and a second continuing east to the Marquesas, both missing the Cooks completely. Now it is thought that the Cooks were discovered during later westward explorations from the Societies, as late as 500 years ago. Cook Islands legend supports this theory, with its frequent mention of the half-sacred "Havaiki," and its well-established tale of the first settlers — a pair of adventurers from Tahiti and Samoa.

For several centuries the Cooks remained untouched by outsiders, and although the islanders may have had some contact with Tahiti, they were isolated enough to develop some unusual cultural traits such as using sandals as protection against the rough coral, and wearing brief loincloths and long feather capes. They wore both ornaments and utensils in their pierced ears, and woven, cone-shaped hats or tall headdresses made of feathers and human hair. They ate coconuts and fish, which they caught with poison, brooms, dams, spears, and their hands. During certain periods called "masanga," the chiefs acted to preserve the islands' ecology by declaring sections of the land and water taboo so the fish and coconut supplies could replenish themselves undisturbed — something modern society has only recently started to do.

According to Peter Buck, who visited the Cooks in 1910 and 1929, the islanders were very fond of games, stilts, and flying kites. At the same time, they were very warlike people. Their history refers to constant fighting among tribes of the same island, between neighboring islands, and with the Tongans. They were adept at making weapons, including slings and elaborately carved or serrated clubs. At one time, at least some of the tribes were enthusiastic cannibals. Missionary W. Wyatt Gill described past raids in which "infants were brained and cooked with their parents." Each time the sharkskin drums of peace pounded after battle, a group of captives was sacrificed to the great god Rongo. Although cannibalism had disappeared by the nineteenth century, Gill reported that the last human sacrifice on Rarotonga took place as late as 1823.

During the eighteenth and nineteenth centuries, European navigators kept finding and losing the Cook islands because they were so scattered, and the last two atolls weren't discovered until 1820, by the Russians. It's possible that early Spanish navigators may have sighted several Cook islands, and in 1765 Englishman John Byron spotted Pukapuka, but found the surf unmanageable for landing. On his second world voyage, James Cook found two islands, which he named after British Admiralty Lord Hervey. Four years later he returned to explore three more: Mangaia, where the natives were "almost naked"; Atiu, where a huge oven made Omai nervous; and Palmerston, where the rich wildlife inspired one crewman to wonder "for what purpose Nature should want to conceal a work so elegant."

Later, there were many undocumented visits from New England whalers and an unhappy period in the 1860s when Peruvians raided the northern Cooks repeatedly for slaves to work the guano deposits in the Chincha Islands and the copper mines in the Peruvian mountains. Eventually, the French Minister at Lima was informed by his Tahitian counterpart of what was going on. The French and other governments then brought world opinion to bear on the Peruvians to stop the practice. Efforts were made to repatriate the captured Polynesians, but by then many had died.

Although Rarotonga is the largest of the Cooks, Captain Cook missed it twice. Later, the *Bounty* mutineers stumbled on it and considered settling there, but eventually decided to move on. Then, in 1814 British Captain Goodenough is said to have landed, tried to carry off some native women, and became embroiled in a bloody brouhaha with island warriors; so much so that he was too embarrassed to report his discovery when he finally escaped and returned home. Some sources even give missionary John Williams, who arrived in 1821, credit for discovering the island, but no one is sure who actually saw it first.

Captain Cook never set foot on Rarotonga, but he did discover five nearby islands, and eventually the British government named all 15 of the "lonely" islands — as the Cooks were sometimes referred to — after him, the greatest navigator, cartographer, and amateur anthropological observer in English history.

Born in a Yorkshire farm village in 1728, Cook left home as a boy, went to work on coal ships, studied math and navigation in his spare time, and enlisted in the Royal Navy at 26. Encouraged by his first commander, Sir Hugh Palliser, he won praise for his work in charting the Newfoundland coast. Later his painstaking surveys of the St. Lawrence River, conducted under cover of night, enabled the British fleet to maneuver up the river and successfully attack Quebec. Then the Royal Society appointed him head of the 1769 expedition to Tahiti, and Cook's sea-roving began in earnest.

During the next 10 years, Cook circled the globe three times. He charted the coasts of Australia and New Zealand and sailed south to the ice, disproving the popular theory of a large, habitable southern continent and rightly concluding that while there might well be land there, it would be too cold for use. Crisscrossing the Pacific many times, he explored dozens of islands, then ducked icebergs to reach through the Bering Strait to within 1,300 miles of the North Pole. He would have done more had he not been murdered in 1779 by nervous Hawaiian natives.

Cook's accomplishments, however, went far beyond mere exploration and discovery. His observations on island life gave the world precious records of Pacific civilization. He perfected the use of the chronometer to reckon longitude, and he pioneered in the prevention of scurvy. Stern and aloof but scrupulously fair, he inspired loyalty among his men, friendship among island peoples, and respect throughout the civilized world. When news of his death reached England, King George III is said to have wept.

As we approached Rarotonga, we realized the harbor was slightly better than what was indicated on the chart, but there was a heavy surge following us right up the harbor, making it difficult to lie comfortably to an anchor. We tried tying up to a pier, but we pitched and tossed constantly, and when chased from there by a steamer we found we had to retreat to the head of the harbor where we were at the mercy of the full force of wind and waves. It was an uneasy berth at best and a rude awakening after the calm anchorages we had enjoyed in the Societies.

No sooner had we tied up than a heavy-set, casually dressed man of about 40 drove up in a Datsun pickup truck and introduced himself as a Dutch Reformed minister. His hobby, he told us, was meeting every yacht that arrived in the harbor, and asking the crew for a page about themselves and their boat to add to his scrapbook. We concocted a page using some of Helen's sketches and giving *Palawan*'s statistics, and he seemed pleased. Then he invited us for a ride around the island in the back of his truck. After a short visit to his house in town, we went to a local rugby game — his second favorite hobby and our first reminder that we were really out of French Polynesia and on an island that had been under British influence for 150 years.

The game — a noisy, no-holds-barred combination of football and soccer — was particularly exciting because it gave us our first and only large-scale contact with the Cook islanders. We were amazed at the players' intensity and vigor and at the spectators' enthusiasm. Uniformed school children stood along the sidelines looking — except for their black hair and brown skin — like British students attending a game at Folkestone. Between plays they crowded around the numerous ice cream wagons, occasionally scattering to make room for the teenaged big shots who roared in and out on their Hondas and Suzukis. Motorcycles were obviously the local status symbol.

Our Dutch friend was in his element, cheering the players by name in Polynesian, but after an hour we hinted that we would like to move on, and the kindly priest loaded up the Datsun and we drove off to see his church. Built of cement and tin, the tiny house of worship couldn't have held more than 60 people. The minister's house was also small and spare, with few material comforts. I couldn't help wondering how he felt about being alone, tens of thousands of miles away from Amsterdam. But in these days of declining interest in religion, perhaps he was glad to be in a place where Christianity still has a firm hold. There were many churches larger than his on Rarotonga, but he seemed to be actively involved in the community, and it was gratifying to see that a variety of religions now flourish on an island once strictly controlled by the English missionaries.

Beginning with John Williams's arrival in 1823, the missionaries quickly gained influence over the Rarotongan people and their leaders. In 1900 a visiting bishop reported finding a "pandemonium of virtue." Native police enforced laws against such crimes as being an unwed mother, consulting a sorcerer, touching a woman in public after dark, receiving a tattoo, and traveling on Sunday. For these offenses, natives were punished by public flogging or imprisonment. In addition, many maraes were destroyed and many traditional customs outlawed. According to F.J. Moss, an early British island official who disapproved of these laws:

The old amusements and dances were sternly repressed... as relics of heathenism. No healthy recreation was given in its place. The minds of the people have become a perfect blank. They have no literature, no books, nothing to move the imagination or please the taste, nothing on which a healthy progress can be based.

The missionaries' grip began to loosen after the islands were annexed to New Zealand in 1901, but their teachings had taken root. Today the islanders have blended Christianity with more colorful, native spiritual teachings. One of the most moving experiences of my whole trip was a visit Jimmy and I made to a church service in Avarua. My sister had told us how beautiful the church singing was at Pitcairn, and I was eager to hear some of it myself. As we rode our bikes up to the church compound near the sea, the priest was welcoming a long line of worshippers at the door. Rarotongans are generally tall and handsome, their bodies less prone to obesity than are their neighbors to the east. Always neat and clean, they were dressed that day with particular care, the women in white dresses and the men in simple khaki pants and shirts.

We went in and the congregation courteously made room for us on the benches where we could see and hear everything. The organist began to play and the singing began. Everyone was seated by vocal sections, and as the Polynesian melodies developed, the voices answered each other in counterpart, from sopranos to tenors and from altos to basses. The congregation began to sway, and the sounds were so harmonious and pure that the scene brought tears to my eyes. When I try to recall it now, it returns not to my eyes but to my ears — an unparalleled musical experience for both Jimmy and me.

After the hectic, distinctly French atmosphere of Papeete, we were happy to discover that Avarua was still a sleepy British trading post. There were a few modest government buildings, a gift shop or two, a pharmacy, some small motels, a museum, and

This evening I took Helen to dinner in a pleasant restaurant outside Avarua. For me, this was one of the most memorable evenings of the cruise, perhaps of my entire life. I am still aware of the petty frictions that have arisen between us occasionally; nevertheless, I feel she has done very well, coming on board a month after the rest of us had settled in, and working her way into everyone's heart by the time she has to leave. Above all, I am impressed by her basic good nature and kindness. I wrote a poem to read to her this evening: it expresses how during my life I have tried to cope with the generation gap, in respect to both my parents and my children, and how much joy she has given me, not only during the past four months but over the past 20 years.

We dined by candlelight, and after the first course and a glass of wine, I read the poem to her. She was very moved, and so was I.

churches, but although a small jet port had been built in 1970, tourism had barely begun to affect island life. The Cook islands have been losing population for many years, and in the last few decades to the sophistication of New Zealand cities and, occasionally, to Tahiti. On the more remote islands, natives still eke out a near-subsistence economy of fishing and erratic copra production. But many reefs have become over-fished, and the Japanese cultured-pearl industry has eclipsed the Cooks' pearl-shell trade, so many northern atolls now rely on food and supplies from New Zealand relief ships.

On the larger, more populated islands of Rarotonga, Atiu and Aitutaki, pearl and copra production have been gradually replaced by plantations of non-native crops — oranges, pineapples, grapefruit, and lemons. These plantations and several canneries employ most of the islands' workers in the production of canned juice.

During our stay in Avarua Harbor, we met yachting people of a different sort from the ones we had encountered at Papeete. We also met several individuals who had escaped civilization to settle in this remote area. One yacht from New Zealand was hardly 30 feet overall and had aboard two children under five years old and four adults. The size of the boat and lightness of her gear indicated that these were indeed clement waters, if sailed at the right time of year. There were also two couples who were sailing around the world alone in 50-foot sloops. Now, a 50-footer is a lot of vessel to be controlled by two middle-aged people. One of the skippers told me that whenever he and his wife, both in their late 50s, sailed island waters, where it was important to remain constantly alert, they usually stayed in port until they were so completely rested they could face a week at sea with very little sleep; then, when the barometer was high and sky blue, off they would go. Both boats were manned by knowledgeable skippers, and both had self-steering devices for use in good weather.

Another unusual expatriate we met was a 75-year-old Britisher, who had sailed to the Cooks 50 years ago and married a Palmerston woman. He visited *Palawan* several times and proved to be an excellent source of information about the area, especially Palmerston's odd history. He told us how William Marsters, with great foresight, had planted 80,000 coconut trees there, how his mixed-breed family lived primitively until the missionaries came, how the native workers rose up against him on one occasion, and how from that day on he always kept a revolver and two black dogs at his side. Our British friend had lived on that isolated island for several years and later brought his wife — a Marsters herself — down to Rarotonga, where he said he now owned a gift shop in Avarua. Marster's descendants have scattered throughout the Cooks and farther, and the settlement there is now very small, with the remaining inhabitants depending on government supplies to survive.

On our second afternoon on Rarotonga, Helen and I took off on our motorbikes and rode around the perimeter of the island. Parts of the road were new, but in other places it was still the original road built at least 400 years ago. These ancient cobbles are the only remaining sign of Rarotonga's first settlers, and our drive through the quiet, green land was fascinating. But even the unusual charm of the island couldn't quell my sadness at the prospect of Helen's imminent departure. I was going to miss her very much.

On our last night, Jimmy and Anne gave a crew dinner which also served as a goodbye party for Jimmy, *Palawan*'s best shipmate and the hardest-working navigator I have ever had the pleasure of sailing with. Jim and I never discussed his relationship with his daughter Anne, and he didn't seem to talk much with her during the voyage. Anne is naturally very quiet and charming but timid as a fawn, perhaps as a result of growing up with a number of brothers. After watching Jim and Anne at sea for weeks, I realized that they had one of those rare relationships where two people commmunicate silently and are quite content with each other's company. As we sat around the cabin table at night, Jimmy's eyes followed Anne, he smiled at her jokes, and his pleasure and pride in his daughter were obvious. On this night, this father-daughter experience — perhaps less dramatic than Helen's and mine, but equally fulfilling and intense — was also coming to an end. I was beginning to wonder how much I would enjoy the rest of the voyage without Jimmy's companionship and without the buoying presence of Helen, for whom the whole idea of a South Pacific cruise had been created.

On 11 May we said our fond farewells, loaded Jim's and Helen's gear onto the pier, and prepared to leave for Niue, 400 miles to the west. We cast off the docklines, but came up short

LOG ENTRY: MAY 11, 1976

I'm sorry Paul is unhappy over my decision to head for Samoa. He has not been his happy self at all lately. I think perhaps that the decade that separates him from Jim and me has left him in a kind of limbo between the younger and older crew segments, and perhaps he resents a little the companionship between Jim and me, especially since Jim's return to the crew after his brother's death. Also, Paul knows that the farther west we sail, the longer it will take him to sail the boat back and get home to his family, and although the pilot charts assure good weather, there is always the possibility of surprise storm. The return crew will not be much more experienced than this one, and there could always be a recurrence of the problems with the gear box or electrical system. These things, I am sure, are all troubling Paul at the moment.

on the beam anchor, which we had been using to hold us off the pier. It was deeply imbedded in mud. Finally we got it up and washed it off as we slowly motored out of the pass. Looking astern, I waved to the two figures on the pier until they faded from view — a tall, tanned girl in faded cut-offs, and a small, wistful man in a sailor's cap.

A hundred yards out of the pass, however, our sentimental departure was rudely interrupted when the boat suddenly began to slow down, even though the engine was still running smoothly and the gear handle was in "forward." Somehow, power was no longer being transmitted from the engine to the propeller. We were uncomfortably close to a coral reef and to the ominous wreck of Irving Johnson's *Yankee*. *Yankee* had been sold by the Johnsons years before to a charter operator, and in 1965, while in that service, had ended her career ingloriously on this reef off Rarotonga. Our crew responded quickly to the emergency, getting the sails up in jig time. Although there was little wind, we were able to work our way under sail into deep water.

We soon diagnosed the trouble. Our old problem of salt water getting into the gearbox had returned to haunt us. This time there could be no temporary solutions. The gear was ruined. According to our manual, the closest major diesel repair facility was in Suva, Fiji. The only alternative was to have a new gearbox flown from home. Our immediate priority was to get to an island that had either reliable air service to Fiji or frequent jet service to the States. I went below to get out the charts and work out the possibilities. Our planned destination of Niue, isolated and tiny, would be of no help. Tonga wasn't too far west, but even its capitol island of Tongatapu had only sporadic flights to Fiji. New Zealand was a tempting idea, but that was more than 1,000 miles away. Finally, I settled on American Samoa, 700 miles to the northwest. As a major stop on transpacific jet routes to New Zealand and Australia, it offered good plane service to Fiji. It also harbored American naval and Coast Guard repair facilities.

Relieved to have a solution to our problem and a course of action to follow, I went on deck and announced it to the crew. Everyone agreed readily except Paul, who voiced some reservations. Wanting to humor him, I sat down and explained all my reasons for choosing to head for Samoa. I then went below again

to plot our new course.

Several months later, after we had all returned home, I found out what else had been troubling Paul — cabin fever. At one point I had switched his bunk from the uncomfortable fo'c's'le to one in the starboard stateroom, where he had to cope with a female world. Sharing the head with four women, he had to fight his way through shampoo bottles, face cream, deodorant, long hairs in the sink, and someone else occupying the head when he wanted to get in there. It began to overwhelm him. Also, for some reason, the women seemed to cluster frequently in the companionway, and in an effort to assert his machismo, Paul finally took to bumping into them slightly when passing. Much of this escaped me at the time, but he mentioned it later, as did the women.

I also found out sometime later why Helen had left the ship at Rarotonga. She called me one evening from California, and after a couple of false starts, she finally blurted out, "Daddy, you know that wedding I said I wanted to leave the cruise early to go to? Well, there really wasn't any wedding. I was just afraid of getting involved on *Palawan* for too long, so I made that up to have a definite departure date. Also, there was someone here I wanted to get back to see. I've been thinking about this ever since and — uh — I had a great time on the cruise, and I knew I wouldn't feel right until I confessed this fib to you."

I thanked her for being so forthright and hung up very deeply touched by this call to set things straight.

CHAPTER 12

SAMOA:

Pago Pago and Apia

As we got underway and discovered some unexpected problems, I found that our careful preparations for the cruise — such as including an SSB — paid off. We could use the single-sideband radio for only one short period each day — when the sun was in exactly the right position. But patience is the key to success with this very-long-range gadget, and with persistence I was able to get at least one call daily through to the States. After 24 hours of analysis and then discussion via SSB with our shipyard in Camden, Maine, we decided it would be less costly to have a new gear flown from home than to risk getting the wrong parts from Fiji. So we arranged to have a mechanic from Southwest Harbor, Maine, bring the gear to Samoa. I was also able to contact Rene and Cheryl Coudert, old ocean-racing friends who had planned to meet us in Tonga, and told them to fly to Samoa instead.

The crew adapted to our new situation well, seemed confident in my decision, and went about their work with a will. Paul recovered from his disappointment over my decision to head for Samoa, and then blamed himself for the engine breakdown, although I tried to reassure him that it couldn't possibly have been prevented.

Even with the difficulty of getting regular sights, our dead reckoning was right on and the navigation went surprisingly well. At mid-afternoon of 16 May we spotted the sharp peak of Mount Matafao, "The Rainmaker," on the island of Tutuila, and several hours later we sailed through a colorful Sunfish regatta and into Pagopago Harbor. This is one of the loveliest harbors in the Pacific, but it was so hot and humid that evening, and the odor from two waterfront tuna processing plants was so overpowering, that we decided for the sake of better ventilation and rest to drop the anchor well out in the harbor.

However, shortly after I retired, a tugboat approached and informed Paul that we were anchored in the path of a cruise ship about to leave the dock. On learning that we were without an engine, the tug crew offered a tow. With the shrewdness of a former freighter captain, Paul shrugged and said, "No money."

LOG ENTRY: MAY 16, 1976

We've made the 700 miles from Rarotonga to Samoa in five days, not bad with no engine and light winds from the start. Later the wind picked up and we ran for hours at eight to nine knots under a small, winged-out jib and main, even using the spinnaker for a while. Skies were overcast most of the time, making regular sun sights difficult; the watch had a standing order to call me whenever it looked as if the sun might appear. We passed through many squalls, with lots of rain and lightning, and one night when Ellie and I were on watch, we encountered a husky blow of 30 to 35 knots. Great sailing! Otherwise, it's been generally easy going on a lonely ocean. We've passed at most three boats at sea since the Galapagos.

This passage made me realize how comforting it is to have a healthy, 170-hp engine under the deck. Now without one we're totally dependent on the elements — like the Polynesian in his canoe or Magellan in his 110-ton ship.

After a long silence from the tug, a string of American four-letter words was followed by, "All right, we tow you free, you stingy bastards!" Thanks to Paul, *Palawan* was towed down to the end of the harbor courtesy of the tug, while I slept.

Samoa consists of seven islands stretched across 300 miles of tropical ocean only 14 degrees below the equator. To the west are the large islands of Savai'i and Upolu, which make up the independent State of Western Samoa. These 1,300 square miles of beach, volcanic peaks, lava plain, and farmland support a growing population of 150,000. Some of the steep hills rise to 6,000 feet, and there are several volcanoes, but none active lately.

To the east is the much smaller U.S. Territory of Eastern Samoa. Its major island, Tutuila, is almost cut in half by Pagopago Harbor. Together with the Manu'a Islands and tiny Rose Island, the 73-square-mile territory is home to 125,000 Polynesians and numerous Americans.

Samoa has been occupied by Polynesians for a very long time, according to the many artifacts that have been carbon-dated to the first century A.D. More recent archaeological excavations have moved the time of known occupation further and further back, perhaps as early as 1000 B.C. Certainly Samoa served as one of the bases for the original occupation of central Polynesia; the name "Savai'i" is a variation of "Havai'iki," the mythical Polynesian homeland. But there is still considerable argument over how the early Samoans got there — whether by migrations eastward from Tonga and Fiji or from the islands to the north. Oddly enough, the average Samoan is a few shades darker than Polynesians farther east. Somehow Micronesian blood was filtered into the Polynesians of Samoa, probably after they had been on Samoa for hundreds of years, and lighter-colored Polynesians had then continued migrating eastward.

The Samoans say simply that they have "always been here." Their myths do not include tales of sea voyages; rather, they feature grotesque tales of men developing from maggots that swarmed on rotting vines when the islands were created. The Samoan word for white man — papapagi — means "sky burster," and it is tradition that the first white visitor "burst" through the known universe to find Samoa, although it may be that the image developed from billowing sails rising over the horizon.

The original sky burster was Jacob Roggeveen, who sighted

Samoan children — bright, lively and curious about us — were typical of the Polynesian youngsters we encountered all during our cruise.

the Manu'a Islands less than nine weeks after he discovered Easter Island in 1722. Going ashore briefly, he was met by a number of "lively fellows, fat and sleek, in colour brownish red with long black rosy hair." (Perhaps their hair had a reddish tinge, or was adorned with bright blossoms.) Forty years later Bougainville came close to Upolu and Savai'i, but found the surf too rough to land. Impressed by the dexterity of the native sailors whose canoes ran rings around his ship, he named the islands the "Navigator Archipelago" and continued on his way. In 1787, La Perouse landed at Tutuila, but lost 12 men when natives attacked a landing party. Three years later, HMS *Pandora* searched briefly for the *Bounty* mutineers along the coasts of Tutuila and Upolu, but no other ships dared return to the site of La Perouse's misfortune until 1824, when Russian explorer Otto Von Kotzebue stopped to trade at Massacre Bay and was greeted without hostility by the islanders.

Whatever their origins, the early Samoans developed some unique traits as they became isolated from other cultures. In contrast to other Polynesian areas, Samoan children were put to work from the age of six, baby-sitting or helping with chores. As anthropologist Margaret Mead wrote in 1923, "All the irritating, detailed routine of housekeeping, which in our civilization is accused of warping the souls and souring the tempers of grown women, is here performed by children under 14." The women spent their time weaving pandanus mats, making bark cloth garments, and working the inland copra and taro fields. The men were responsible for building houses, making and repairing canoes, and fishing. In the evening, villagers of all ages often gathered to dance the "Siva," and sometimes they dropped work altogether to go on a "malaga," a singing and dancing procession from village to village.

Samoans are known to display an exaggerated respect for ceremony and rank, and a casual irreverence for spiritual and political authority. Instead of major Polynesian gods, they worshipped local ones. On the other hand, they handed down many of the same myths: for example, the lovers who jumped off a sea cliff to become the first turtle and shark, and the eel that died for the love of a princess and turned into the first coconut palm. Despite their practical approach to religion, the Samoans were terrified of ghosts. And some of their customs were very harsh, particularly a ban on brother-sister contact and the defloration of brides by lucky village chiefs.

Samoans have always loved partisan politics and elaborate plots to unseat local chiefs — hence their nickname, the "Irishmen of the Pacific." Yet, they have always paid great attention to etiquette and title. Each village was led by a powerful chief — matai — who could be approached or petitioned only through his "talking chief," or what Dr. Mead called a combination "major-domo, assistant, ambassador, henchman and councilor."

Masters of protocol, these assistants spoke only in a special, flowery language. The system of elaborate social ritual also extended to kava-drinking — only maiden daughters of chiefs were allowed to prepare the pepper plant root by chewing it and spitting the juice into a bowl, which was later passed solemnly around the village leaders. And the flair for public courtesy even spilled over into everyday life where, as Robert Louis Stevenson wrote, "terms of ceremony fly thick as oaths on board a ship; commoners 'my lord' each other when they meet, and urchins as they play marbles."

As we came on deck our first morning at Pagopago, a large cable car was swinging across the harbor, on its way from the center of town to the top of a high peak to the north. To us it seemed a superfluous piece of equipment, but later we were given various reasons for its construction: as a tourist attraction, to bring villagers down from the hills, and to service the TV antenna atop Mount Alava. Actually, it was the result of an energetic American governor's effort during the Kennedy administration to improve Samoan education. The idea was to build TV antennae on a number of mountains, and then keep all the good teachers in a central location to broadcast their classes to local schools. The idea proved controversial, and it was clearly a mistake to spend so many tax dollars installing a system that had failed in U.S. schools. Today most Samoan schools have their own teachers again, but the cable car remains as a symbol of bureaucratic blundering on the part of well-meaning American officials.

The more we saw of Pagopago during our five-day stay, the more we realized how Americanized the town of 20,000 had become since the U.S. Navy first leased some land to build a coaling station there in 1872. There were government employees everywhere. Many native men wore business coats and ties over their dark formal skirts. In the markets and shops, people were pleasant but aggressive; they were impatient to sell their merchandise rather than answer our questions.

Obviously, the Americans brought money to Pagopago. Most houses have a TV antenna, and the roads are well paved and filled with automobiles. We talked with a Los Angeles lawyer whose client, the wife of a native chief, had local investments of more than $1,000,000. Yet, what the Samoans have gained economically as they have come to depend more and more on the U.S., they have lost in native pride and heritage. As in Tonga, we found few traces of ancient history here, even though Samoa was close to the birthplace of the Polynesian race. The local musuem featured American whaling lore. And according to a *National Geographic* writer who visited a large marae there, his local guide turned to him sadly and said, "It means nothing to us."

On the other hand, it wasn't hard to picture Pagopago as it had been 100 years ago, when Robert Louis Stevenson wrote his Pacific yarns; or later, when W. Somerset Maugham described the bustling seaport in his 1920 short story, "Rain," which I reread one rainy afternoon in the Pagopago library. If I closed my eyes and pretended that the tourist shops, new government buildings, and post office weren't there, I was back in a classic tropical town like New Orleans or Galveston of many years ago.

There were many old, lovely buildings and churches and a particularly dignified edifice impressively labelled "The High Court of Samoa." Wooden and weathered, it conjured up all sorts of visions of what had been our American ideas of how to "get these people in line."

Towering over everything was Rainmaker Mountain, at the eastern end of the island. The trade winds blow constantly up and over the mountain, frequently dropping light rainshowers into the harbor, oddly enough missing the shore most of the time. One morning Anne, Ellie, and I drove a rented car to the eastern end, and the farther we got from Pagopago the more primitive and thus more interesting the villages became, and the happier the people seemed. Finally, we turned onto a narrow, muddy road running along the northern coast. Bumping up a

---

LOG ENTRY: MAY 17, 1976

I've taken a room in the Rainmaker Hotel to catch up on my notes, rest and spend some time alone. This famous hotel is lovely from the outside and has a beautiful location on the western end of the harbor, but inside it is badly deteriorated. So far, Samoa has left me with mixed feelings — ugly modernization on top of so much beauty. I've concluded that the time to have visited here was back at the turn of the century.

steep, rutted hill, we slithered down the other side into the heart of another village.

Here a violent sea crashed against black volcanic rock, and dense growth rose abruptly from the shallow beach into the hills. Randomly perched along the water were large fales, the unique Samoan houses developed over centuries as protection from the hot, humid climate. Elevated on log foundations, the oval, thatched-roof huts used pandanus mats in place of side walls; the mats could be rolled down in case of rain, but rolled up to admit breeze. Along the dusty streets, the natives walked quietly about their business, neither welcoming nor shunning us. They were unusually tall, slightly darker than their neighbors to the east, with broad, flat faces. Thair hands and feet were large and slightly splayed, and most of those over 30 were overweight, but all carried themselves with marked dignity.

We got back over the hill and had just descended to the beach on the other side when the car ran out of gas. Anne and Ellie boarded a passing bus and went back to the village to find some fuel while I stayed with the car. Soon, two native boys of about 18 sauntered by with fishing rods and stopped. After asking me a few questions about the car, they suddenly threw open the hood, despite my protest that we were merely out of gas, and said they were going to try to fix the car. Then they began to shake it, and when I asked them to stop, they shook it still harder, banging on the doors and hood viciously. Then they taunted me in English, saying "I wonder if it's as safe out here in Samoa as it is in Harlem?" Cursing the rental agency, I was nervously considering retreating to the car and locking the doors when another bus came by and the driver stopped to chat. To my relief, the boys went on their way.

I finally got a ride back to the village, where I found Anne and Ellie chattering away with the residents, Ellie making good use of her French and a few words in Polynesian to make new friends. Eventually, we took a taxi back to town and the boat, leaving the car where it was for the rental agency to deal with. It was an ignominious end to the day's adventure.

That night I thought about the incident with the boys, and it brought home to me the paradox of the American welfare state in Samoa. I believe it developed in the mid-1800s, when German, British, and American firms began competing for con-

trol over production and trade of copra, bananas, and other crops. These three powers began throwing their weights behind rival native chiefs, until they nearly provoked an international incident in 1888. Luckily, just when ships of the three western powers were poised for battle to assume control of the islands, a hurricane intervened, sinking all but one ship. The three foreign governments then backed down and agreed to a pact instead of a battle to divide up the islands.

Western Samoa went to the Germans, who ruled firmly until World War I, when New Zealand made a military stand there and took over trusteeship of the islands under the League of Nations. New Zealand remained in control for the next 40 years.

From the beginning, the natives refused to work exclusively on German plantations, and developed their own tracts for raising coconuts, bananas, cocoa, coffee, and cattle. During New Zealand's rule, 30,000 acres of former German cropland were turned over to the islanders. Despite political infighting, the Samoans built up a strong nationalistic movement over the next decades, and in 1962 Western Samoa became an independent nation. Fifteen years later it became the 147th member of the United Nations, and today the islands' 9,000 "matais" elect a general assemby and appoint a small cabinet.

At the time of the pact, Eastern Samoa went to the U.S. and was administered for the next 50 years by the Navy, which left local politics alone but took control of agricultural exports. Although there were complaints of dictatorship, the real problem was Tutuila's growing financial dependence on the U.S. In the 1950s the Interior Department took over, and during the next decade the U.S. governors built schools, roads, reservoirs, a hospital, and an excellent airport. Soon the U.S. government was pumping $4 million a year into Samoa. Today, native authority in legal and political matters has increased. However, life in Pagopago bears the unpleasant stamp of a welfare state — with all the hurt pride and resentment such dependency fosters among its beneficiaries.

During all that time of foreign dominance, however, the proud Samoans never gave up their heritage to the white man's religious, economic, or political control. The strong sense of identity that kept Western Samoa from foreign political control also kept its religious heritage from being destroyed by zealous missionaries. When British minister John Williams arrived in 1830, he found a self-confident, calmly spiritual people who simply incorporated the new Christian beliefs into their traditional customs.

Even in American Samoa, where she lived in 1923, Dr. Mead found that the native pastors had surpassed the enthusiasm of the foreign clergy, making it "impossible" for them to "establish the rigor of Western Protestantism with its inseparable association of sex offenses and an individual consciousness of sin." No one would suggest that the missionaries in Samoa suffered from the tropical weakness of Somerset Maugham's self-righteous reverend, who was seduced by an American prostitute in Pagopago and promptly killed himself. When Pope Paul IV was traveling in 1970, the Samoans were not at all surprised when he stopped to visit them, bypassing other Pacific nations. "Naturally the Pope has come here," one native churchman reportedly said. "This is God's country."

Trying to stick as closely as possible to our original timetable, I had decided to head directly for Vava'u, in Tonga, on the twenty-second. But when I broached this to the women, they protested strongly. They wanted to visit Western Samoa and thought I was being unfair not to stop there. Also, that evening as we were dining at the Rainmaker Hotel, Victoria Branch, a young novelist who had arrived on the plane with the Couderts, stopped by to chat. She mentioned that she was on her way to Apia, the capital of Western Samoa and final resting place of Robert Louis Stevenson, to stay at the famous Aggie's Hotel. She painted such an interesting picture of the place that I couldn't resist the double pressure. I agreed to set a course for Upolu and Apia instead of Tonga.

The 65-mile night run across to Western Samoa was uneventful. We nosed into port about 0800, and as soon as we were moored I went ashore for our clearances. Then, after breakfast aboard, I decided to ride over to Aggie's and find Victoria Branch. A day of sightseeing with this near-stranger seemed to me the perfect way to take a break from *Palawan*, distract me from my worries over whether the new gearbox would really get the boat to Fiji and then home, and give the three women and me a day's vacation from each other.

Aggie's Hotel, a rambling building surrounded by luxurious

LOG ENTRY: MAY 20-22, 1976

Our new gear and competent mechanic from Maine — Walter Leighton — and his wife arrived at 4 A.M. at Tutuila airport, where I met them. After a rest, Walter went to work, and within a day he had the engine running again. He will do a series of four-hour gearbox tests today at full speed to be sure all is well.

Rene and Cheryl Coudert, who will spend the last three weeks of the cruise with us, have just arrived on the early morning plane. I hope to leave here tomorrow.

flowers and shrubs, had been built by a spunky Samoan-American woman named Aggie Grey in the 1930s. It was popular with GIs during World War II — in fact, it's said that James Michener modeled his character "Bloody Mary" after Aggie. Victoria said she would like to see the island, but wouldn't be ready for an hour, so while I waited I browsed in the local marketplace. It was amusing to see the native policemen wearing British bobbies' hats above their skirts and sandals. This was going to be quite a change from American Samoa!

I rented a car and eventually picked up Victoria at Aggie's. We drove up the steep hill to Vailima, the sprawling and beautifully planted bungalow where Robert Louis Stevenson lived the last six years of his life. The estate was being used as the White House of Western Samoa. Hoping to cure his chronic tuberculosis, Stevenson moved to Apia in 1888 and spent his time writing stories about the Marquesas, Societies, and Samoa. He described the islanders with sympathy and accuracy, and they grew to love the man they called "Tusitala," or "Teller of Tales." When he died in 1894, barely 50 years old, a procession of natives hacked their way up a "Road of Loving Hearts" into the jungle behind Vailima, carrying his coffin on their backs and laying it to rest among garlands of flowers. On his hillside tomb, the headstone is carved with two versions of his poem, "Requiem," ending with these lines:

Under the wide and starry sky
Dig my grave and let me lie,
Glad did I live and gladly die,
And I laid me down with a will.
This be the verse you grave for me:
Here he lies where he longs to be,
Home is the sailor, home from the sea,
And the hunter home from the hill.

Stevenson was not the only writer to describe the beauties of Samoa. Rupert Brooke called it an island "lovely and lost, and half a world away," where one could "slice thin golden white shavings off" the moonlight. Maugham wrote of Upolu natives washing in a forest pool; a scene much like "Devonshire among the hills, but with a tropical richness, a passion, a scented lan-guor which seemed to melt the heart."

Stevenson took great interest in island politics, which he called "a wretched business, with fine elements of farce...involving many dark and many moonlit rides, secret councils which are at once divulged, sealed letters which are read aloud in confidence to the neighbors, and a mass of fudge and fun."

While he was intrigued with the constant feuds, gossip, and plots of Samoan politics, Stevenson had harsher words for the traders and large German copra companies — particularly the mammoth Godeffroy and Son — that exploited native and imported laborers. He became heavily involved in the secession struggle that led to the formation of the three-nation pact in 1888, and after Germany took over Western Samoa he championed the cause of Samoan independence until local officials tried to deport him. In "The Beach at Falesa," he told of traders who treated the islanders as dirt, and thought of them as children. As his character, trader John Wiltshire, expounded:

I know how to deal with Kanakas. Give him plain sense and
fair dealing, and — I'll do them that much justice — they'll
knuckle under every time. They haven't any real government or
laws; that's what you've got to knock into their heads, and even
if they had, it would be a good joke if it was to apply to a white
man. It would be a strange thing if we came all this way and
couldn't do as we pleased.

Leaving Vailima, we drove over the top of Mount Vaea and down the other side to a magnificent waterfall nearly obscured in the mist, then on to the south coast, where we stopped at a beachside hotel for lunch. Thus far, our conversation had been relaxed and pleasant. Victoria had talked of her father, a former Hollywood screenwriter, and we each remarked how strongly our fathers had affected our lives. She described her job as publicist for Northrop Aircraft Company and expressed some interesting views on the aerospace industry. But soon she began to speak of more personal convictions, and the more interested I became in the discussions, the more I realized my plans for a tranquil day were to remain unfulfilled. Victoria was very outspoken of her feelings about feminism and other relatively new ideas. Fascinating as these ideas were, they didn't provide me with a peaceful change of pace, but rather emphasized the difference in age and so, perhaps, philosophy between us.

After lunch we circled the western tip of the island, passing through numerous seacoast villages that appeared not to have changed in a thousand years. Along the roads and set back among the trees were fales arranged some distance from each other for privacy. Through the airy open sides, the spotless interiors were plainly visible. The bedding was rolled up for the day. There was an occasional mirror and bureau, but no chairs; most daily activity seemed to take place on the woven frond floors. A short distance from each fale was a small cookhouse from which the aroma of broiling chicken rose temptingly. Off the beach some little fales were raised on stilts over the water, although the Peace Corps had done much to make these island outhouses obsolete. In the center of each village was a large fale for entertainment and political gatherings.

As we passed slowly from village to village, we were greeted with smiles, quite in contrast to our experience in American Samoa. Mothers interrupted their weaving or coconut pounding and pushed their children out in front of their fales to pose for pictures. Others tended the coconut-husk fires in the cookhouses while the children played among the chickens and pigs in yards littered with coconut shells and an occasional tin can. Most of the women were very dignified, and some were quite beautiful — a result of the gradual intermingling of Polynesian, Asian, and European blood on these islands. From the road, we watched many fishermen making good catches with hand-thrown nets, but the only other visible economic activity was copra-making, and the villages seemed close to subsistence-level living. Yet, the people were neatly dressed, generally well-fed, and cheerful, and

they manifested a kind of dignity and pride that had been lacking in the more affluent American Samoans.

Toward the end of the afternoon, people began flocking to the water for daily baths, chatting and laughing without embarrassment as they washed over and under their pareus. In one fale we came upon a grandmother who was resting on some pillows and watching a small baby. She talked to us and posed for a photo with poise that radiated both dignity and strength.

The atmosphere here was very different from Samoa's eastern islands. Withal, I had to concede that the detour to Apia had been worthwhile, especially for the visits to Aggie's Hotel and Stevenson's home.

We departed for Tonga late in the afternoon of 23 May, switching on the radar and coasting under power along the northern coast of Upolu to the Apolima lighthouse on a tiny island past Upolu's western tip. We then turned south through the Apolima Strait and headed for Vava'u, the northernmost point in the Tongan Islands, 300 miles away.

On watch as we headed south, I looked at the dimming beach and hills, and these lines from Rupert Brooke came to mind:

It's all true about the South Seas! I get a little tired of it at moments, because I am just too old for romance [Brooke was less than 25 years old at the time!], but there it is; there it wonderfully is — heaven on earth, the ideal life...people of incredible loveliness, a divine tropical climate....If you ever miss me, one day...you'll know I've got sick for the full moon on these little thatched roofs, and the palms against the morning, and the Samoan boys and girls diving 30 feet into a green sea or a deep mountain pool under a waterfall — and that I've gone back!

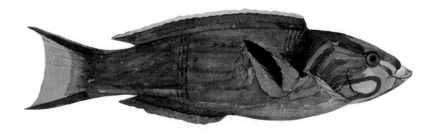

In a tropical rainstorm,
David Flanagan steers while
Paul Wolter and Carter
Christiansen, off watch, keep
him company.

CHAPTER 13

FEASTS AND NEW FRIENDS:

The Kingdom
of Tonga

Soon after we anchored at Neiafu, three polite, helpful officials came aboard and cleared us, informally, into the Kingdom of Tonga. Tall and straight, and speaking very good English, they were obviously proud of their island and seemed delighted that we had chosen to visit there. Over the past few years, they told us, only two or three other cruising yachts had stopped by, and they hoped that in the future Vava'u would become a popular port for the cruising fraternity.

I am sure that it will. It was one of the best harbors we visited. The main island of Vava'u surrounded us on all sides, and the hills are high, so that while there were refreshing breezes from time to time, we were free of a constant heavy wind. Looking ashore at the town to the north and noting trading vessels at the wharf, I felt sure the scene would not have been very different had we been anchored there 100 years ago.

Shortly after the island officials departed, a small fleet of canoes and other assorted small craft approached. They were laden with various local products and came alongside to ask permission to tie up and offer their wares, which included everything from melons and taro root to assorted woven baskets and intricate primitive carvings. We made some careful selections and they departed, always very polite.

We spent a couple of very pleasant hours in this kind of restful, post-passage relaxation, then turned our attention to *Palawan*, opened up all the hatches, and got busy cleaning up and drying out the boat and gear. With everything shipshape once again, we sat down to a well-deserved roast beef dinner and turned in early, looking forward to a good night's sleep before exploring the island in the morning.

Only 46 square miles in area, Vava'u is the second largest of the 150 islands that make up the Tongan archipelago. Three separate clusters of islands emerge from the long shoal that stretches north and south here along the International Dateline — the Vava'u Group in the north, Ha'apai in the center, and Tongatapu to the south. It is 150 miles as the crow flies from Vava'u — the only fertile and formerly volcanic island — to Tongatapu, the 100-square-mile capital that supports more than half of Tonga's 90,000 inhabitants, but the islands and reefs are so numerous that it's impossible to sail a straight course. Only about 45 of the islets are inhabited, and except for Vava'u, all have developed from coral outcroppings

LOG ENTRY: MAY 25, 1976

Early this morning the cliffs of Vava'u appeared right on schedule. We cruised along the steep northern side of the island and then turned southwest and wended our way east, then north into the lovely landlocked harbor at the capital of Neiafu. We dropped anchor at noon and are now relieved to be at rest in four fathoms of calm water.

It's been a rough 300-mile passage and an unusually heavy-weather introduction to Pacific cruising for the Couderts, although they are experienced enough in that to even enjoy it. The wind came up as we left Upolu, Western Samoa, and stayed at 15 to 25 knots for the next three days. Our direct course to Vava'u was southwest and we knew that the wind would eventually go from east to

south. So, as we left we tried to hold somewhat east of south, so that when it started to head us, we would have made sufficient southing to fall off on a WSW course and make Vava'u without difficulty. That's the way it worked out, but it was heavy going at times.

and have poor soil. The word "tonga" means "south" in many Polynesian dialects, but it also means "garden" in Samoan. No one knows which is the correct interpretation, but both names would accurately describe these well-cultivated islands lying far south of the rest of Western Polynesia.

The Tongan Archipelago has been inhabited for several thousand years, and recent archaeological finds have dated occupations as far back as 1000 B.C. Much evidence comes from a trail of "Lapita-style" pottery shards leading down from Fiji and other Melanesian islands. For some reason, the trail ends at Fiji and Tonga and doesn't continue through to eastern Polynesia. Those who believe the original settlers followed a Micronesian path to Polynesia blame this dead end on the lack of clay for making the pottery to the east. But it could also support the theory that they descended instead along the northeastern fringe of Melanesia and split somewhere north of Fiji, with one branch moving directly east to the Marquesas, the other moving south several thousand years before Christ to colonize the western triangle.

Europeans first came to Tonga in 1616, when Dutch explorers Schouten and Le Maire anchored of Niuatolputau in the Vava'u Group and had to defend themselves against a furious native attack. Twenty-seven years later another Dutchman, Abel Tasman, charted the islands around Tongatapu during his search for "Terra Australis Incognita." For more than 100 years after that, the islands lay untouched. Then Wallis stopped briefly in 1767, and on three separate visits during the next decade Captain Cook visited Tongatapu and Eua, and discovered most of Ha'apai. Vava'u wasn't discovered until 1781, when Spaniard Francisco Maurelle and his starving crew stumbled on a tiny, barren islet nearby. Moving on to Vava'u's west coast, they found a welcoming "Port of Refuge" — our own anchorage — where the natives fed and entertained them for three weeks. Maurelle was so impressed with the neat croplands that he called them "worthy to be imitated by the most polished nations."

Circumstances were less pleasant for William Bligh, whose crew mutinied off Tufua in the Ha'apai Group in 1797. Reaching the island in his longboat, he had to flee after relations with the natives deteriorated into a pitched battle. During the next century a growing number of explorers, whalers, missionaries, and slave-raiders visited Tonga, and the papalangi invasion was on.

The people of the Kingdom
of Tonga are poor, and life
is somewhat primitive. But
they are cheerful, warm and
hospitable — as we were to
discover when we became
their guests.

The natives of Nomuka and Tongatapu welcomed Capain Cook so warmly that he christened the area the "Friendly Islands." Yet, he also reported unsavory sights and practices among the inhabitants. They often chopped off their little fingers in mourning. Many were disfigured by leprosy or syphilis. Cook's crew witnessed the brutal beating of a man who had committed adultery, and Cook noted that the whole race seemed addicted to fighting. His mixed assessment was accurate. The Tongans had always shown a strange mix of generosity and savagery, and their history included continual wars and truces among the three island groups.

Not until the mid-1800s, when the missionaries had been established and the islands had been adopted by England, did total peace reign in Tonga.

Our first day ashore, I wandered alone around the town of Neiafu, which looked like a Hollywood reconstruction of a two-centuries-old South Sea island trading village. Very few buildings had been built in the last 50 years, and although the few government buildings nestled in the trees were in good repair, the paint had worn off the shop fronts and the lettering on the signs was nearly gone. The proprietors were either Chinese or Indian.

The townspeople were carefully dressed, but there was an atmosphere of lethargy about the place, due perhaps to its proximity to the equator and the constant heat and humidity. Many villagers spoke adequate English, and I soon found that even in this remote spot I could rent a car. At the rental agency the taciturn and rather mysterious owner said that for a small consideration he could arrange for us a traditional Tongan feast with music and dancing on a small island nearby, which he owned. I knew the crew could use some of this kind of morale-building, so I signed him up at once for a few days hence. Then the Couderts and I took off in a small Japanese car to explore Vava'u.

Driving out of town, we were soon moving through a series of small, primitive villages. Each had a church, a dozen or so modest cottages surrounded by neat yards and abundant flowers, and a few tall shade trees. The majority of homes were made of rough woven-palm mats, and they ranged from small and primitive to rather elaborate. On either side of the road, cultivated patches of taro and coconut covered most of the land — some owned by native co-ops, others divided into the eight-acre lots that the government gives to every Tongan man on his sixteenth birthday. Fat

pigs and small children clad only in shirts — to eliminate the need for diapers — ran about in the unfenced yards. A few dogs skulked in the shadows, probably left to forage for themselves now that they no longer need to be fattened for the Polynesians' table. Occasionally, bony horses plodded by hauling ancient wagons filled with copra or vegetables.

Yet, despite this meager existence, people waved happily at us everywhere we went. Often, their ever-present grins were startlingly marred by missing teeth. Dentistry was still a luxury here. Now that we were moving closer to Melanesia, the natives were darker, with kinkier hair and more Negroid features. All the adults were neatly dressed: the men and some of the older women wore a blouse and tapa skirt, over which was a short woven bamboo-mesh apron or a long straw sash wrapped around the waist several times. Without doubt, these were the friendliest and most charming of any islanders we had met so far.

On our second night in Vava'u, we were just sitting down to a twilight chicken dinner — prepared in Dave's famous jelly-smothered style — when we heard a very American-sounding woman's voice calling from the water, "How's everything up in North Haven, Maine?" I stuck my head out of the companionway to see two ladies sitting in an old, heavy Tongan rowboat with a Seagull outboard, and quickly asked them aboard.

The woman who had called out was Bethany Shuster from Riverside, Connecticut, and she had an interesting story to tell. She and her husband had sailed through Vava'u a year earlier on their way to Australia. While there, they had been thrown up on a beach near Brisbane during a typhoon and had nearly lost their boat, the *To and Fro*. Beth's husband had taken up world sailing in his 60s, and she had been good sport enough to accompany him. Together they had seen the Azores, sailed up a river in Gambia, rounded Cape Horn, and continued into the South Pacific. But the near-disaster at Brisbane had proved too much for Beth, so she had returned to Vava'u to stay with a friend while her husband continued around the world. She was to meet him later in the Mediterranean.

Beth's companion, Pat Matheson, had served as a WAC in WWII and had gone to Vava'u in 1950 to spend a year as a headmistress of a mission-run girls' college. Before the year was over, she had fallen in love with Tonga and a Scottish government doctor named Farquhar Matheson and settled down for good. She had now been a widow for many years, and it was easy to see that she was independent and resourceful.

After she had lived on Vava'u for five years, Pat wrote a book about her experiences that painted a complimentary portrait of the islanders, but a less flattering one of the whites who had come to Tonga over the years. She described the natives as generous, curious, and shy, often bringing her gifts and stories. Among the white inhabitants, however, she found colonial snobbery and an attitude that all natives "are in reality nothing more than servants." But she reserved her harshest words for the missionaries, whom she called condescending, haughty, and expecting the natives to be grateful and eager for their tutelage. "I soon discovered that their main idea in running a college was not to educate the girls, but to keep them from falling into the clutches of rival sects," she wrote. As a result, the overemphasis on religion and the neglect of the girls' social lives turned them into "dark, docile lumps of clay."

The history of Tonga's missionaries is a stormy one. In 1797, the good ship *Duff* landed at Tongatapu, leaving ten British clerics who had no idea the natives were on the brink of another civil war. By 1800 three missionaries had been killed and the remaining seven sensibly departed. It wasn't until 20 years later that a group of Wesleyan missionaries from England established a permanent base on Tonga. They were greatly helped by a young Ha'apai chief who embraced Christianity and went on a pious rampage to convert and unify Tonga. By 1845 he had succeeded, and in 1875 he and the Wesleyans created the first Tongan constitution.

The Tongan mission was not entirely free of criticism. There are stories of "plate days" — church-sponsored contests to see who could donate the most money from the copra harvest. And there was the Rev. Shirley Baker, the flamboyant evangelist who became an adviser to the king, gained power and titles, and became embroiled in local politics until he was finally removed in 1900.

In many villages I had seen hollowed-out logs that looked like poi-grinding receptacles. During one afternoon's walk, I stopped and asked a New Zealand priest what they were. He told me they were native drums, some several hundred years old, and he asked two members of his congregation to drum out a demonstration rhythm for me. It was exciting to realize that these same drumbeats had gone out for 2,000 years — formerly to alert islanders to outside invasions or civil wars, but now to call them to worship. The priest himself bore little resemblance to his fiery, zealous predecessors. He was much more concerned with improving the natives' hygiene, housing, and education, and increasing the annual copra yield, than he was with how often they attended church. He was not planning to stay in Tonga forever, he told us, but considered his stint there important to his clerical career; altogether he was a very practical fellow.

During our stay at Vava'u, one of the more interesting Tongans we met was a friend of Pat's, a princess about 60 years old, whose bearing and low, mellifluous voice were distinctly regal. Tonga has been ruled by a royal dynasty for several thousand years, and even its current king can trace his ancestry back through generations to the first king, Tui Tonga, whose mother was said to have mated with the god Tangaloa.

From 1918 to 1965 the presiding monarch was gentle Queen Salote, who made headlines by going to England to represent her country at Queen Elizabeth's coronation. All London was impressed by her kindly, reserved manner and imposing six-foot frame. Two years after her death, the Tongans crowned her son — 330-pound Taufa'ahau Tupou IV — the new king, with world dignitaries attending the Fourth of July ceremonies. Although the Tongan constitution actually governs the people, and the islanders' traditional obsession with title and a rigid caste system have given way to somewhat more democratic principles, the massive Tupou remains a symbol of royal authority and the pride of the only Pacific island group never to have come under foreign control.

Later we met and became friends with an equally gracious Tongan woman from quite a different social background. Nancy Finau was a curio-seller from the village of Makave, a mile west of Neiafu. She went about her business of selling curios so charmingly that we took to her at once. After we'd bought a few items from her on the street and engaged her in conversation, she invited the crew to her house for a visit and dancing that evening. We accepted with pleasure, and so that night, after dining rather well aboard *Palawan*, we climbed into the dinghies and headed for shore. We walked to Nancy's house by flashlight, and as we approached the villagers pointed us in the right direction; obviously, the whole town was expecting us.

Nancy welcomed us into her family home, which was small,

LOG ENTRY: MAY 27, 1976

Tonight at dinner, Paul and Dave presented me with an interesting five-foot carving of local origin, accompanied by a poem. I was especially touched by this gesture from Paul. Our recent differences were still on my mind, and this gift indicated that they were also still on his and that he, as I, did not want them to affect our relationship. The more I learn about his problems below decks living among the girls, and the more I think about how much we all depend on his mechanical knowledge, the more I understand him.

very neat, and lighted by two pressure gasoline lamps. To our surprise and chagrin we then realized that we had not fully understood her invitation: she had laid out a full dinner for us on the floor, with dozens of steaming dishes surrounding two small suckling pigs. A crowd of friendly faces gathered around — Nancy's dignified mother, her austere school-teacher aunt, who looked and spoke as if she had just graduated from Radcliffe, and the usual assortment of children, grandchildren, and other relatives. Touched by the elaborate welcome and not wanting to seem ungrateful, we sat down to our second sumptuous meal in 70 minutes and everyone made a superhuman effort to cram down the delicious food before us. As we finished, Nancy brought out tapa cloth to sell us, and we all bought more than we wanted, because she had gone to so much trouble on our behalf.

After dinner we were steered toward a nearby assembly hall, lighted by the only electric lights in the village and pulsing with boisterous music from the dancing already in progress.

Encouraged by the local people's friendliness and the relative darkness of the room, we soon ventured out on the dance floor. It was a rare chance to mingle with the Tongans in their own relaxed element. The dance was a very informal affair, with small children, old men, and people of every age dancing alone, in couples, or in groups. During the evening Rene and I had acquired various articles of Tongan costume; I wound up wearing a tapa skirt, numerous cloth necklaces, and several ovalas — woven straw aprons — around my waist, and I had a great time. At one point a heavy middle-aged woman, who was amazingly adept at wiggling her hips to the music, asked me to dance. Her good teaching inspired me to extreme efforts, to the delight of the onlookers, especially my crew. It was an evening to be remembered and a great morale-builder for all.

May twenty-ninth dawned sparkling clear with light winds. It was our last day at Vava'u and the day of the feast that I had arranged to be catered by Mr. Paea. Our party had now expanded to 14 guests, including Beth and Pat, the Tongan princess, four Peace Corps volunteers, "Tapa" Nancy, and a friend of hers. We moved *Palawan* to the pier about 11:00 A.M., and soon Mr. Paea appeared, followed by a horde of, we surmised, participants — band members with their instruments and then a dozen or so giggling girls and young men, whose function I didn't quite understand, but did not question. "No beer for orchestra," Mr. Paea admonished, sternly, "makes poor music." Shortly, we got underway for Mr. Paea's island six miles away, breaking every Coast Guard regulation in the book with 60-odd bodies filling every available square foot of space on deck. But some people found room enough to dance, and others just sat and swayed to the music as we moved slowly through the lovely archipelago to the rhythm of guitars from the foredeck.

Going below for a moment, I found Nancy and her friend sitting in the cabin looking unhappy. I then realized with a shock that there were still class barriers, even out here in paradise. The various Tongans on board had divided into several distinct social groups, communicating little with each other. Obviously, Nancy and her friend felt inferior; they stayed below and aloof from the others during the passages to and from the island. There seemed no way to break the code.

I was surprised to see how many Tongans began to look seasick during the calm passage over to the island. It certainly didn't fit my image of the ancient Tongans' seamanship and navigational feats, such as the historically documented incident in 1820 when King Taufu'hau's fleet of canoes became lost while returning from a ceremony in Samoa. The crew appealed to an ancient, blind navigator sitting in the stern of one canoe. Turning into the wind until his craft stood still, the old man climbed out on the outrigger and dipped his hand into the sea. "Tell the king we're in Fijian waters," he said. Then, asking for the location of the sun, he guided the fleet to the Lau Islands, east of Fiji, whence they were able to make their way home.

When we reached the island, we found that a crew of islanders had been at work there for some time preparing fires and food, and when we went ashore we were greeted with leis by Mr. Paea's daughter, who ushered us to our places around the sandy dance floor and described the dances we were about to see. Then the band struck up a strong rhythm, and the dancing began. It was unlike any we had seen before. The women were chunkier than the Tahitians, but their movements were far more subtle and beguiling, without the violent hip movements of the hula or tamure. With heavily oiled bodies and bright flowers woven into their hair and around their necks, they danced with a snap of the head, a suggestive expression in their eyes, and flirtatious beckoning

---

LOG ENTRY: MAY 28, 1976

This morning I asked Rene to ferry me to Pat Matheson's house on the point at 'Utulei overlooking the harbor. On climbing the rough path from the beach, I found that Pat was not there, but Beth showed me around the bungalow. It was obvious that Pat had put down roots here and would never leave. The study was crammed with books and recordings of native chants and legends. Pat speaks Tongan fluently and has so many friends among the islanders that I couldn't imagine her being lonely here, even as a widow. But there was no road to her house, and it saddens me to think of her growing older here all alone, with no means of getting supplies except with the heavy boat and the hard-to-handle Seagull engine. When I get back to the States, I will send her the most foolproof outboard I can find — a small token indeed for her boundless kindness and friendship to us.

movements of the hands. Needless to say, they mesmerized and charmed us.

When they finished, men began carrying in the eight-foot long, woven-palm platters that held the feast. A small suckling pig served as centerpiece on each platter, surrounded by heaps of food — broiled chicken, roasted chickens, coconut creams and marinades, pineapples and taro, yams and breadfruit — each dish cooked in its own palm-leaf bundle so its juices and aroma were contained.

Mr. Paea asked me to give a blessing, and then we all fell to in Tongan style — without using knives or forks — and feasted well indeed. This was followed by more music and dancing until 4:00 P.M., when we were summoned to start back to the boat in the dinghy, to be sure that the return passage could be made in daylight.

Seating our guests of honor — Pat and Beth — in the dinghy, I climbed in after them with Cheryl and Rene. What with our cameras, tape recorders, and passengers, there was a slight overload, but the water was so flat it seemed safe enough to me. Rene drove the outboard at full speed, and we were about halfway to *Palawan* when a fishing boat passed, throwing a huge wake. Suddenly, a pleasant ride turned into panic as we found ourselves flailing about in the water, trying to retrieve our sinking cameras and drifting hats. Our first thought was of Pat, but we needn't have worried. She was floating happily with her straw hat drooping down around her ears, trying to decide whether to stay where she was or swim the quarter-mile back to shore.

Ever-efficient Paul, who had witnessed the mishap from *Palawan*'s deck, soon arrived in the other dinghy, so we helped each other on board and dripped all the way back to the boat. As soon as we had changed into dry clothes, and the orchestra had reassembled, the party started up again on deck. This time Paul was the center of attention, led into a lively dance by a pretty, dark-eyed Tongan lady, and I was glad to see him get so thoroughly into the spirit of the day.

It was dark by the time all guests had gone ashore from *Palawan*, but I wanted to get an early start in the morning for the 60-mile run to Lifuka, capital of the Ha'apai Group. We crept out of the harbor by radar and anchored where we could have free access to the open sea in the morning, and then tucked in for the night. Departing at dawn, we reached Pangi Harbor about 1400,

maneuvering slowly through the difficult, shallow entrance to the harbor and anchored to await official clearance.

Although later several of us took a long walk to the northern end of the island, sightseeing one more Pacific island was beginning to lose its charm for me, and I found myself quite content to spend the afternoon in the cockpit watching native boats and harbor activities. That evening I asked Stephanie and Wayne Witzell, a Peace Corps couple stationed at Lifuka, over for dinner, and — to our delight — they arrived bringing two large lobsters with them. An interesting couple from Woods Hole Oceanographic Institute, they were trying, with little success, to change traditional native fishing methods, which were adequate for a subsistence economy but not likely to create a surplus and raise island living standards. For 1,000 years the Tongans have fished with spears or small nets, politely inviting the fish to "come and eat" as they worked. In one ceremonial fish roundup, they chase the fish into palm enclosures (much like a Maine fish weir), drug them with shredded kava bark, then scoop them up in baskets. According to Tongan legend, even sharks will allow themselves to be caught if the fisherman sings to them. The Witzells were finding it difficult to change local customs, and I wondered whether they would ever succeed.

Our next course was a 100-mile run to Tongatapu, but the numerous reefs and bars made the going so slow that we were only halfway there by nightfall. I was not anxious to sail at night in these waters, so we anchored between two islands until dawn. As we left the next morning in early light, the easterly came in, giving us a broad reach at nine knots all the way to Tongatapu, where we arrived about noon.

I slept away the afternoon and evening at Tongatapu, hoping the feeling of fatigue and apprehension would pass. The next day, when I finally went ashore, I spent the time running around on a moped finding a bank to cash my traveler's checks, and a supplier who could sell us some fuel. Although I rode by the elegant white, red-roofed palace of the king, surrounded by exquisite Norfolk pines, I never did dress up and go present my letter. Nor did I take the time to drive out to the coast and watch the famous blowholes — geysers that spurt high in the air when surf becomes trapped in hollows in the coral bed and is forced upward dramatically through holes in the formation. For the time being, I had seen and experienced enough.

On our last night at Tongatapu, I took Paul, Anne, and the Couderts to dinner at Nuku'alofa's only western-style hotel — the International Dateline — which was built in 1967 for guests who attended the King's coronation. During dinner we saw one of the booths was curtained on three sides, and learned that the king's eldest daughter was seated inside with friends. The curtain allowed her to move out on the dance floor, but protected her from the stares of the audience. After we had watched her dance several times, Paul, apparently emboldened by his success on the day of the feast, asked her to dance, and the two of them managed a lively combination of traditional island and more contemporary steps. Again, I was glad to see him enjoying himself, even though I knew his exuberance might have been due to the imminence of the end of the cruise.

Although none of us really took advantage of everything Tonga had to offer, it is a delightful stop. However, exposure to the outside world has begun its erosion of the dream of a modern paradise here. In the early 1970s, the nation was shaken by its first strike, and many younger natives have begun to yearn for the sophistication of the cities.

But as we left Nuku'alofa on 5 June I couldn't help but feel we were leaving one of the unspoiled spots on earth; a place where, as a visitor once remarked, people can still "live on love and oranges."

LOG ENTRY: JUNE 3, 1976

There is much to see here, especially in the capital town of Nuku'alofa, but somehow none of us has the strength or inspiration to plunge into another day of sightseeing. We are all suffering from end-of- the-cruise syndrome, I guess. Everyone is reaching the end of his or her emotional rope — which manifests itself differently with each individual — and all seem now to be focussing on the next activity. Ellie, who is winding up her cruise report for the Cincinnati paper, is anxious to get on with her career and plans to begin an educational program in Massachusetts. Anne seems a little homesick. Paul has bounced back a bit since Tahiti, but he won't be totally happy until he has a long vacation from me after Palawan *is home in Maine. The Couderts are still fresh from their late entrance to the voyage, and have proved great assets. Cheryl has endeared herself to everyone on board*

and has been wise in not trying to inject herself into the now strongly formed female clique in the crew.

As for me, I feel a deep fatigue, which has robbed me of my desire to take anything more than a cursory look at Nuku'alofa, even though I've come all this way with a letter of introduction to the king from a museum director in the States. I'm a little undone at the prospect of leaving this mobile lifestyle and returning to the routine responsibilities of husband, father and semi-retired businessman.

At a Tongan feast we were entertained by the native dancer above. The feast was arranged by S.F. Paea, a businessman of Neiafu, and we were accompanied to Mr. Paea's small island by his three daughters, shown at far left.

CHAPTER 14

THE ADVENTURE'S END:
Fiji and Farewells

Ongea Levu had been recommended by Lord Riverdale and, knowing him to be a great seaman, I had to find out why the bearing seemed wrong. After we got underway for Totoya, I went back to chart and book and found that I had made a mistake. I had read the 160 degrees to be a magnetic bearing, although, as I well knew, pilot book bearings are always true. That was the reason for my error; not an excuse. I just blew it — a major navigational error — but only my third in 11,000 miles from the Panama Canal. A fair amateur average.

We arrived at Ongea Levu, one of the easternmost of the Fiji islands, after an uneventful 220-mile passage from Nuku'alofa. A southerly set put us four miles south of our desired course and made it difficult to identify the island for a time. But sun line, radar, and reef soon gave us a positive fix. The *Fiji Coast Pilot* told me the Barracouta Passage into the lagoon was only 150 feet wide and tortuous. We lay to off the entrance for a time to look the situation over. Two men in an outrigger canoe beckoned us in, but I held back, again referring to the British and U.S. pilot books. Each said, "Bearing 160 degrees on outstanding small islet easily identifiable. This identifies the entrance."

I thought I had calculated correctly, but whether the bearing was right or wrong, the entrance did not look inviting, and a Japanese fishing boat hulk perched on the reef was an ominous warning not to make a mistake. Nothing seemed to fit, so I decided to forego the pleasures of Ongea Levu and head instead for Totoya, 80 miles west, which meant another night at sea.

We arrived at Totoya under power about dawn and sailed up the western side of the offshore reef, admiring the rugged hills beyond through intermittent rainshowers. The reef was fairly clear of obstructions, but it had few passes; we used the only one that was clearly navigable and safe. Lying-to off the pass, we looked it over and found it wide and well marked, so that if we lined up 1,000-foot Mount Numbuni with the center of the Nai Vaka Gap on a bearing of 103 degrees true (which I now correctly translated to 090 degrees magnetic — there being almost 13 degrees easterly variation), everything fitted into place. We followed that bearing and despite the rain had no difficulty finding our way between reef and island, with Dave in the spreaders giving us instructions via walkie-talkie. Entering Herald Sound about breakfast time, we cruised south slowly and carefully, and then Dave conned us through the Gullet, a narrow opening into the lagoon.

The scene was remarkably beautiful. The Polynesians had certainly been there for centuries, for the island was covered with palm trees. High green land, formed by a volcano, surrounded the lagoon on all sides except the south, and thatched huts were clustered here and there along the shore. We emerged from the Gullet just off a small village, then motored at full speed to

Ndravualu, a more substantial settlement with several dozen huts and a church, and anchored behind a coral head, just below the green mountains. This was by all odds the least settled, most primitive and — after four days — the most memorable island of our entire Pacific cruise.

The history of early European contact with Totoya is obscure. I have a chart that was made by HMS *Herald* in 1855, and it's likely that by then other British, as well as French, Spanish, or Dutch ships had passed nearby or visited here. Abel Tasman sailed through the archipelago in 1643, and Captain Cook passed south of it 100 years later; neither made landfalls. In fact, it was only because of the *Bounty* mutiny that the Fiji archipelago was finally explored in the late eighteenth century. After being put off the ship in his small launch, William Bligh made his way west and decided to press past the thick reefs of eastern Fiji. He passed 75 miles north of Totoya, then through a wide strait between the two largest islands, later named Bligh Water, before being chased into a storm by two canoes of warriors. Although he was too busy surviving to explore, he kept a detailed notebook and returned two years later to make the first careful survey of the archipelago.

Bligh's charting efforts ended Fiji's isolation from the world. First came a colorful decade of sandalwood traders, who introduced guns into local wars and turned villages into rough waterfront centers. The first Wesleyan missionaries arrived from Tonga in 1835, and five years later Charles Wilkes thoroughly mapped the islands and set up commercial port regulations. After decades of confused, sometimes violent relations between natives and whites, Fiji became a British colony in 1874. The sugar industry began to thrive, and by the early 1900s Fiji had become a crossroads of Pacific travel and trade.

Yet, even in 1976 many Fiji islands had rarely been visited by westerners, and this was the charm of Totoya. The sight of white people was unusual to the natives, but once we had established ourselves as friends they went out of their way to make our stay pleasant and memorable. The appearance and physical carriage of the Totoyans was distinguished. Although their faces had retained distinct Polynesian features, their skin was the darkest of any islanders we had seen — proof that we were now entering Melanesia, the long chain of islands reaching back to New Guinea. Their hair was slightly kinky and their build robust.

There was something initially forbidding about this combination of features, but that emotion quickly vanished and we found the Totoyans to be very warm and friendly.

Most spoke good English, which had been taught in British government schools there for decades, and the children were particularly talkative after we had made a lollipop distribution. The adults seemed happy and communicative, and many invited us into their homes, but we were reluctant to intrude. Peeking through the windows of several huts, we saw that they were immaculately clean, with mat-covered floors and many bead ornaments and photographs of relatives for decorations. There were a few metal cooking pots and chipped plates, and some of the houses were made of clapboard or stone block, but most people lived in thatched huts at close to subsistence level. Their food came from the lagoon or the small farm plots behind the village, and any foreign exchange they earned to supply gas for their outboards and other luxuries had to come from the laborious task of making copra.

After we had been at Totoya two days, a young man named Bale came to me and said, "Skipper, we're glad to have you here, but you are doing everything wrong."

I asked him why, of course, and he replied, "This island is ruled by a chief and that chief is my brother. It's the custom in Polynesia to ask the chief's permission to go ashore, and not to set foot on the ground except to get to his house, until you have spoken with him. This is because the chief owns the land and is therefore the king."

I apologized for our lack of sensitivity, and immediately made up a gift box and proceeded ashore to pay my respects properly to the chief. When I arrived at his house, I was surprised to find that he spoke less English than many of the villagers. He was an attractive fellow, with a regal bearing that would have made him a good leader anywhere. However, once we had observed the required formalities, the chief and his brother became warm hosts and friends and remained so throughout our stay.

On our third day, several of us walked through taro plots and coconut groves to the top of the 1,200-foot mountain behind the village. The path was well worn, but difficult because it was very steep and muddy. But when we reached the top the view of the lagoon was breathtaking. As we rested in the grass admiring it,

Coconut shells dry in the sun on the island of Fiji — one step in the labor-intensive business of supplying dried coconut — copra — to the world's soap factories.

we were joined by a native man and two women who had followed us up, anxious to chat. The man said he was 32, although he looked much older; the women were his wife and sister. Actually, there were very few people over 50 living in Ndravualu. According to the islanders, many people there die before they reach that age, not from bad health but from a curse put on them by someone else. This inadequate explanation wasn't easy to accept, but there was no one to offer a better one. Perhaps, we concluded, the islanders' life expectancy is shortened by inadequate diet and hard work; and the end, when it comes, is simply blamed on tabu, the handiest traditional explanation.

From the top of the mountain we could see the copra groves below on the northern side of the island. Our friends explained that the village had been placed on the lagoon side so the trade winds blowing in from the sea would keep it cool. This meant that workers going to collect copra had to climb over the mountain to get to the groves, although there were primitive overnight facilities there to let them stay a night or two before climbing back again. A narrow-gauge railroad, apparently built by a former copra company, ran from the groves around to the port. The dried copra was loaded onto the small cars and pushed by hand around to the port, where it was then loaded on the occasional small freighters from Suva. This was primitive enough, but better than carrying it over the mountain.

We had heard that the local children were curious about *Palawan*, so we asked our friend Bale if some of them would like to come aboard. The next afternoon, 75 slim brown youngsters in blue cotton uniforms filed down to the beach accompanied by two native schoolmasters. Unfortunately, it was a windy day, and their launch, although seaworthy, was not really adequate to take so many people the distance out to *Palawan*. Reluctantly, we told the teachers we would have to limit the group. I felt badly seeing the disappointment on the younger faces as the teachers announced in their clipped British accents, "Limited to the three upper classes only, please."

The youngsters were well behaved as they climbed over the ship, and I was impressed with their intelligence. Later during our stay, many of them dove for shells and brought them out to the boat to trade for frisbees, chocolate bars, and anything else we could spare. One boy in particular stood out in the crowd: alert, good-looking, and quick to smile, he had an ephemeral quality of leadership stamped all over him. His shells were no more beautiful than the other boys', but he was so charming that he ended up with more of *Palawan*'s spoils than the others.

One evening, Bale and the chief came for dinner. The handsome young chief wore a mixture of Fijian and European clothing, but Bale sported the bright yellow pants and blue shirt of a well-dressed man from Suva. Leaving Totoya as a youth, he had worked as a policeman in Suva for several years, but had eventually returned to the quieter life of Totoya to act as a communications

liaison for his brother. When they both sat down to dinner with us, Bale called for silence, the chief expressed his pleasure at having *Palawan* in his harbor, and then, to my immense surprise, he presented me with a rare gift — a whale's tooth strung on woven sennit. This was the ancient money of Fiji, in use until 100 years ago; its symbol still appears on modern Fijian coins. This tooth was probably from the chief's own treasured family archives. Deeply touched, I tried to respond in kind by saying how glad we were to be in Totoya, and how this above all other islands would always remind us of the great charms of Polynesia, but I knew no words could match this extraordinary demonstration of friendship and hospitality.

Although Totoya has probably been continuously occupied for well over 2,000 years, we found once again that its history had largely been lost, and that the otherwise talkative islanders were not particularly anxious to discuss their former gods or religious way of life. For example, directly inland from part of the beach where we landed was a marae hidden in the underbrush. I stumbled about in the woods examining the massive platform surrounded by huge, upright stones. It looked a great deal like those we had seen on Raiatea and in Tonga. But when I asked about it none of the natives would make any comment other than to agree that it had once been a religious place. Questions about other spiritual sites on the island met with similarly vague answers. The Totoyans were simply no longer interested in their heritage.

Perhaps, in one sense, it was just as well. From ancient times until well into the nineteenth century, the Fijians were known as cannibals and cruel warriors. "They are much dreaded...from the

The chief's family on Totoya — including our friend Bale in orange shirt at far right.

unnatural practice of eating their enemies whom they kill in battle," wrote a member of Cook's crew after talking with the Tongans. "They deem a jolly good carcass of a man the most delicious fare in the world," added another. Early missionaries were forced to watch cannibal feasts, and sometimes found chunks of human flesh hung ominously on their fences. Forever at war with their neighbors, the Fijian warriors cultivated a terrifying appearance. They dyed their bushy hair shades of red and purple, painted themselves red from the waist down and "a fearsome black above through which their teeth and eyes gleamed savagely," according to historian Stanley Brown. Waiting in ambush, they would attack suddenly, yelling fiercely and brandishing huge carved clubs. Yet some experts say that all the hoopla was more a sign of bravado than bravery. And it was one of the most notorious cannibal chiefs of all — Thakombau — who first became a Christian and peacefully united Fiji under Queen Victoria.

Traditional life in Fiji was not always gruesome. When a Fijian was not your enemy, the saying went, he made the best friend in the world. So automatic was generosity among the ancient islanders that they had no words for "thank you." Although some of their gods were macabre — such as Maintavasera, the "god who had just come from the slaughter" — their morality was quaint and strict. All unmarried men lived in separate, communal houses, and all girls were guarded until their wedding day. If found not to be virgins, they were ostracized. Curiously, Fijian women were tattooed rather than men, and according to the Melanesian custom of "vasu," the lines of authority and descent were traced through the female household heads. The ancient Fijians were experts at building long double canoes, designing beautiful tapa, and carving huge kava bowls. For entertainment, they performed a long, seated dance called "meke," and the men of some islands practiced fire-walking, or treading barefoot on hot stones. When not at war with the Tongans, the Fijians welcomed neighbors who came to trade for precious scarlet parrot feathers, and their kingdom functioned as a cultural and trading center for all of western Polynesia.

On our final day at Totoya we sailed around to the point where the chief's wife lived in the village of Na Vesi. The chief had greatly admired our motorbikes and asked if we would bring one ashore to show the children, saying that none had ever seen a self-propelled vehicle like that. We obliged, riding a motorbike around the schoolyard as the youngsters and their parents watched and marveled. When we finished, a young Totoyan presented himself, stated with great conviction that he was an experienced motorbike rider, and asked if, just for nostalgia's sake, he could please borrow one for a five-minute ride. Again we obliged — with near disastrous results, which we witnessed moments later. He hopped on the bike, opened the throttle wide, zipped across the open space in the center of the village and smashed resoundingly into a wall on the other side. Neither he nor the bike was seriously hurt — fortunately it was not very high-powered — but we quickly got it into the dinghy and back to *Palawan* before anything else could happen to either the bike or the local population.

Just before our departure, Bale took us to a thicket near the waterfront, where he showed us Totoya's last seagoing canoe. It wasn't much to look at — probably just big enough to hold two or three people. But Bale told us that once it had made frequent trips to Suva and back, although it had not been used for the last 30 years — yet another token of a fast-disappearing native heritage.

Although it had been raining when we entered Totoya, our departure that afternoon came at the end of a beautiful clear, dry day. After numerous farewells to our hosts, we powered quietly up the lagoon to the Gullet and, feeling like pilot veterans by now, turned westward on the bearing that would take us safely through the reef on our way to Suva, our final port.

It was a straight, easy 120-mile sail to Suva on the southeast corner of Viti Levu. Three-quarters the size of Connecticut, this huge island houses more than four-fifths of Fiji's population, more than half a million people, and its terrain ranges from dense rain forest on the moist windward side, over thick hills to the dry plains and dark beaches of the leeward shore.

"It was seldom a thing of beauty," Harry L. Foster said of Viti Levu's shore in his book, *A Vagabond in Fiji*, published in 1927. "Generally soft black mud, pierced by jagged mounds of coral — an oozy, evil-smelling place, yet abounding in curious treasures" — among which were blue starfish, octopi stranded among mangrove roots, and bright crabs scurrying into their holes. He was equally intrigued with the island's interior and described one trek through the hills and "tropic dells where streams...ran

LOG ENTRY: JUNE 8, 1976

The sea is smooth, the sky crystal clear, the wind favorable and light. As the sun sets on our last night at sea together, we are quiet, each of us alone with our thoughts. My thoughts turn to my soon-to-be-disbanded crew and how we have all reacted to one another. Ellie and Anne have become introspective; they spent a lot of time ashore with the Totoyans and I think they are feeling the tensions of returning to the real world again. The Couderts, sophisticated and self-sufficient, have obviously enjoyed themselves immensely; they are buoyant. Carter remains an enigma — so helpful and lovable at times, so thoughtless at others. David is unflappable and still the ship's diplomat. Paul and I are both tense, because I must leave Palawan *in his hands and he must assume the entire responsibility for taking her home.*

Although he knows that any sea accidents would not be blamed on him, the new command must be weighing heavily on his subconscious.

With Suva only hours away, I am thinking back over three years of planning and four months of voyaging. Have the fulfillments outweighed the disappointments? Has it all been worth it? As far as I am concerned, the voyage has been a 90% success. Of course, there have been minor problems — some were expected — but my major aims — reaching Fiji safely and on a relatively rigid schedule, and keeping the crew reasonably happy — have been achieved. I've visited places I have dreamed of for 45 years. I now know that I can navigate with reasonable accuracy and dependability anywhere on the high seas. And, considering the length and monotony of parts of the voyage and variety of personalities, I think the crew has worked together extremely well, considering how closely we have lived for these months. However, I'm sure some of them could write pages on how I could be improved upon as captain. Perhaps now I could, too.

In some ways I would like to keep this cruise going forever, although I now realize that four months at sea is about all I can manage. I do not have the emotional stamina to travel for several years on a boat, as I once thought I would like to do. Every minute has been enjoyable, but in the past few weeks I've often found myself feeling lonely or bored. With Jimmy, both Helens, and Robin gone, I've been rather restricted to a steady diet of conversation with people less than half my age; while stimulating, it does not provide sufficient companionship.

Mostly, however, the tedium is due to the everlastingly benign weather in the South Pacific. After years of challenging conditions and the stimulation of racing — from Bermuda to Denmark or Buenos Aires to Rio — or of cruising hazardous

sweetly beneath overhanging beds of palm and lichen. Giant fern trees abounded…groves of bamboo formed lofty arches…and one could see for miles over the virgin wilderness of rolling green, dotted with splashes of scarlet."

We entered Suva harbor on the morning of 10 June with a light rain falling. An erroneous radio bearing had confused my navigation and put us somewhere north of the entrance, but we soon noted the error and sailed southward to correct it. The wide, deep-water harbor was crowded with passenger steamers, freighters, small motorboats, native sailboats, and canoes. At last we had reached civilization, and it was not entirely a welcome sight. After passing the rows of commercial wharves, we anchored off the Suva Yacht Club.

Suva has an interesting history, an unusual mixture of population, several colleges, huge public gardens, and a lovely old hotel called the Grand Pacific. Ten stories high and built around a courtyard, it is much like the famous Raffles Hotel in Singapore. But I had little time for sightseeing, and Suva's status as the most modern, complex city in the Pacific islands has hardly left it the ideal spot for tropical tours. A particularly pressing problem is tension between the natives and the growing population of Indians originally imported to work on the colonial copra and sugar plantations in the late 1880s. Now they outnumber the Fijians. Although they are hard workers, many Fijians blame them for most of the crime and moral decay in Suva. As the Indians have begun to climb in social, financial, and political stature, the problem of prejudice has grown more intense. It is South Africa in microcosm.

Paul and I were very busy in Suva. *Palawan* needed maintenance, minor repairs, and a thorough cleaning before we could turn her over to her new crew for the return voyage. While we were completing these chores, I got surprising assistance from Carter. Ever since our initial disagreements in the Galapagos, our relationship had been sort of an affectionate armed truce. On this rainy afternoon, however, her sweetness appeared once more, and I searched my memory to find out why I hadn't been able to bring it out more during the cruise. Most of the crew had gone ashore, and I decided this would be a good time to clean up the ship in anticipation of the arrival of daughter Susan, 24, who was part of the return crew. Carter was reading in one of the forward bunks and she called out to ask if I needed help. I said yes, and for the next six hours we worked together without stopping, and she did it with a cheerfulness I hadn't seen since leaving Tahiti. It was very rewarding to me, even though some of her exuberance also may have been due to the imminence of returning home.

The next day the new crew began to assemble. Susan brought a friend, and the two Smith brothers from Camden added some welcome brawn. One of my oldest friends, Pan Am pilot Bill MacDougall, would be joining them for a few weeks, and I had given my secretary, Marie Smith — who had helped make many of the arrangements for the trip — plane tickets out to Fiji and home from Tahiti, so she could sail with *Palawan* between the two island groups. That afternoon we all met aboard the ship, and almost immediately Paul busily began briefing the new crew. The rest of us — the old crew — suddenly felt unneeded and in the way. Attention had switched from us — our contributions, our authority, our personalities. It was a natural change, but we were shocked by its abruptness. Another lesson learned about shipboard relationships.

Our last night together in Fiji was, unfortunately, something of a disaster. I had thought Paul might feel a little nostalgic about the departure of his old crew, but he had already turned his mind totally to the tasks ahead. Carter had disappeared with Dave, so I hoped the Couderts, the other women and I could have a nice quiet final dinner in my hotel. Apparently, however, Ellie and Anne misunderstood my invitation, and we waited an hour for them. Because of the impending leave-taking, everyone's emotions were already high, and when they finally arrived to say they were eating elsewhere, tension mounted. Thinking about it later, I realized I simply should have dropped anchor, left appropriate orders in Paul's capable hands, stepped off the vessel, and gone home rather than staying and trying to oversee the difficult moment of changing command and the uneasy intermediate period between voyages.

On the fourteenth, the Couderts and I rented a car for the 100-mile drive from Suva to Nandi, a winding difficult route that took us six hours. However, we eventually arrived at Nandi airport, which I had last seen in 1945 when flying home from the war. After a night in the hotel, we boarded a 707 for home.

The mission had ended, but not the dream.

waters such as the North Sea or Greenland coast, I find the sameness of these cloudless, hot, and often windless days getting on my nerves. Despite the titillation of new faces and experiences at each island, the sameness of it all — the swaying palms, the white beaches, the rather simple navigation — has finally become monotonous.

Epilogue

A s I reread and relive the log of this four-month cruise fifteen years after the fact, I am extremely happy that we made the cruise no later than we did. If anything, I regret that I did not make it fifteen years earlier. Thirty years ago the vast reaches of the South Pacific were still shrouded in the myth and mystery of the unexplored, heightened by tales of idyllic islands from returning World War II servicemen. Still in their infancies, rapid communication and transportation had not yet enabled the voluminous westward flow of tourism that has now left its mark forevermore on South Sea island cultures.

One of the lasting treasures of the South Seas voyage for all of us on *Palawan* was the background reading we did beforehand and en route, which made us aware as we approached each island of its place in time, legend, and history: Cocos's pirates, the Galapagos's turtles, Easter's enigmatic monoliths, Pitcairn's *Bounty*, and others. We learned of ancient economic needs that created a race of instinct-driven navigators as native populations pushed eastward, relentlessly seeking new atolls to call their own. We also dug deeply into the chronicles of Captain James Cook and other European adventurers into the Pacific, and we read about and witnessed the varied social effects of the insistent spread of Christianity throughout the area. We were able to link that history to the recent past with visits to Stevenson's home on Apia, Gauguin's haunts in Tahiti, the homes of Fletcher Christian's descendants on Pitcairn, an afternoon with James Norman Hall's widow and daughter in the Hall home on Tahiti, and finally a visit to Aggie's hotel of (Bloody Mary)

World War II fame. These visits were thrills and unforgettable experiences for us all. We all returned home with a far greater appreciation of the meaning of "Polynesia" and Polynesians than we had imagined possible when we started out. That reason alone made the cruise well worthwhile, but there were other benefits as well.

Although I had carefully planned our cruise dates — January to June — to coincide with favorable weather in the Pacific, particularly in view of my relatively untried crew, I had not anticipated that the weather would turn out to be quite as "pacific" as it was. Occasionally the glassy seas, heavy heat, and droning engine made me long for a rail-down breeze on my summer-home waters of Maine's Penobscot Bay, or for the cool damp mist of a three-day New England northeaster. However, I realized that I had much to be thankful for in our calm weather. During many years of racing and cruising, I had left the navigation to others. In the Pacific I did most of the navigating myself, and it took me several hundred miles of plotting — before Jimmy Madden left the cruise — to get back into the swing of it under his watchful eye. When approaching reef-ringed islands, I was grateful that I did not have to contend with heavy weather as well as tricky currents and hidden reefs. Thus, one more benefit of the cruise for me was that during those 15,000 miles I fully regained confidence in myself as a navigator.

Looking back at my crew for the cruise, I often think that I could not possibly have assembled a more disparate group of individuals for a four-month voyage into unknown waters. Yet, relationships on the whole were compatible, with remarkably little petty sniping, and moments of tension usually dissipating quickly and leaving no verbal scars. We got to know and appreciate each other in spite of age and interest differences; it's even possible that those differences contributed to our overall compatibility. We learned to live, work, and play together in the small confines of the ship, and I think we each came to know ourselves a little bit better in those four months.

Again looking back, it's interesting to note how those varied personalities blended into the future. The alert and ever-inquiring Ellie Lazarus completed the graduate studies she was headed for at cruise end. She is now working in a museum in Boston, spreading her intellectual abilities across interesting new fields. She is successful and we correspond frequently.

Carter Christensen was going through a difficult time in her life when the cruise took place, with the result that she was exasperating at times. However, in spite of her stubborness about instruction in seamanship, in the end she did try to learn, and we all appreciated the turnaround. It pleases me that, following the cruise, she went back to Easter Island and worked as a midwife for a while, later going elsewhere to work with third-world communities. Carter was happiest when she was dedicating her efforts to someone else in an area where she knew more than the person she was working with, and her subsequent occupations have borne this out.

Quiet, resourceful Anne Madden is happily married and raising a family of three children. The delight Jimmy took in her presence on the cruise delighted me, and delights me still in retrospect as we now know that Jimmy was carrying his final illness at that time. One of the warmest friends that I will ever have, Jimmy has passed on to a better sailing ground off this earth, a victim of Parkinson's disease. It had been diagnosed when we made the cruise, but he was able to cope with it with the aid of medication and by resting when necessary. His assistance to me as friend and navigation mentor was invaluable. He did not always feel well, but with his tremendous courage he kept us all amused and himself cheerful until he left the cruise at Rarotonga. He passed away a few years later.

The indomitable Robin Balfour, Lord Riverdale, continues to thrive in Sheffield, England. He cruises every winter, sometimes on a small boat, sometimes on a slow freighter, but he leaves time as well for rebuilding old cars and hunting. Now 89, he is very lively and an inspiration for me since

Outrigger canoes of the Marquesas.

he is ten years older than I am. I am in touch with him frequently, and when we were cruising in England after the delivery in Germany of *Palawan VI* in 1984, Robin sailed with us from Cowes to Lands End, and again I listened to a story or two of his adventures with *Bluebird* .

Dave Flanagan, our diplomatic, strong-armed assistant to Paul Wolter, returned to Camden, Maine, and took over his father's lumber business. It has been a great success; so much so that I have not been able to pry him away for another cruise. I still hope to do so in the future.

Unfortunately for me, my great skipper of 27 years, Paul Wolter, has swallowed the anchor. Long periods of separation from his wife, daughter, and grandchildren when off cruising became a burden. Then, when he almost fell overboard while delivering *Palawan VI* from Bremen to Helsinki, he decided that it was time to step ashore. This was a shock to me. He had become a close friend in whom I had complete confidence. He had done such a superb job handling and ferrying the boat for so many years that I dreaded his departure. He now lives in a splendid house above Camden, with a sea captain's view of lower Penobscot Bay and Matinicus Island, and he acts as a consultant on all things maritime for people in the area. He has his own cruising boat in which he and Barbara head down the inland waterway each year to winter in the Bahamas. I felt very fortunate to have him join the crew when we took *Palawan VI* from Maine to Antigua in the fall of l988. It was heavy going for a while, and Paul's assistance was as always invaluable.

Last but far from least is Helen, for whom the cruise was designed — you'll remember that she deflected its course from the Strait of Magellan to the Panama Canal and into the Pacific. In spite of my occasional concerns as she was growing up, she has developed into a remarkably responsible and beautiful wife and mother of three. We are in close contact with her family, as we are with the families of all our children, each of whom has a summer home in the vicinity of ours in Maine. Grandchildren are a constant delight, and I have high hopes of making sailors out of some of them.

Although I felt that I was operating on borrowed time when I planned the cruise to Fiji, subsequent cruising has taken me again transocean and almost to the ends of the earth north and south. After Olive and I returned from a tour of duty as Ambassador to Russia from 1979 to 1981, I embarked on a single-handed passage from Bermuda to Antigua and back in our 50-foot *Palawan V*, inspired by the then-recently-completed Naomi James circumnavigation. Then, after *Palawan VI* was built in 1984, we sailed her back across the Atlantic, stopping at the Canaries for supplies and continuing on to the Cape Verde Islands. From there it was a 4,000-mile passage to Montevideo, Uruguay, and on to the Strait of Magellan, Tierra del Fuego, the Strait of Le Maire, and a vicious 48-hour beat with engine to Cape Horn. Once in the vicinity, and having photographed the Cape and carefully established the fact that it bore east of north, we stated that we had rounded and retreated to a small port and finally to Ushuaia, Patagonia, for a trip home. When I returned, we sailed from there to the Antarctic and then back up the west coast of South America to Puerto Montt, Chile.

Many years ago I compiled a list of cruises I wished to make, and after the Antarctic only one remained. After the boat was brought home from Chile, and in between trips to the Mayo clinic for nips, tucks, and repairs, in 1986 I embarked on the last of my dream cruises: to Churchill, on the western rim of Hudson Bay, and back. The voyage involved considerable preparation, including briefing from an ice pilot and securing further ice data from the U.S. Hydrographic Office. Finally, fully provisioned and equipped, the boat was ferried to Corner Brook, Newfoundland, where the crew assembled and we headed north. One other yacht had made the passage to Churchill but, since she was shipped home from there, *Palawan VI* was the first yacht to make it to and out of Churchill on her own bottom. And a thrilling passage it was — tough sailing under difficult weather conditions.

The Churchill voyage ended in the culmination of my fondest sailor's dream. Jimmy Madden, I found out some years after his death, had put me up for the Cruising Club of America's Blue Water Medal when I sailed to Fiji. Well, I did considerable additional sailing before the ruling powers decided the award should go to me, and I think the additional sailing was really necessary to put me into consideration for the medal. In any case, I received it. It hangs in the cabin of *Palawan VI*, and I look at it with great pride whenever I go aboard.

I now figure that I have sailed somewhere between 100,000 and 200,000 miles — not much for sailors of centuries ago, but perhaps more than adequate for someone who has spent most of his life in active business. I still hope there are a few thousand miles left to me as I look forward to another cruise that will take me to St. John's, Newfoundland, over to the Faroe Islands, down the Irish Sea and to each of the Azores, then to the Canaries and home.

God and the Mayo Clinic willing, I will sail it.